FLASH Review

for

Psychology

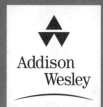

Addison
Wesley

Boston San Francisco New York
London Toronto Sydney Tokyo Singapore Madrid
Mexico City Munich Paris Cape Town Hong Kong Montreal

Vice President and Publisher: Alison Pendergast
Senior Production Manager: Susan Brown
Production Editor: Michelle Limoges
Project Coordination, Text Design, and Electronic Page Makeup: TechBooks
Cover Design Manager: Barbara Atkinson
Cover Design: Night & Day Design
Manufacturing Buyer: Chris Marson
Printer and Binder: Courier, Kendallville
Cover Printer: Coral Graphic Services, Inc.

Library of Congress Cataloging-in-Publication Data

Flash review for psychology.
       p. cm. -- (Flash review)
    Includes index.
    ISBN 0-205-3500-X
     1. Psychology.   I. Series.

BF121 I57 2002
150--dc21   2001056562

Please visit our website at http://www.flashreview.com

ISBN 0-205-35100-X

1 2 3 4 5 6 7 8 9 10 – ptr code – 04 03 02 01

CONTENTS

FOREWORD

Dear College Student:

Congratulations on purchasing your *Flash Review*. The fact that you purchased it indicates that you know there's an easier way to make good grades in college—and that you have decided to pursue it. This is the first and most important step you can take to start excelling in your academic efforts.

You see, making good grades in college has more to do with your attitude, determination, and knowledge of how to excel academically than with your level of raw intelligence. I am living proof of that principle.

How a Struggling High School Student Became a College Star

As a high school senior, I had no desire to do well in school, and my grades reflected my bad attitude. As a freshman I had tried to study and make good grades, but my test scores were always disappointing. After my sophomore year I essentially gave up. After all, spending time with my friends was a lot more fun than staying home and studying. As a result, I graduated at the bottom of my class—497th in a class of 512 students. In fact, my poor academic performance almost kept me from graduating altogether.

My parents constantly reminded me how important my education was. They often told me it would determine what types of jobs I would get and how much money I would make. My education would even affect how happy I was, they said. Unfortunately, their advice fell on deaf ears. I was having fun with my friends, and homework seemed like a waste of time.

I underwent an attitude adjustment after high school. I took odd jobs such as shoveling asphalt to fill potholes, offloading semi trucks at a loading dock, flipping burgers at a fast-food joint, and delivering stacks of newspapers to paperboys on street corners. Now don't get me wrong—there's nothing wrong with good, honest hard work. I felt, though, that I was capable of doing more.

When I turned 27, I decided it was time to get a college education, so I took some refresher classes at a local community college to boost my grades. Eventually, I was accepted into a four-year college. Five years later I graduated at the top of my class with bachelor's and master's degrees in business. How did I do it? I learned how to be a smart student rather than a student who is smart.

Study the Habits of the Best Students

I knew I couldn't compete with the top students in terms of raw intelligence, so I started observing their study habits. Then I began to use all the tips, tool, and tactics they used to get straight A's. I asked a friend who was a great student to let me in on his secret. He said, "David, you need to look at your education as though it were a full-time job." He went on to ask, "Are you ever late for your regular job?" I wasn't. "Do you ever just skip work because you don't feel like going?" I didn't. Then he asked, "When your boss gives you an assignment, do you ever just blow it off?" Of course not—I'd get fired. "Exactly," he concluded. "You'd get fired. Why should your job be any different from your college education?"

That very day I decided I would take my education seriously and treat it as though it were a full-time job. I never skipped another class; I arrived on campus at 7:30 AM and didn't leave until I finished my work for the day; and I turned in every assignment that was given to me, even all the optional and extra-credit assignments.

I continued to gather information about study techniques from many other sources and started to figure out what worked for me and what didn't. Finally, I condensed all the advice into a few effective techniques, and I implemented them one by one. For example, I learned that studying in the same place at the same time every day helps one focus and get more done. So I found a spot in the corner of the campus library and made it my "office." Sure enough, I was able to concentrate better and get my work done faster.

Another powerful tip helped me boost my math and science scores. While most study-skills books tell you to stop studying a couple of hours before a test to clear your mind and help you relax, this technique had never worked for me. A friend advised me to do just the opposite—to spend the hour before the test memorizing the formulas. "Forget about how to apply them," he said. "Just organize them and write them down on paper several times. Keep studying them until the test starts. When the test begins, pull out a fresh piece of paper and write down all the formulas, just like you've been doing for the past hour." I tried this technique, and it worked. At the start of my next math exam, I had all the formulas I needed right in front of me—it was almost like an open-book test. That one tip increased my math and science test scores by a full grade.

Flash Review will help you put this tip into practice because it provides all the formulas in one compact, easy-to-study place. With *Flash Review*, you'll breeze through quick, comprehensive reviews before taking your tests.

Academic Success Is Mainly a Function of Knowing How to Make Good Grades

When my scores started to improve, I began to realize that academic success has more to do with knowing how to make good grades than with being a genius. Let me explain. When I started college I spent hours on end studying in the library. I tried to memorize information and cram for tests, but my grades were mediocre. I became frustrated and depressed.

Then a friend taught me some techniques for memorizing facts and figures using word-picture associations. I began to practice these and suddenly started to ace my daily quizzes. Then I bought an organizer and began to schedule my time and develop daily to-do lists. My productivity soared, and I was completing tasks in half the time they took previously. I formed a couple of study groups for some of my harder classes and found myself teaching others the material I was learning. My comprehension of the material improved dramatically. I started to visit my professors during office hours and developed trusting relationships. As a result, they always went the extra mile to help me when I had trouble. I went to the academic skills office and took a short course on taking tests. The course gave me a host of test-taking techniques, and my grades started to improve immediately.

Are you getting the picture? You must learn *how* to be a good student. Most of you will be in college for at least two years; some will be in college for more than eight years. That's a long time. Doesn't it make sense to invest some time in learning how to be an exceptional student?

Using *Flash Review* Will Help You Grasp Topics Quickly

Flash Review is an excellent study tool to help you learn your assigned topic quickly and easily. It is also an effective tool to use when preparing for exams. I'll never forget when I was assigned to do a report on Shakespeare's classic work *The Taming of the Shrew*. I read the first twenty pages and was completely lost. I kept trying to follow the story, but it was useless—I just wasn't getting it.

Finally, I decided to talk to the teacher's assistant, and he suggested that I buy a study guide similar to *Flash Review*. After reading the first few pages, the mystery unfolded, and I finally understood what the story was about. I went on to get an A in that class. After that experience, I purchased a study guide for every topic my classes covered.

Using *Flash Review* will help you grasp difficult and complex topics in record time. It will make you more productive, and when used in conjunction with your regular reading and homework assignments, it will help you master the material you are studying.

Flash Review has also developed a companion Web site that will dramatically improve your comprehension of the materials and shave time off your learning curve. The *Flash Review* Online Study Center (*http://www.flashreview.com*) is a fully interactive learning environment that allows you to take practice quizzes. It provides immediate feedback, enabling you to use your time wisely. Interactive quizzes are only one example of what the *Flash Review* Online Study Center offers to help you learn the material and become a top student. I urge you to visit Flashreview.com and start benefiting from its rich set of interactive learning tools.

I wish you success in your academic endeavors.

David Frey
Author, *Make Straight A's in School: 50 Proven Secrets for Making the Grade!*

INTRODUCTION

Welcome to the world of psychology! Psychology is a fascinating topic that will be of value to you not only in your life as a student but also in your everyday exchanges with others. Psychology is the scientific study of human behavior and cognitive (thought) processes. You will read a more comprehensive introduction in Psychology as a Field of Study in the following pages. In your introductory psychology course, and in the pages of this *Flash Review for Psychology*, you will learn not only the basic principles of psychology but also how to think like a psychologist. This includes developing your critical thinking skills, so you will be able to evaluate information, apply psychological theory to everyday facts and stories, question commonly held assumptions, and ask challenging questions. The study of psychology has many applications to everyday life, including learning about how we think, study, and retain information; how our personalities develop; and how we attract and are attracted to others. Your introductory psychology course will open up a new world of information that can be applied to many other aspects of your life.

Overview of *Flash Review for Psychology*

Flash Review for Psychology is a resource that can aid you in your understanding of psychology and in learning to think like a psychologist. This resource was designed for students taking an introductory psychology course. It can be used as a companion to an assigned textbook, in distance-learning courses, or as a refresher course for those who want to review concepts learned in a previous psychology course. The Introduction contains a section of tips that may help you succeed in your psychology course. This is followed by a section on how *Flash Review for Psychology* can be used in relation to these tips for success. A table mapping the contents of *Flash Review for Psychology* to commonly used textbooks is located at the end of the Introduction.

In addition to the Introduction, there are five content units contained in *Flash Review for Psychology*. This course content offers five units of study divided into fourteen topical "chapters." With some variation in sequence, the content and progression of chapters generally match the way most introductions to psychology are taught in lecture courses. Each chapter is divided into terms of significant subheadings and offers the following resources:

	Flash Focus	Chapter objectives and list of Core Concepts
	Flash Link	Recommended web sites for particular topics
	Flash Summary	Summaries of the main points of the chapter
	Flash Review	Applications of Core Concepts to cases or practice
	Flash Test	Practice tests with multiple-choice and essay questions, with Answer Explanations at the end of each test

Each chapter begins with the Flash Focus component, followed by Flash Summary and Flash Review components; each chapter ends with the Flash Test component. The Flash Focus and Flash Link tables, as well as some of the Flash Review exercises, include space for you to add information provided by your instructor, your text, and your own exploration.

Tips for Success

Many factors affect the success of an individual in any course. These may include attitude, communicating with your instructor, class attendance, class preparation, note taking, study habits, test preparation, and exam-taking strategies. Although these factors are discussed with relation to an introductory psychology class, the tips listed here can be helpful in any course.

Attitude

✓ Keep it positive—It may seem odd that attitude is listed as the first factor in improving your success in your introductory course in psychology. However, if you approach the course and the topic with a positive attitude, you will have a more positive experience.

✓ The course is not a waste of time—Learning about psychological theories and research can be both interesting and useful. Have you ever taken a course that made you wonder why it was required because you don't think you will ever see the material again? Introductory psychology not only is fascinating in and of itself but also has multiple applications to your daily life and study habits.

Communicating with Your Instructor

✓ The syllabus—Most instructors will provide a syllabus for the course at the beginning of the semester. Read the syllabus to familiarize yourself with your instructor's policies. Keep the syllabus in your notebook, and refer to it before asking the instructor about topics such as attendance, homework, quizzes, exams, and grading. If the syllabus does not answer your question, then ask your instructor for the information you need.

✓ Mode of communication—Determine your instructor's preferred mode of communication—in person, by telephone, and/or by e-mail. If you want to see your instructor in person, try to go by their office during posted office hours. If you have a conflict with those hours, make an appointment. When telephoning or e-mailing your instructor, identify yourself by name and by the course in which you are enrolled at the beginning of the communication.

✓ Asking questions—Determine your instructor's preference for the timing of questions. Do they only take questions at the beginning or at the end of the class period? Is it permissible to ask a question during the middle of a lecture? Ask questions as soon as it is feasible. Remember that the only stupid question is one you fail to ask because failing to ask means you do not receive the information you need.

Class Attendance

✓ Go to class—Information not contained in other sources, such as your text, may be covered in class; if you miss that lecture, you miss that information. While you should borrow notes if you must miss class, your own notes will generally make more sense to you than notes you obtain from a classmate. Class attendance is required by some instructors, because missed classes may also affect your grade.

✓ Be on time—Students who are consistently late for class miss material and irritate the instructor. If you have a scheduling conflict that causes you to be tardy on a regular basis, discuss the problem with your instructor.

✓ Making up work—Your instructor's policies on making up homework assignments, quizzes, and exams are often included in the syllabus. If they are not, and you must miss class, contact your instructor **prior** to the missed class period to determine the make-up policy. If permissible, ask a classmate or a friend to deliver homework assignments on time if you are unable to attend the class period when it is due.

Class Preparation

✓ Read the text—Make an attempt to read the text prior to the class lecture in which a topic is discussed. You may not understand all the material the first time you read it; however, the topic will be familiar when you hear the instructor discuss it. When reading the text, pay particular attention to boxes and bold faced print, as these often contain important concepts, definitions, and formulas.

✓ Review your lecture notes—Read your lecture notes from the previous class and make a list of questions about concepts you do not fully understand.

Note Taking

✓ Keep it organized—Keep a separate notebook for your psychology class, or use dividers to keep your class notes separated if you have one notebook for several classes. Structure your notes sequentially in a manner that makes them easy to understand when you read them, such as by outlining or keeping lists of definitions and examples.

✓ Material—Many instructors will write on the board or use overheads for major concepts. Much of this information should go into your notes. You may also want to include explanations that follow formal definitions.

✓ Incomplete notes—If you find that your notes are not as useful, because you feel they should be due to missing information, ask your instructor if you may tape-record the class. Leave a blank space in your notes during class, and fill in missed material when you listen to the recording of the lecture. You might also compare your notes with those of a classmate to see whether that student included material that you did not.

Study Habits

✓ Time—Be sure you allot enough time in your schedule to study. A general rule of thumb is to spend an average of 3 hours per week studying for a class for every hour of credit.

✓ Read resource material—Read the text, both before a topic is covered in class and after the instructor presents the topic in lecture. Compare your lecture notes to the text to help you decide what concepts to emphasize during your study time. Other sources of material can be utilized for topics that are particularly difficult for you and for those topics that you find interesting.

✓ Study groups—Studying with classmates can be very beneficial for all the students involved. Other students may have a better understanding of certain concepts or notes that cover different aspects of a concept from your own notes. Ask other students for help, but be sure you do your own work. Remember that you will not be able to rely on your study partner during an exam.

✓ Ask for help—If you are having difficulties with the material, try to identify the source of the problem. Providing you with assistance will be easier for your instructor, and you can ask specific questions rather than just saying, "I don't understand." If you continue to have difficulties, you may want to consider finding a tutor.

Test Preparation

✓ Time—Be sure to allow plenty of time to study for an exam. A rule of thumb is to begin to review the oldest material to be covered on the exam 1 week prior to the exam date. Cramming the night before a test is not the most effective way to perform well; however, reviewing the night before (or earlier the same day if it is a late class) can help you to remember material and feel less stressed.

✓ Take practice exams—The practice exams in this *Flash Review Introduction to Psychology*, as well as the questions that may be included in your text, will help you to familiarize yourself with key concepts and both objective (multiple choice) and subjective (essay) question formats.

✓ Review concepts—Make a list of important concepts, definitions, and formulas. Try to condense your notes for these topics into one or two sheets of paper, and study from these sheets.

✓ Information from your instructor—Utilize any information your instructor provides such as study guides or sample tests. If your instructor schedules a review session, make a list of questions prior to attending.

✓ Chapter reviews—If your textbook includes a review section at the end of each chapter, read the information provided. Take any sample tests that are included.

✓ Ask for help—Make a list of any problem areas, and ask your instructor for help well in advance of exam time.

Exam-Taking Strategies

✓ Be on time—Arriving late for an exam is disruptive to you and to your classmates.

✓ Be prepared—Take all materials with you that you will need for the exam such as pencils and erasers, and make sure your pencils are already sharpened.

✓ You don't have to start with question 1—Look through the entire test when you receive it to familiarize yourself with the types of questions asked. Start with questions that you feel confident about being able to answer correctly. This will boost your confidence and keep you from using too much time at the beginning of the exam.

✓ Pace yourself—Work as quickly and steadily as you can. Don't rush, but don't spend an excessive amount of time on one problem. Read all essay questions and jot down some notes for your answers; remember not to spend all your time on only one question; allow enough time to cover all questions.

✓ Don't panic—If you get stuck on a particular question and start to panic, go on to another question; then return to that question when you have finished the rest of the exam.

✓ Check your work—If you complete the exam before the allotted time is up, go back and check your work.

Flash Review Introduction to Psychology can be a valuable resource for improving your success—your knowledge, understanding, and performance—in your introductory psychology course. The following suggestions may help you to utilize this resource effectively.

Flash Focus

✓ Class preparation—Flash Focus provides a list of important concepts, key terms, and important people discussed in that chapter. Previewing these terms and names prior to the lecture for a particular topic will familiarize you with the vocabulary.

✓ Study habits—Compare the concepts in the Flash Focus table to those in your text and your lecture notes. Add any items from lectures or your text that you feel are important but are not included in the list. As you complete a unit, go back to the Flash Focus component and review the objectives. If you cannot meet any of the objectives, review the appropriate sections.

✓ Test preparation—The Core Concepts table in the Flash Focus component is an excellent resource for preparing for an exam. Use the objectives in the Flash Focus component to focus your test preparation time.

Flash Link

✓ Study habits—The recommended web sites provided in the Flash Link sections provide resources for additional material including definitions, alternative explanations, and extra examples. In addition, some sites provide demonstrations of concepts to strengthen your understanding.

✓ Test preparation—The web sites listed in the Flash Link sections can be used to provide extra information and examples that could be helpful in exams.

Flash Summary

✓ Class preparation—Summaries of the main points of the chapter topics provided in the Flash Summary component can be used as a preview of topics to be presented in future lectures.

✓ Note taking—In some introductory psychology classes, it will be possible to take class notes directly in the Flash Summary component of a chapter or section. These components include definitions, explanations, information about important individuals in the field, and examples. Use the margins to add concepts and examples.

✓ Study habits—The Flash Summary components are a useful study tool. If you take class notes in a separate notebook, compare your lecture notes to the information provided in Flash Summary.

✓ Test preparation—The Flash Summary sections provide basic information that you will need in preparing for exams.

Flash Review

✓ Study habits—The Flash Review sections provide exercises or applications that will help you to review key concepts or provide additional information or examples.

Flash Test

✓ Test preparation—The practice test in the Flash Test component is an excellent resource for preparing for exams. Since different instructors may ask that you demonstrate your knowledge in different ways on exams, the practice test includes both multiple-choice and essay questions. Detailed explanations of the correct answers, called Answer Explanations, are provided following the test. For any questions you miss, be sure to review the explanation carefully and reread the appropriate portion of the section to which the question applies. If you still do not understand the correct answer, review the concept in your text and/or ask your instructor for assistance.

Mapping *Flash Review for Psychology* to Introductory Psychology Texts

A table which maps the chapters and/or sections contained in *Flash Review for Psychology* to the analogous sections of six commonly used introductory statistics texts is provided on the next pages. The textbooks are listed in the table by author.

Baron, R. A. 2001. *Psychology.* 5th ed. Boston: Allyn and Bacon.

Lefton, L. A. 2000. *Psychology.* 7th ed. Boston: Allyn and Bacon.

Wood, S. E., and Wood, E. G. 2002. *The World of Psychology.* 4th ed. Boston: Allyn and Bacon.

Coon, D. 2001. *Introduction to Psychology: Gateways to Mind and Behavior.* 9th ed. Stamford, CT: Wadsworth.

Davis, S. F., and Palladino, J. J. 2002. *Psychology—Media and Research Update.* 3rd ed. New Jersey: Prentice Hall.

Gray, P. O. 2002. *Psychology.* 4th ed. New York: Worth Publishers.

Flash Review for Psychology	**Baron (2001)**	**Lefton (2000)**	**Wood and Wood (2002)**	**Coon (2001)**	**Davis and Palladino (2002)**	**Gray (2002)**
Unit I: The Study of Psychology						Part I: Background to the Study of Psychology
Chapter 1: Psychology and Psychological Research	Chapter 1: Psychology: A Science . . . and a Perspective	Chapter 1: What Is Psychology?	Chapter 1: Introduction to Psychology	Chapter 1: Psychology: The Search for Understanding	Chapter 1: Psychology, Research, and You	Chapter 1: The History and Scope of Psychology

				Chapter 2: Research Methods and Critical Thinking		Chapter 2: Methods of Psychology
Chapter 2: Biology and Psychology	Chapter 2: Biological Bases of Behavior	Chapter 2: The Brain and Behavior	Chapter 2: Biology and Behavior	Chapter 3: The Brain, Biology, and Behavior	Chapter 2: Biological Foundations of Psychology	Chapter 3: Genetic and Evolutionary Foundations of Behavior; Chapter 5: The Nervous System
Unit II: Basic Psychological Processes						Part II: The Adaptiveness of Behavior; Part III: Physiological Mechanisms of Behavior; Part IV: Sensation and Perception
Chapter 3: Sensation and Perception	Chapter 3: Sensation and Perception Making Contact with the World Around Us	Chapter 3: Sensation and Perception	Chapter 3: Sensation and Perception	Chapter 6: Sensation and Reality; Chapter 7: Perceiving the World	Chapter 3: Sensation and Perception	Chapter 7: Overview of Sensory Processes; Chapter 8: Vision
Chapter 4: States of Consciousness	Chapter 4: States of Consciousness	Chapter 4: Consciousness	Chapter 4: States of Consciousness	Chapter 8: States of Consciousness	Chapter 5: States of Consciousness	Chapter 6: Mechanisms of Motivation, Sleep, and Emotion; Chapter 9: Memory and Consciousness

Chapter 5: Learning and Memory	Chapter 5: Learning: How We're Changed by Experience; Chapter 6: Memory: Of Things Remembered . . . and Forgotten	Chapter 5: Learning; Chapter 6: Memory	Chapter 5: Learning; Chapter 6: Memory	Chapter 9: Conditioning and Learning; Chapter 10: Memory	Chapter 6: Basic Principles of Learning; Chapter 7: Memory	Chapter 4: Basic Processes of Learning; Chapter 9: Memory and Conciousness
Chapter 6: Language and Thought	Chapter 7: Cognition: Thinking, Deciding, Communicating	Chapter 7: Cognition: Thought and Language	Chapter 7: Cognition and Language	Chapter 11: Cognition, Language, and Creativity	Chapter 8: Thinking and Intelligence	Chapter 11: The Development of Thought and Language
Chapter 7: Motivation and Emotion	Chapter 10: Motivation and Emotion	Chapter 9: Motivation and Emotion	Chapter 11: Motivation and Emotion	Chapter 13: Motivation and Emotion	Chapter 4: Motivation and Emotion	Chapter 6: Mechanisms of Motivation, Sleep, and Emotion
Unit III: Human Development						Part VI: Growth of the Mind and Person
Chapter 8: Human Development	Chapter 8: Human Development I: The Childhood Years; Chapter 9: Human Development II: Adolescence, Adulthood, and Aging	Chapter 10: Child Development; Chapter 11: Adolescence and Adulthood	Chapter 9: Child Development; Chapter 10: Adolescence and Adulthood	Chapter 4: Child Development; Chapter 5: From Birth to Death: Life-Span Development; Chapter 14: Gender and Sexuality	Chapter 9: Developmental Psychology I: Conception through Childhood; Chapter 10: Developmental Psychology II: Adolescence through Old Age; Chapter 11:Sex and Gender	Chapter 12: Social Development

Chapter 9: Personality	Chapter 12: Personality: Uniqueness and Consistency in the Behavior of Individuals	Chapter 12: Personality and Its Assessment	Chapter 14: Personality Theory and Assessment	Chapter 15: Personality	Chapter 12: Personality	Chapter 15: Personality
Chapter 10: Intelligence, Intelligence Testing, and Creativity	Chapter 11: Intelligence: Cognitive, Practical, Emotional	Chapter 8: Intelligence	Chapter 8: Intelligence and Creativity	Chapter 11: Cognition, Language, and Creativity; Chapter 12: Intelligence	Chapter 8: Thinking and Intelligence	Chapter 10: Intelligence and Reasoning
Unit IV: Variations on Normal Functioning						Part VIII: Personality and Disorders
Chapter 11: Stress, Coping, and Health	Chapter 13: Health, Stress, and Coping	Chapter 14: Stress and Health Psychology	Chapter 13: Health and Stress	Chapter 16: Health, Stress, and Coping	Chapter 15: Health Psychology	
Chapter 12: Psychological Disorders	Chapter 14: Mental Disorders: Their Nature and Causes	Chapter 15: Psychological Disorders	Chapter 15: Psychological Disorders	Chapter 17: Psychological Disorders	Chapter 13: Psychological Disorders	Chapter 16: Mental Disorders
Chapter 13: Therapies for Treating Mental Disorders	Chapter 15: Therapies: Techniques for Alleviating Mental Disorders	Chapter 16: Therapy	Chapter 16: Therapies	Chapter 18: Therapies	Chapter 14: Therapy	Chapter 17: Treatment
Unit V: Interacting with Others						Part VII: The Person in a World of People
Chapter 14: Social Psychology	Chapter 16: Social Thought and Social Behavior	Chapter 17: Applied Psychology	Chapter 17: Social Psychology	Chapter 19: Social Behavior; Chapter 20: Attitudes, Culture, and Human Relations	Chapter 16: Social Psychology: The Individual in Society; Chapter 17: Industrial and Organizational Psychology	Chapter 13: Social Perception and Attitudes; Chapter 14: Social Influences on Behavior

Good luck with your course, and remember to enjoy the journey!

PSYCHOLOGY AS A FIELD OF STUDY

Overview of Psychology as a Field of Study

Psychology is the scientific study of **human behavior and cognitive processes.** Psychologists study a very broad field that is concerned with such topics as sensation and perception, memory, learning, consciousness, stages of the human life cycle, personality, intelligence, health, mental disorders and their treatment, and more.

The scientific discipline of psychology is descended from the disciplines of philosophy and physiology. In philosophy, philosophers attempted to pose some "ultimate" questions about the meaning of life, but they also tried to answer questions about the human mind: How do we perceive the world around us? What is involved in the process of thinking, or in self-awareness? How do we learn, and how does memory work? In the discipline of physiology, scientists were constructing a model of the human body and its functions, including the nervous system and the brain. Physiologists like **Johannes Muller** and **Hermann von Helmholtz** showed how the senses operated to transmit sensations to the brain. The birth of the modern discipline of psychology is usually given as 1879, the year in which **Wilhelm Wundt** founded the first formal research laboratory in psychology at the University of Leipzig.

Thinking Like a Psychologist

Psychologists find the study of human behavior and mental processes fascinating and exciting. Psychologists are investigators, who carefully and systematically attempt to discover the underpinnings of human behavior and mental processes. Psychology is increasingly becoming a biological science, and is more and more interdisciplinary.

Developing good critical thinking skills is important in thinking like a psychologist and being a wise consumer of information from a variety of sources. **Critical thinking** enables you to:

✓ Identify and challenge commonly held assumptions.

✓ Receive content from popular media with more insight.

✓ Evaluate the adequacy and accuracy of evidence used to support an argument.

✓ Reach well-reasoned conclusions and make appropriate generalizations.

✓ Grasp the complexity of causal relationships.

✓ Recognize the implications and applications of psychological theory and research.

✓ Develop metacognitive skills (thinking about thinking as a problem-solving process).

✓ Apply psychological knowledge and thinking skills to advantage in everyday life.

✓ Apply psychological knowledge and thinking skills to current issues and social problems.

"Pure" or basic psychologists tend to focus on psychological research for its own sake. **Applied psychology** focuses on the application of theory and research to practical areas such as health and medical care, education, the organization or workplace, and the improvement or implementation of mental health in clinics, hospitals, and other settings.

Doing Research in Psychology

Psychologists utilize the scientific method in a search for understandings about behavior and thought processes. The **scientific method** entails utilization of three basic principles:

✓ **Objectivity**—Objectivity is the principle of evaluating research results without preconceived ideas. Psychologists do not rely on anecdotal evidence of behavior or thought processes; they attempt to develop research findings that will enable them to both describe and predict aspects of behavior.

✓ **Accuracy**—Psychologists learn to gather data in precise, accurate ways. Rather than relying on limited data samples or questionable methods, as scientists, psychologists base their analyses on thorough, detailed, and accurate studies.

✓ **Skepticism**—When they learn of a reported "miracle cure" or strange phenomena, psychologists, like other scientists, retain a healthy skepticism. Psychologists are interested in data that can be verified and research results that can be reproduced.

The **scientific method** in psychology, as in many other disciplines, consists of a number of steps:

1. **State the problem.** The problem must be stated in such a way that it can be investigated.

2. **Develop a hypothesis.** A **hypothesis** is a tentative statement or idea expressing a causal relationship between two events or variables that can then be evaluated in a research study.

3. **Design the study.** The study must be designed in such a way that the results will be consistent, accurate, statistically meaningful, and repeatable by other scientists.

4. **Collect and analyze the data.** Data obtained through experimentation must be organized, coded, and evaluated in such a way that conclusions can be drawn.

5. **Replicate the results.** It is important that a particular experiment can be reproduced, either by the same group of psychologists or by others; the results must be shown to be reliable and repeatable.

6. **Draw conclusions and report results.** Psychologists must be careful to limit their conclusions to only what has been proved by their research; they can also begin to relate their results to those of other studies. At the conclusion of this process, psychologists report their results to the scientific community by publishing them in a reputable journal or other scientific arena.

Conducting a primary or secondary psychological research project on your campus might be an assignment in the course you are taking.

✓ See Chapter 1 for more information on designing a research project.

✓ Check out your library's holdings psychology and any special collections. What sources on theory and research in psychology are available to you on campus?

✓ Survey any books your instructor has placed on reserve for the course.

✓ For information on doing online research in psychology, see the section Psychology Wired.

Core Concepts in Psychology

Core Concepts in Psychology as a Field of Study includes the important ideas and key terms bold faced in this Introduction, Psychology as a Field of Study, and in each chapter of this book. The following table identifies the important ideas and Core Concepts in this section. Use a highlighter to identify terms and concepts your instructor chooses to emphasize, and add terms to the chart as needed.

Core Concepts in Psychology as a Field of Study

Important Ideas	Key Terms	Important People
Psychology	Objectivity	Johannes Muller
Human behavior	Accuracy	Hermann von Helmholtz
Cognitive processes	Skepticism	Wilhelm Wundt
Critical thinking	Hypothesis	
Applied psychology	Theory	
Scientific method	Data	
	Replication	
	Variables	

PSYCHOLOGY WIRED

Researching Online

Online research in psychology calls for you to evaluate the sources of your information. Here are some guidelines for the questions you should ask.

✓ Is the information really relevant to your research question or project?

✓ Do you think it meets the same basic standards of authenticity and reliability of a college library?

✓ Is the information complete and accurate, including supporting documents, figures, or tables?

✓ Who is the author? Does the author have academic or professional affiliations?

✓ Is enough information given about the author to determine if the material is authoritative?

✓ Is there a link to the author's homepage or is e-mail contact information provided?

✓ Who is the sponsor of the resource or site? Is it an academic institution? A business? A government agency? Sponsorship affects content.

✓ Who is the intended audience for this side? Audience affects content.

✓ What is the purpose of the site? To inform? To argue a point of view? To solicit business or charity? Purpose affects content.

✓ How comprehensive is the site? Is it regularly updated?

✓ How are sources on the site documented? Is documentation thorough?

✓ On what basis are links selected? Are links up to date?

✓ Are articles reviewed by peers? By users?

✓ Is the site easy to navigate and use?

✓ Does the site follow good basic principles of composition and design?

✓ What is the relative value of the online resource compared to other information resources on your topic that are available to you? Would a print resource be better?

For additional information on **Evaluating Sources** for online research, check out the Using Cyber-sources Web Site at http://www.devry-phx.edu/lrnresrc/dowsc/integrty.htm and the Argus Clearinghouse at http://www.clearinghouse.net.

To do key word searches on your research subject or topic, use **Subject Directory Indexes,** often found on Search Engine homepages, such as The Internet Public Library at http://www.ipl.org/, the Librarian's Index to the Internet at http://www.lii.org/, and the WWW Virtual Library at http://www.vlib.org and Yahoo at http://www.yahoo.com.

Try **Search Engines** such as AltaVista http://www.altavista.com/, Google http://www.google.com/, Infoseek http://www.infoseek.go.com/, Lycos http://lycos.com/, and several others. Each search engine has particular features that may appeal to you. In AltaVista, for instance, you can find out all the sites that are linked to a particular site you are interested in by using the Link Command. Type link:http:/ and add the URL of the site you're in and click on the search button.

Use **Online Reference Materials.** For example, visit the Library of Congress at http://lc.Web.loc.gov/ and search *Encarta,* http://encarta.msn.com/, or *Encyclopedia Britannica,* http://www.britannica.com/. Use an information clearinghouse for college students, such as CRESCA, http://www.cresca.com/, which provides in one place a rich collection of for-free and by-subscription services, including direct academic support, an encyclopedia, a dictionary, a world atlas, almanacs, and a searchable research library in your subject.

Survey **Online News Sites and Services,** such as *CNN Digest,* http://cnn.com/DIGEST; *Jerusalem Post,* http://www.jpost.co.il; *Mojo Wire* (Mother Jones Interactive), http://www.mojones.com; *National Public Radio Online,* http://www.npr.org; *NY Times* Fax (subscription needed), http://nytimesfax.com; *Public Broadcasting System* (PBS) Online, http://www.pbs.org; *Seattle Times,* http://www.seatimes.com; *the Times and the Sunday Times,* http://www.the-times.co.uk/news/pages/home. html?000999; *USA Today,* http://www.usatoday.com; *ABC News,* http://www.abcnews.com/; *MSNBC,* http://msnbc.com; *Time Magazine,* http://pathfinder.com/time/; and *Washington Post,* http://www.washingtonpost.com/.

Explore the features and functionalities of the Internet and World Wide Web as possible resources for **Your Research Project in Psychology.** In each case note how you might use the type of resource to conduct research or gather information. For instance, would you help your project by administering a questionnaire online? Use this chart to record your discoveries and strategies for researching online. For more information on the types of resources the Internet and World Wide Web have to offer, see *Learn the Net,* http://www.learnthenet.com, and the *HTML Reference Manual,* http://www.sandia.gov/sci_compute/html_ref.html.

Research or Term Paper Topic:

Working Thesis Statement:

Internet or WWW Resource	Possible Use in Your Term Paper/Research Project
WWW search capabilities	
E-mail	
Listservs	
Chat room message boards	
Internet relay chats	
Multiuser virtual environments	
WWW news sites	
WWW reference sites (online dictionaries, encyclopedias, libraries)	
Online information clearinghouses	
Online audio and video	
Newsgroups	
Creating a web page or publishing your own documents on the web	

FLASH LINKS FOR PSYCHOLOGY

To help you get started on your research paper, here are some general online resources for psychology, some research sites in the social sciences, and some sources of psychological data. Use links at these sites to find further information and bookmark or record your finds. Keep in mind that URLs frequently change or disappear. If you can't find a site, use a search engine to look for it by name.

General Resources for Psychology

American Psychological Association, www.apa.org/

American Psychological Society, www.hanover.edu/psych/APS/aps.html

Society for Neuroscience, www.sfn.org

The Federation of Behavioral, Psychological, and Cognitive Sciences, www.am.org/federation/

The National Honor Society in Psychology, www.psichi.org/intro.asp

Canadian Psychological Association, www.cpa.ca/

British Psychological Society, www.bps.org.uk/index.cfm

Psychology site from the United Kingdom: www.psychnet-uk.com/

Australian Psychological Society, www.psichi.org/intro.asp

International Mental Health Site, www.mentalhealth.com

Encyclopedia of Psychology: www.psychology.org/

World Lecture Hall, www.utexas.edu/world/lecture/

Psychology Central: www.psychcentral.com/

Mental Health Net: http://mentalhelp.net/

WWW Virtual Library: U.S. Government Information Sources, http://iridium.nttc.edu/gov_res.html

Psychwatch, www.psychwatch.com/index.htm

Real Psychology, www.realpsychology.com/

CogPrints, http://cogprints.soton.ac.uk/view-psyc.html

Psychology Departments on the Web, www.psychwww.com/resource/deptlist.htm

Tools for Research in Psychology

Glossary of Online Psychological/Psychiatric Terms, www.priory.com/gloss.htm

Ejournal Links to Electronic Journals, www.edoc.com/ejournal

Psychological Research on the Net, http://psych.hanover.edu/APS/exponent.html

American Statistical Index, www.fedstats.gov

Bureau of Census Reports, www.census.gov

Statistical Resources on the Web, www.lib.umich.edu/libhome/documents.center/stats.html

Statistic Glossary, www.cas.lancs.ac.uk/glossary_v1.1/main.html

National Center for Health Statistics, www.cdc.gov/nchs/default.htm

Research Resources for the Social Sciences, www.socsciresearch.com

Research Methods, www.siu.edu/~hawkes/methods.html

Research Engines for Social Sciences, www.carleton.ca/~cmckie/research.html

Internet Research Journal, www.mcb.co.uk/cgi-bin/journal3/intr

Steele's Quantitative and Qualitative Tool Shed, www.clark.net/pub/ssteele/home.htm

Experimental Psychology, www.york.ac.uk/depts./psych/www/etc/whatispsych.html

Ethics in Research, http://methods.fullerton.edu/chapter3.html

Applied Ethics Resources on WWW, www.ethics.ubc.ca/papers/AppliedEthics.html

Institute for Global Ethics, www.globalethics.org/

Psychological Databases and Statistics

CyberPsychLink, http://cctr.umkc.edu/user/dmartin/psych2.html

Brief History of Web Experimenting: www.psychologie.uni-bonn.de/sozial/birnbaum.html

Cogprints: http://cogprints.soton.ac.uk/view-psyc.html

Zeus: Eurobarometer, http:/zeus.mzes.uni-mannheim.de/datasets

Service-Learning Resources

Does your college encourage service learning? Consider looking for a way to integrate a service-learning experience or perspective into the research or term paper requirements for your introduction to psychology course. Following are some links sites to help you explore the possibility of whether service learning is appropriate for your situation.

National Service-Learning Clearinghouse
http://www.etr.org/NSRC/newsletter.html

Service-Learning Links Pages
http://www.med.wright.edu/som/comminv/CHC/sllink.html
http://www.csusm.edu/ocsl/links.htm
http://www.serviceleader.org/manage/servicel.html
http://www.cns.gov/resources/links.html

Links and Guide to College and University Service-Learning Programs
http://csf.colorado.edu/sl/academic.html
http://www.upenn.edu/civichouse/other_campuses.html

Tips on Reading Electronic Sources

✓ Pay attention to sound, graphics, and animation as well as words; however, if you are distracted by them, check to see if a text-only version of the site is available.

✓ Note if information is chunked in screen-sized areas intended to stand alone. If you need background information or a context for reading, screen-size-based electronic information may not be the best choice.

✓ Note if information appears as a group of topic sentences without details. If to make sense of information you need a traditional organization of a topic sentence or main idea followed by supporting details, electronic information may not be the best choice.

✓ Apply different reading strategies that are multidirectional rather than lineal. When reading web sites you essentially are creating your own text through your choices of what to look at and what to ignore. Electronic sources are great for exploration, but not necessarily the best for exposition.

✓ If you are distracted by the need to be making choices and sacrifices constantly as you navigate the site, a printed text might be a better source for you.

✓ Because of the flexibility of working with online resources, you can decide how you want to learn. You may want to work systematically one step at a time by clicking through a menu in sequence, or you may want to go directly to supporting examples or start by taking the test! Take advantage of this flexibility to develop your own strategies for learning online.

✓ When working online, stay focused on your purpose. Familiarize yourself with the site's design and layout and how the information is organized.

✓ Take the time to learn the symbol systems, abbreviations, conventions, and navigation tricks, such as searches and site maps, that are part of an online learner's tool kit.

✓ Bookmark both the original site and the links that you find useful. If you get lost, use the "Back" feature on browsers to trace the history of your search. Print out and read long documents offline.

Documenting Online Sources

A journal article exists, either in print or on microfilm, virtually forever. A document on the Internet can come, go, and change without warning. Because the purpose of citing sources is to allow another scholar to retrace your argument, a good citation allows a reader to obtain information from your primary sources, to the extent possible. This means you need to include not only information on when a source was posted on the Internet (if available) but also when you obtained the information.

The two arbiters of form for academic and scholarly writing are the Modern Language Association (MLA) and the American Psychological Association (APA); both organizations have established styles for citing electronic publications. Style guides for citing both print and nonprint sources are available online at the following sites:

Modern Language Association, http://www.mla.org/set_stl.htm

American Psychological Association, http://www.apa.org

Columbia Online Style Web Site, http://www.columbia.edu/cu/cup/cgos/

MLA Style

In the fifth edition of the *MLA Handbook for Writers of Research Papers,* the MLA recommends the following formats:

URLs. URLs are enclosed in angle brackets (<>) and contain the access mode identifier, the formal name for such indicators as "http" or "ftp." If a URL must be split across two lines, break it only after a slash (/). Never introduce a hyphen at the end of the first line. The URL should include all the parts necessary to identify uniquely the file/document being cited.

<http://www.csun.edu/~rtvfdept/home/index.html>

An online scholarly project or reference database. A complete online reference contains the title of the project or database (underlined); the name of the editor of the project or database (if given); electronic publication information, including version number (if relevant and if not part of the title); date of electronic publication or latest update; name of any sponsoring institution or organization; date of access; and electronic address.

The Perseus Project. Ed. Gregory R. Crane. Mar. 1997. Dept. of Classics, Tufts U. 15 June 1998 <http://www.perseus.tufts.edu/>.

If you cannot find some of the information, then include the information that is available. The MLA also recommends that you print or download electronic documents, freezing them in time for future reference.

A document within a scholarly project or reference database. It is much more common to use only a portion of a scholarly project or database. To cite an essay, poem, or other short work, begin this citation with the name of the author and the title of the work (in quotation marks). Then include all the information used when citing a complete online scholarly project or reference database; however, use the URL of the specific work and not the address of the general site.

Cuthbert, Lori. "Moonwalk: Earthlings' Finest Hour." Discovery Channel Online. 1999. Discovery Channel. 25 Nov. 1999. <http://www.discovery.com/indep/ newsfeatures/moonwalk/challenge.html>.

A professional or personal site. Include the name of the person creating the site (reversed), followed by a period, the title of the site (underlined), or, if there is no title, a description such as *Home page.* (Such a description is neither placed in quotes nor underlined.) Specify the name of any school, organization, or other institution affiliated with the site, and follow it with your date of access and the URL of the page.

Packer, Andy. Home page. 1 Apr. 1998. <http://www.suu.edu/~students/packer.htm>.

Some electronic references are truly unique to the online domain. These include e-mail, newsgroup postings, MUDs (multiuser domains) or MOOs (multiuser domains, object oriented), and IRCs (Internet Relay Chats).

E-mail. In citing e-mail messages, begin with the writer's name (reversed) followed by a period, then the title of the message (if any) in quotations as it appears in the subject line. Next comes a description of the message, typically "E-mail to," and the recipient (e.g., "the author"), and finally the date of the message.

Davis, Jeffrey. "Web Writing Resources." E-mail to Nora Davis. 5 July 2000.

Sommers, Laurice. "Re: College Admissions Practices." E-mail to the author. 12 August 2000.

List servers and newsgroups. In citing these references, begin with the author's name (reversed) followed by a period. Next include the title of the document (in quotes) from the subject line, followed by the words "Online posting" (not in quotes). Follow this with the date of posting. For list servers, include the date of access, the name of the list (if known), and the online address of the list's moderator or administrator. For newsgroups, follow "Online posting" with the date of posting, the date of access, and the name of the newsgroup, prefixed with news; enclose in angle brackets.

Applebaum, Dale. "Educational Variables." Online posting. 29 Jan. 1998. Higher Education Discussion Group. 30 January 1993 <jlucidoj@unc.edu>.

Gostl, Jack. "Re: Mr. Levitan." Online posting. 13 June 1997. 20 June 1997. <news:alt.edu.bronxscience>.

MUDs, MOOs, and IRCs. Citations for these online sources take the form of the name of the speaker(s) followed by a period. Then comes the description and date of the event, the name of the forum, the date of access, and the online address prefixed by "telnet://".

Guest. Personal interview. 13 August 1999 <telnet//du.edu 8888>.

APA Style

The *Publication Manual of the American Psychological Association* (Fourth Edition) is fairly dated in its handling of online sources, because it was published before the rise of the WWW and the generally recognized format for URLs. The format that follows is based on the APA manual, with modifications. It is important to remember that, unlike the MLA, the APA does not include temporary or transient sources (e.g., letters, phone calls, etc.) in its "References" page, preferring to handle them as in-text citations exclusively. This rule holds for electronic sources as well: e-mail, MOOs/MUDs, list server postings, etc. are not included in the "References" page, merely cited in text; for example, "But Wilson has rescinded his earlier support for these policies" (Charles Wilson, personal e-mail to the author, 20 November 1996). But also note that many list server and Usenet groups and MOOs actually archive their correspondences, so that there is a permanent site (usually a Gopher or FTP server) where those documents reside. In that case, you would want to find the archive and cite it as an unchanging source. Strictly speaking, according to the APA manual, a file from an FTP site should be referenced as follows:

Deutsch, P. (1991). "Archie—An electronic directory service for the Internet" [Online]. Available FTP: ftp.sura.net Directory: pub/archie/docs File: whatis.archie.

However, the increasing familiarity of Net users with the convention of a URL makes the prose description of how to find a file ("Available FTP: ftp.sura.net Directory: pub/archie/docs File: whatis.archie") unnecessary. Thus, modification of the APA format, citations from the standard Internet sources, would appear as follows.

FTP (File Transfer Protocol) Sites. To cite files available for downloading via FTP, give the author's name (if known), the publication date (if available and if different from the date accessed), the full title of the paper (capitalizing only the first word and proper nouns), the address of the FTP site along with the full path necessary to access the file.

Deutsch, P. (1991) "Archie—An electronic directory service for the Internet." [Online]. Available: ftp://ftp.sura.net/pub/archie/docs/whatis.archie.

WWW Sites (World Wide Web). To cite files available for viewing or downloading via the World Wide Web, give the author's name (if known), the year of publication (if known and if different from the date accessed), the full title of the article, and the title of the complete work (if applicable) in italics. Include any additional information (such as versions, editions, or revisions) in parentheses immediately following the title. Include the full URL (the http address) and the date of visit.

Burka, L. P. (1993). A hypertext history of multi-user dungeons. MUDdex. Retrieved January 13, 1997, from the World Wide Web: http://www.utopia.com/talent/lpb/muddex/essay/.

Tilton, J. (1995). Composing good HTML (Vers. 2.0.6). Retrieved December 1, 1996, from the World Wide Web: http://www.cs.cmu.edu/~tilt/cgh/.

Synchronous Communications (MOOs, MUDs, IRC, etc.). Give the name of the speaker(s), the complete date of the conversation being referenced in parentheses (if different from the date accessed), and the title of the session (if applicable). Next, list the title of the site in italics, the protocol and address (if applicable), and any directions necessary to access the work. Last, list the date of access, followed by the retrieval information. Personal interviews do not need to be listed in the References, but do need to be included in parenthetic references in the text (see the *APA Publication Manual*).

Cross, J. (1996, February 27). Netoric's Tuesday cafe: Why use MUDs in the writing classroom? MediaMoo. Retrieved March 1, 1996, from File Transfer Protocol: ftp://daedalus.com/ pub/ACW/NETORIC/catalog.

Gopher Sites. List the author's name (if applicable), the year of publication (if known and if different from the date accessed), the title of the file or paper, and the title of the complete work (if applicable). Include any print publication information (if available) followed by the protocol (i.e., gopher://) and the path necessary to access the file. List the date that the file was accessed in parentheses immediately following the path.

Massachusetts Higher Education Coordinating Council. (1994) Using coordination and collaboration to address change. Retrieved July 16, 1999, from the World Wide Web: gopher://gopher.mass.edu:170/00gopher_root%3A%5B_hecc%5D_plan.

E-mail, Listservs, and Newsgroups. Do not include personal e-mail in the list of References. Although unretrievable communication such as e-mail is not included in APA References, somewhat more public or accessible Internet postings from newsgroups or listservs may be included. See the *APA Publication Manual* for information on in-text citations.

Bruckman, A. S. MOOSE crossing proposal. mediamoo@media.mit.edu (20 Dec. 1994).

Heilke, J. (1996, May 3). Webfolios. Alliance for Computers and Writing Discussion List. Retrieved December 31, 1996, from the World Wide Web: http://www.ttu.edu/lists/acw-1/9605/0040.html

Other authors and educators have proposed similar extensions to the APA style, too. You can find URLs to these pages at www.psychwww.com/resource/apacrib.htm and www.uvm.edu/~ncrane/estyles/apa.htm.

Remember, "frequently referenced" does not equate to "correct" or even "desirable." Check with your professor to see if your course or school has a preference for an extended APA style.

UNIT I: THE STUDY OF PSYCHOLOGY

CHAPTER 1—PSYCHOLOGY AND PSYCHOLOGICAL RESEARCH

 FLASH FOCUS

When you complete this chapter, you will be able to:

✓ Define psychology, and describe the major movements or schools of thought that have developed in the history of the discipline

✓ Describe the scientific method and how it is applied in the field of psychology

✓ Compare and contrast some of the varying research methods used in psychology

✓ Discuss some major ethical issues in psychological research and how they have been addressed by the American Psychological Association

✓ Define multiculturalism, and describe how this perspective, as well as new scientific considerations, is currently influencing the discipline of psychology

Review the Core Concepts in Psychology as a Field of Study in the Introduction to this book. Chapter 1 includes those core concepts, in addition to the ones listed in the following chart. Use a highlighter to identify ideas, terms, and people that your instructor refers to in lectures or emphasizes in the course. Add to the charts any other ideas, terms, or people that your instructor discusses.

Core Concepts in "Psychology and Psychological Research"

Important Ideas	Key Concepts	Important People
Psychology	Introspection	Wilhelm Wundt
Physiology	Structuralism	Ernst Weber
Scientific method/	Functionalism	Gustav Fechner
Experimental method	Evolution	Hermann von Helmholtz
American Psychological	Gestalt Psychology	Edward Bradford Titchener
Association (APA)	Behaviorism	Charles Darwin
	Psychoanalysis	William James
	Neo-Freudians	Max Wertheimer
	Humanistic psychology	Kurt Koffka
	Cognitive psychology	Wolfgang Kohler
	Descriptive research	John B. Watson
	Experimental/scientific	Ivan Pavlov
	Method	B. F. Skinner
	Naturalistic observations	Sigmund Freud
	Case study	Carl Jung
	Survey research	Alfred Adler
	Representative sample	Karen Horney
	Correlational studies	Abraham Maslow

	Experiments Hypothesis Theory Variables Independent variable Dependent variable Experimental group Control group Reliability Random assignment Single-blind Double-blind Placebo Single-subject research Case study Retrospective study Informed consent Confidentiality Debriefing Diversity Multicultural perspective Evolutionary psychology Neuroscience Clinical psychologists Counseling psychologists Physiological psychologists Experimental psychologists Developmental Psychologists Educational psychologists Social psychologists Industrial/organizational Psychologists		Noam Chomsky

The Development of Psychology

FLASH SUMMARY

Psychology is the discipline that studies both behavior and mental processes; in other words, psychologists attempt to understand how human beings think, feel, and why they behave in certain ways. Psychology is a relatively recent science that developed from roots in both *philosophy*, the search for basic truths and principles about the universe, and *physiology*, the study of the bodies of living organisms. *Wilhelm Wundt* (1832–1920) is generally considered the "father of psychology." His establishment of a psychological laboratory at the University of Leipzig in Germany in 1879 is considered the beginning of psychology as an academic discipline. Wundt and his followers studied the elements of consciousness by the process of *introspection*, or self-examination, of their own conscious processes.

Other German physiologists, *Ernst Weber*, *Gustav Fechner*, and *Hermann von Helmholtz*, were also pioneers in the application of experimental methods to the study of psychological processes. One of Wundt's students, *Edward Bradford Titchener*, brought the new field of science to the United States, where he set up a laboratory at Cornell University. He developed a method of analysis that he termed *structuralism*, since it was aimed at analyzing the basic structure of consciousness.

Another school of thought that developed in the United States was termed *functionalism*, since it was concerned with how mental processes function, that is, how they are used by both humans and animals to adapt to their environments. This school was very much influenced by the work of *Charles Darwin* and his theories of the *evolution* of species. The well-known American writer and psychologist *William James* was a proponent of functionalism; his textbook, *Principles of Psychology,* was published in 1890.

In 1912, the field of *gestalt psychology* was developed in Germany by psychologists who included *Max Wertheimer, Kurt Koffka,* and *Wolfgang Kohler.* "Gestalt," a German word that means "whole" or "pattern," refers to humans' tendency to see objects as patterns or whole units.

A later psychologist, *John B. Watson,* could not accept either the structuralist or the functionalist perspective; he felt that the scientific method should be more rigorously applied to the processes of mental functioning. He proposed a new school, *behaviorism,* to study behavior as it could be observed and measured in a scientific, objective manner. *Ivan Pavlov* was a pioneer researcher in the field of behaviorism. Behaviorism, particularly under its proponent *B. F. Skinner,* became the prevalent school of thought in the United States through the 1960s.

In contrast to the behaviorists, *Sigmund Freud* emphasized the importance of unobservable, unconscious forces on behavior. Freud developed the process of *psychoanalysis* to attempt to bring these unconscious forces into the conscious mind. Student of Freud's, including *Carl Jung, Alfred Adler,* and *Karen Horney,* developed their own theories of personality that attracted a number of followers; collectively, they have been called *neo-Freudians.*

Humanistic psychology developed as a reaction to both behaviorism and psychoanalysis; humanistic psychology focuses on the uniqueness of human beings and their capacity for psychological growth and health. *Abraham Maslow* was one of the proponents of humanistic psychology. Beginning in the 1950s, *cognitive psychology,* which focuses on mental processes, was developed, influenced in part by linguist *Noam Chomsky.*

 ## FLASH REVIEW

Complete the following chart, including the proponents of each school of psychological thought, and write a sentence or two characterizing each perspective. Include any additional information or perspectives that your instructor emphasizes in your class.

Schools of Thought in Psychology

School	Proponent(s)	Key Features
Structuralism	E. B. Titchener	Goal of analyzing the basic elements, or structure, of conscious mental experience
Functionalism		

Gestalt		
Behaviorism		
Psychoanalysis		
Humanistic		
Cognitive		
Other		

Principles of Psychological Research

FLASH SUMMARY

Psychology employs the *scientific method,* or a set of rules that scientists observe in conducting research. The scientific method is intended to be objective, or free of bias, and to produce results that can be reproduced by other researchers. The two major types of scientific research are *descriptive research* methods and the *experimental* or *scientific method.* Descriptive research methods provide descriptions of behavior rather than explanations of the causes of behavior. Descriptive research includes *naturalistic observations,* or observations of people or animals in their natural environment; the *case study* method, in which one individual or a small group of individuals are studied over time; and *survey research.* Survey research can consist of interviews or questionnaires that are intended to gather information about the attitudes, beliefs, experiences, or behaviors of a group of people. In survey research, experimenters select a *representative sample* of the population they wish to investigate; *correlational studies,* or more formal measurements of events, characteristics, and behaviors; and *experiments,* or scientifically controlled observations.

The *experimental method* of psychological research generally consists of five different parts:

1. Identify the problem and formulate a hypothesis of cause-and-effect.
2. Design the experiment.
3. Perform the experiment.
4. Evaluate the hypothesis by examining the data from the experiment.
5. Communicate the results.

In an experiment, scientists attempt to prove or disprove a *hypothesis,* or statement about a possible cause-and-effect relationship between two or more events. The scientist may propose a *theory,* or set of statements designed to explain certain phenomena. Research is then constructed so that different *variables,* or factors, can be manipulated by the researcher. The *independent variable* is the element that is systematically changed by the researcher, while the *dependent variable* is the variable that is measured.

Subjects for the experiment are chosen to be part of either the *experimental group,* the group that will be exposed to a particular value assigned to the independent variable, or the *control group,* which will be exposed to a naturally occurring or zero-value–independent variable.

In performing an experiment, researchers are looking for high *reliability,* that is, consistency of results. Subjects for the experiment must be carefully selected and distributed between the two experimental groups, the experimental and the control group, by the method of *random assignment,* so that the researcher does not unintentionally build in a bias or prejudice.

Experiments may be organized as either *single-blind,* in which the experimenter but not the subject knows the value of the independent variable, or as *double-blind,* in which not even the experimenter knows the value of the independent variable. For example, if the experiment is organized to test the effectiveness of a certain drug, the control group will receive a *placebo,* or harmless substance, whereas the experimental group will receive the actual drug; if the experimenter does not know which group received the placebo, it is a double-blind study.

Ethics in Psychological Research

FLASH SUMMARY

Ethics are of concern in any research that is conducted on either human or animal subjects. The *American Psychological Association (APA)* has developed a set of guidelines for ethical research in psychology. These guidelines mandate that participants must give their *informed consent* to research before they participate in a study; this usually consists of providing a written statement about the research requirements, compensation, and any aspects of the research that would affect a subject's willingness to participate. The guidelines also specify that subjects should be provided *confidentiality,* or protection of their privacy; and they must receive a *debriefing,* or full disclosure of the nature and purpose of the experiment after its conclusion.

Research with animals is supposed to be justified as being both humane and worthwhile. Scientists justify research with animals as providing valuable insights into human health and behavior that could not be obtained in any other way. Animal rights activists point out that animals are sentient beings with their own thoughts and feelings who should not be subjected to imprisonment, pain, suffering, and finally death at the hands of researchers.

Issues in Modern Psychology

FLASH SUMMARY

Psychology through the 1960s included little consideration of or appreciation for *diversity*, or the spectrum of differences in individuals from different cultural or ethnic groups, or of different sexes. Today, psychologists adopt a *multicultural perspective* that evaluates and appreciates the value of these differences. The American Psychological Association's guidelines now mandate that psychologists recognize cultural diversity and take it into account in their activities. For example, to many early psychologists, men were considered "normal," and women were considered "abnormal," or less than equal, where their behaviors or attitudes differed from those of male subjects. Also, women were often not included in studies at all, and generalizations about both sexes were made from studies of male subjects.

A new branch of psychology that has recently developed is called *evolutionary psychology*. This study suggests that evolutionary traits evolved to help human beings survive in their environment, and that these surviving traits may now either help or hinder our lives in modern society. A new interdisciplinary field that has influenced psychology is *neuroscience,* or the study of the structure and function of the nervous system. Neuroscience includes contributions from psychologists, biologists, biochemists, medical researchers, and others; it has been greatly aided by the development of new medical technologies such as brain scans.

Psychologists now work in many different areas of specialty; for example *clinical psychologists* diagnose and treat mental disorders; *counseling psychologists* help people with less severe adjustment problems; *physiological psychologists,* or neuropsychologists, study the relationship between physiological processes and behavior; *experimental psychologists* specialize in experimental research; *developmental psychologists* study the growth and development of human beings through the life cycle; *educational psychologists* study how people learn; *social psychologists* study individuals' interactions within social settings; and *industrial* or *organizational psychologists* study people's behavior in work environments.

FLASH LINK

All websites are not created equal; some sites provide scientific or credible information, while some dispense opinions and, in some cases, propaganda. It is important to develop a framework to evaluate the credibility of different sites. You may wish to review the Psychology Wired section of the Introduction to this manual.

As an exercise, visit two contrasting sites: first, the official site for the Center for Research on Concepts and Cognition, www.cogsci.indiana.edu/; and second, the site for the Thinking Page, www.thinking.net. Then record your observations in the following chart.

Evaluating a Website

URL: Who Owns the Site?	Observations
www.cogsci.indiana.edu	

FLASH TEST

Review the information in the preceding Core Concepts chart and in the Introduction to this guide. Then, take the Practice Test on the pages that follow, and rate your performance.

PRACTICE TEST

(Chapter 1—Psychology and Psychological Research)

Multiple Choice (3 points each)

1. What types of behaviors do psychologists study?
   a. strange behaviors
   b. unusual behaviors
   c. normal behaviors
   d. strange, unusual, and normal behaviors

2. Wilhelm Wundt asked trained participants to look inward to examine their own conscious experiences. This method used in the early days of psychology was called
   a. introspection.
   b. structuralism.
   c. mentalism.
   d. conscious observation.

3. John B. Watson and B. F. Skinner are associated with the period in psychology known as
   a. behaviorism.
   b. functionalism.
   c. structuralism.
   d. humanism.

4. If you were trained in this area of psychology, you would learn about unconscious motivations and the importance of early childhood experiences. This area is called _____ psychology.
   a. cognitive
   b. evolutionary
   c. sociocultural
   d. psychoanalytic

5. Who established the first psychological laboratory in 1879 in Leipzig, Germany?
   a. Ernst Weber
   b. William James
   c. Wilhelm Wundt
   d. Sigmund Freud

6. The major emphasis of psychoanalysis is
   a. the uniqueness of human beings and their capacity for conscious choice and growth.
   b. the perception of whole units or patterns.
   c. the scientific study of behavior.
   d. the unconscious.

7. Whereas structuralism focused on the basic elements of consciousness, Gestalt psychology focused on
   a. the basic elements of perception.
   b. the basic elements of personality and disorders.
   c. the whole person, including emotion and judgment.
   d. how whole patterns and forms are perceived.

8. A focus on brain structure, neurotransmitters, hormones, and genes marks the _____ perspective in psychology.
   a. biological
   b. behavioral
   c. cognitive
   d. evolutionary

9. Behavioral psychology is more _____ in its approach, while humanistic psychology is more _____.
   a. objective; subjective
   b. subjective; objective
   c. eclectic; pragmatic
   d. pragmatic; eclectic

10. The school of psychological thought emphasizing each person's unique individuality and our control over our own lives is
    a. humanistic psychology.
    b. Gestalt psychology.
    c. cognitive psychology.
    d. behavioral psychology.

11. Cognitive psychology was influenced by the work of
    a. psychoanalyst Sigmund Freud.
    b. linguist Noam Chomsky.
    c. behaviorist B. F. Skinner.
    d. neo-Freudian Carl Jung.

12. For a class project, Sheila is watching preschool children at play in a daycare setting. Sheila records the number of times the children share toys and the number of times they take toys from others. By collecting these data, Sheila is conducting a
    a. case study.
    b. survey study.
    c. laboratory study.
    d. naturalistic observation study.

13. The _____ variable is manipulated by the researcher to determine if it causes a change in behavior.
    a. control
    b. dependent
    c. independent
    d. confounding

14. In conducting a survey of the sexual behaviors of young adults, which sampling technique would be the most "scientific?"
    a. taking a random sample of 2,000 young adults
    b. polling 10,000 young adults who volunteer for the survey
    c. polling readers of magazines like *Playboy*
    d. polling college students at a nearby campus

15. Which of the following statements is *not* true about an experimental group?
    a. It should be similar to a control group.
    b. It is exposed to the independent variable.
    c. At the end of the experiment, it is measured on the dependent variable.
    d. It is exposed only to the dependent variable.

16. In medical or pharmaceutical tests, the control group receives a harmless substance called a(n)
    a. unknown substance.

    b. placebo.

    c. passive drug.

    d. vitamin.

17. Which of the following is *not* true about a control group?

    a. It should be similar to an experimental group.

    b. It is exposed to the treatment being tested.

    c. At the end of the experiment, it is measured on the dependent variable.

    d. It is used for purposes of comparison.

18. In an experiment on auto safety, researchers drove cars into a wall at 35 miles an hour and varied the angle at which they hit to see what effect the angle had on the "injuries" to the crash dummies. In this experiment, the angle of impact would be different levels of the _____ variable.

    a. confounded

    b. independent

    c. hypothetical

    d. dependent

19. Which of the following is an important weakness of questionnaires?

    a. strict limits on how much information can be collected

    b. the inability to measure relationships between variables

    c. difficulty in processing the amount of data received

    d. concerns that people might lie when answering questions

20. If a research participant is given full information before an experiment begins concerning what is going to happen, the procedure is called

    a. naturalistic observation.

    b. debriefing.

    c. deception.

    d. informed consent.

21. The most important thing to remember about diversity is that

    a. theories developed in different times are relevant today.

    b. the factors which apply to one group of people most likely apply to other groups with only minor modifications.

    c. individual behavior reflects common life experiences.

    d. there are usually more differences within a group than between groups.

22. The oldest and largest professional organization for psychologists is the

    a. Psychological Research Foundation (PRF).

    b. Behavioral Scientist's Club (BSC).

    c. Master Psychologist's Foundation (MPF).

    d. American Psychological Association (APA).

23. Which of the following individuals would most likely write a book entitled *How to Change Problem Behaviors and Improve Your Mental Functioning?*

    a. a psychiatrist

    b. a psychoanalyst

    c. a clinical psychologist

    d. a developmental psychologist

24. A psychologist who focuses on how to make machines easier for people to use is called a(n) _____ psychologist.

    a. medical

    b. engineering

    c. behavioral

    d. cognitive

25. The study of _____ psychology suggests that particular traits may help or hinder individuals in modern society.

    a. neuroscientific

    b. evolutionary

c. behavioral

  d. cognitive

Essay Questions (5 points each)

1. Describe some of the major developments in the history of psychology, and the proponents of those developments.

2. Name the two major types of psychological research, and describe the salient components of each type of research.

3. Discuss the major ethical concerns in conducting psychological research with both animal and human subjects. What are the main ethical guidelines for conducting psychological research?

4. Why are considerations of diversity important in psychology and in psychological research?

5. What are some examples of different occupations within the field of psychology?

ANSWER EXPLANATIONS

Multiple-Choice Questions

1. d

Psychologists study all types of behavior, including strange and unusual and also normal behavior; they are interested in how human beings think and feel, as well as how they behave.

2. a

Wilhelm Wundt pioneered the method of introspection; he and his followers studied the elements of consciousness by examining their own conscious processes via self-examination or introspection.

3. a

Watson and Skinner are associated with the behaviorist school of psychology, in that they were particularly interested in scientific observations of behaviors that could be measured. Another pioneer in behaviorist research was Ivan Pavlov.

4. d

The unconscious motivations of individuals is the focus of psychoanalytic psychology, which was pioneered by Sigmund Freud in Vienna. Freud developed the process of psychoanalysis in an attempt to help his patients bring their unconscious motivations into the conscious mind.

5. c

Wilhelm Wundt established the first psychological laboratory in Leipzig, Germany, in 1879; this event is considered the beginning of psychology as an academic discipline.

6. d

Psychoanalysis focuses on the unconscious, the vast store of impulses, thoughts, wishes, and desires that are hidden from conscious thought. Freud believed that individuals are, to a large extent, controlled by the thoughts, feelings, and behaviors that originate in the unconscious mind.

7. d

Gestalt psychology focuses on how whole patterns and forms are perceived. The word "gestalt" is a German word for "whole" or "pattern," and refers to the fact that humans tend to see objects as patterns or whole units. Gestalt psychology is particularly influential in the fields of perception and learning.

8. a

The biological perspective in psychology is prevalent today, in the advent of modern technologies that allow radically new perceptions of the brain and its functioning.

9. a

Behavioral psychology focuses on observable behaviors; it is objective in its approach, whereas humanistic psychology focuses on subjective areas of psychology, such as psychological growth and health.

10. a

Humanistic psychology is the school of psychology that, in reaction against behavioral and psychoanalytic approaches, focuses on the uniqueness of human beings and on their capacity for psychological growth and health.

11. b

Cognitive psychology, which focuses on mental processes and the thinking process, was influenced by linguist Noam Chomsky, as well as by developments in computer science, neuroscience, and other fields.

12. d

A study in which the researcher observes individuals or groups in their own setting is called a naturalistic observation study.

13. c

The independent variable is the factor that is systematically changed by the researcher to determine if it effects a change in the subject's behavior.

14. a

In this instance, the most "scientific" result would be obtained by a random sample of 2,000 young adults. The other choices all indicate some type of bias, either in the population sampled (such as only college students, or only readers of *Playboy*) or in the method of selection (since volunteering for the study might indicate bias either in favor or against the subject matter).

15. d

The experimental group is exposed not only to the dependent variable but also to the independent variable. In other respects, the experimental group should be similar to the control group (since the groups should be selected through random assignment), and at the end of the experiment, the experimental group and the control group are measured on the dependent variable.

16. b

The correct term for the harmless substance given to a control group is a placebo. If the control group were given a drug, even if it were considered a "passive" drug, or even a vitamin, the results of ingesting that substance might have an effect on the control group and could skew the experiment.

17. b

The control group is *not* exposed to the treatment being tested; the experimental group is the group that is given the treatment, while the control group receives a placebo.

18. b

The variable that is manipulated by the researcher is the independent variable. Other variables, such as whether the crash test dummies were wearing seat belts, would remain constant; thus, researchers could be sure that the independent variable was the only factor influencing the results.

19. b

One of the primary weaknesses of questionnaires is the inability to measure relationships between the variables. There is no way to control any one or all of the variables; thus, the results may be uncertain and inconclusive.

20. d

Informed consent is the process of providing full information to the participant before the research study begins, so the participant can make an informed decision to determine whether to participate.

21. d

There are usually more differences within a group than between groups. However, this does not discount the fact that there are cultural differences between groups, and these cultural differences should be valued and respected.

22. d

The American Psychological Association (APA) is the largest and most prestigious professional organization for psychologists in the United States. The APA has adopted guidelines for professional conduct for its members, as well as ethical guidelines for conducting psychological research.

23. d

A clinical psychologist focuses on mental and behavioral disorders and treatment. Most clinical psychologists work in clinics, hospitals, and private practice, and many hold professorships at colleges and universities.

24. b

A psychologist who focuses on how to make machines easier for humans to use is called an engineering psychologist.

25. b

The current study of evolutionary psychology suggests that evolutionary traits that developed in order to aid adaptation to the environment may now be working against people in modern society, such as the "flight-or-fight" response that can be triggered by everyday events such as traffic jams.

Essay Questions

1. Describe some of the major developments in the history of psychology, and the proponents of those developments.

   Psychology developed out of the pursuits of philosophy and physiology, in an attempt to explain processes of thought, emotion, and behavior. The "father of psychology," Wilhelm Wundt, established an experimental laboratory at the University of Leipzig in 1879. Other major developments in the history of psychology have included Edward Titchener's structural analysis, which was aimed at analyzing the basic structure of consciousness; Freud's development of the process of psychoanalysis and his theories of the id, ego, and the unconscious; proponents of functionalism, including William James, who were concerned with the functioning of mental processes; the development of gestalt psychology, or seeing a pattern in individual perceptions of objects; and John Watson's pioneering of behaviorism, along with B. F. Skinner and Ivan Pavlov.

   More recent developments have included humanistic psychology, which focuses on health and positive psychological adaptations, propounded by Abraham Maslow; cognitive psychology, which focuses on mental processes, influenced by Noam Chomsky; and evolutionary psychology, which studies the evolutionary traits that developed to assist human beings and may now, in modern society, be hindering or actively harming them.

2. Name the two major types of psychological research, and describe the components of each type of research.

   The two major types of psychological research are descriptive methods and the experimental method. Descriptive methods include naturalistic observation, a method in which a trained observer watches and records the behavior of individuals or groups in their natural setting; case studies or case histories of one individual or a small number of individuals observed over time; and survey research, or obtaining interviews or questionnaires from a statistically significant population of individuals. An example of the descriptive method would include developmental researchers who observe the behavior of children in play groups; another example would be a case study of an individual who had been severely abused, and who had developed multiple personalities.

   The experimental method, also called the scientific method, is the only method that can identify a cause-and-effect relationship. In this method, the researcher follows a set pattern of steps, including creation of a hypothesis, establishment of independent and dependent variables, selection of a population for the experiment, and assigning the population to either an experimental or a control group. In the experimental method, the researcher must be aware of any potential problems of bias, the "placebo effect," or experimenter bias. An example of the experimental method would be drug testing, in which the control group is given a placebo or harmless substance and the experimental group is given the actual drug, and both groups are then monitored for changes in the original condition (say, arthritis pain) that the drug is intended to affect.

3. Discuss the major ethical concerns in conducting psychological research with both animal and human subjects. What are the main ethical guidelines for conducting psychological research?

   A major consideration for both human and animal subjects is avoidance of harm, danger, and discomfort, with stricter guidelines for human research. With humans, deception must be minimized and justified by a board that regulates research. Debriefing after an experiment is as necessary as informed consent before a study is conducted.

4. Why are considerations of diversity important in psychology and in psychological research?

   Although psychologists still attempt to develop a body of knowledge that is applicable to all, they have become increasingly aware of the importance of diversity, or differences between groups due to culture or biology. For example, many early experiments in psychology did not use women as subjects; instead, the results of experiments with male subjects were generalized to women as well. Similarly, researchers often did not seek to include individuals of different cultures in the populations they studied. In some cases, such as the development of standardized intelligence tests, this led to the discounting of certain types of cultural knowledge that were valuable within certain ethnic communities. As a result of these past biases, researchers are now attempting to include a cross section of appropriate populations in their research to make sure that their findings are applicable across different cultures.

5. What are some examples of different occupations within the field of psychology?

Psychologists can specialize in clinical psychology, or the diagnosis and treatment of mental and behavioral disorders, and work in clinics and hospital settings, as well as in private practice or at colleges and universities. Counseling psychologists can help individuals or groups with adjustment problems that are less severe than those handled by clinical psychologists. Physiological psychologists study neuroscience, or the relationship between physiological processes and behavior. This specialty is especially pertinent today, with the development of new medical methods for viewing and analyzing brain function. Experimental psychologists specialize in conducting research not only in colleges and universities but also in industrial or business settings.

Developmental psychologists study human development, including the process of learning; they may specialize in one particular aspect of development, such as language or cognitive development, or they may specialize in a particular age group such as child psychology or gerontology. Educational psychologists specialize in the study of teaching and learning, in school or administrative settings. Social psychologists study people in groups; industrial or organizational psychologists study the behavior of people in a work environment.

UNIT I: THE STUDY OF PSYCHOLOGY

CHAPTER 2—BIOLOGY AND PSYCHOLOGY

 FLASH FOCUS

When you complete this chapter, you will be able to:

✓ Define heredity, and describe the study of genetics

✓ Discuss the field of sociobiology and why it is controversial

✓ Describe the components of the central nervous system, and how neurons communicate messages to the brain

✓ Describe the structure of the brain and the makeup of the cerebral cortex

✓ Name several ways in which brain activity can be measured

Use a highlighter to identify ideas, terms, and people that your instructor refers to in lectures or emphasizes in the course. Add to the chart any other ideas, terms, or people that your instructor discusses.

Core Concepts in Biology and Psychology

Important Ideas	Key Terms	Important People
Heredity	Enzymes	William D. Hamilton
Genetics	Sex/X and Y chromosomes	E. O. Wilson
Genes	Dominant allele	Paul Broca
DNA (Deoxyribonucleic Acid)	Recessive allele	
Chromosomes	Homozygous	
Alleles	Heterozygous	
Nature–nurture controversy	Polygenic control	
Heritability	Down syndrome	
Mutations	Huntington's chorea	
Chromosomal aberration	Phenylketonuria (PKU)	
Genetic counseling	Twin studies	
Reproductive strategies	Concordance research	
Sociobiology	Monogamy	
Central nervous system	Polygyny	
Peripheral nervous system	Polyandry	
Spinal cord	Polygynandry	
Nerves	Incest	
Synapses	Taboos	
Brain	Altruism	
Brain Stem	Inclusive fitness	
Cerebellum	Kin selection	
Cerebral hemispheres	Neurons	
Cerebral cortex	Glia	
Corpus callosum	Soma	

Frontal lobe	Dendrites	
Parietal lobe	Axon	
Temporal lobe	Terminal buttons	
Occipital lobe	Transmitter substance or	
Broca's area	Neurotransmitters	
Wernicke's area	Myelin sheath	
Electroencephalography (EEG)	Multiple sclerosis	
Computerized tomography (CT)	Presynaptic neuron	
Magnetic resonance imaging (MRI)	Postsynaptic neuron	
Superconducting quantum	Motor neuron	
interference device (SQUID)	Excitatory synapses	
Positron emission tomography (PET)	Inhibitory synapses	
	Reuptake	
	SSRI (selective serotonin	
	reuptake inhibitors)	
	Sensory neuron	
	Interneuron	
	Neuromodulators	
	Endorphins/opioids	
	Meninges	
	Cerebrospinal fluid (CSF)	
	Primary visual cortex	
	Primary auditory cortex	
	Primary somatosensory cortex	
	Primary motor cortex	
	Contralateral connection	
	Anterior cerebral cortex	
	Posterior cerebral cortex	
	Hypothalamus	
	Thalamus	
	Limbic system	
	Prefrontal cortex	
	Wernicke's aphasia	

Heredity and Genetics

FLASH SUMMARY

Heredity is defined as the sum of all the traits we inherit from our parents and other biological ancestors. Understanding the biological basis of heredity involves the study of *genetics*, or the structure and function of *genes*, and the ways in which genes are passed along from one generation to the next. Genes are segments of the genetic material called *DNA (deoxyribonucleic acid)*. The configuration of human DNA is the familiar "twisted ladder" shape; the particular location of genes on the ladder acts to direct the synthesis of proteins and enzymes that regulate the cellular and other physiological processes of the body. Thus, the genes act as a "recipe" to determine how our bodies are constructed and, to a certain extent, our capabilities and behaviors. Genes also direct the action of *enzymes*, which govern the processes that occur in every cell of the body.

Genes are located within *chromosomes*, or rodlike structures that are found in the nucleus of every cell. Human beings inherit twenty-three sets of chromosomes from each of their parents, for a total of forty-six individual chromosomes. One pair of chromosomes, the *sex chromosomes,* contain instructions for the development of either male or female sex characteristics, also called the *X* and *Y* chromosomes. Females have two X chromosomes, whereas males have an X and a Y chromosome. All human beings except for identical twins have different combinations of chromosomes. Identical twins, who are created when a fertilized egg splits in half, share the exact same chromosomes.

Alternative forms of genes are called *alleles.* For example, if parents each contribute the same allele for eye color to their child, the gene combination is called *homozygous,* or the same, and the child's eye color will be the same as that of the parents. However, if the parents contribute different alleles, the combination (called *heterozygous*) will be controlled by the *dominant allele.* Since the allele for brown eyes is dominant, the child of a blue- and brown-eyed parent will have brown eyes. The blue eye color is controlled by the *recessive allele.* However, the action of genes is frequently more complex, with protein synthesis under *polygenic control,* so that many human factors, and particularly behaviors, are influenced by more than one pair of genes. Thus, many hereditary factors are difficult, if not impossible, to predict.

There is also an ongoing controversy about how much of human potential and behaviors are inherited, and how much are the product of the environment; this is called the *nature–nurture controversy.* Scientists create group estimates of how much of a trait comes from genetic contribution; this is called the *heritability* of a specific trait.

Many kinds of accidents or dysfunctions can occur within genetic material. For example, *mutations* are accidental alterations in the DNA code within a single gene. While some mutations may be harmful, others may prove to be helpful in certain environments. Another type of genetic change is *chromosomal aberration,* changes in parts of chromosomes or in the number of chromosomes, which can cause physical or developmental problems. Other genetic disorders include *Down syndrome,* a chromosomal aberration that produces an extra twenty-first chromosome and causes individuals with the syndrome to develop a unique appearance, with round faces and broad skulls, and to have impaired physical, psychomotor, and cognitive development. Other examples of genetic disorders include *Huntington's chorea,* a genetic aberration that causes degeneration of certain parts of the brain, beginning when an individual is 30 to 40 years old; and *phenylketonuria (PKU),* a gene responsible for the inability to break down an amino acid found in many foods. While Huntington's chorea cannot be cured, physicians can test infants for PKU and place them on a special diet that minimizes, and potentially eliminates, the effects of the disorder.

Today, couples who are aware of family genetic disorders can obtain *genetic counseling,* or scientific advice about the likelihood of their children inheriting a specific genetic disorder. Scientists study genetic influences through the breeding of animals, which have been selectively bred by farmers and others for hundreds of years, and through *twin studies,* which study similarities in appearance and behavior, called *concordance research.*

The Study of Sociobiology

FLASH SUMMARY

Sociobiology is the study of the genetic bases of social behavior. Sociobiologists study the evolutionary bases of social behavior in both animals and humans. Sociobiology's "official" beginning was in 1975, with the publication of E. O. Wilson's book, *Sociobiology: The New Synthesis.*

Sociologists examine all types of social behaviors related to the survival of a species, including considerations of *reproductive strategies,* or the systems of mating and rearing offspring, adopted by both humans and animals. Scientists have identified different mating patterns, including *monogamy,* or one male and one female; *polygyny,* or one male mating with more than one female; *polyandry,* or one female mating with more than one male; and *polygynandry,* or several females mating with several males. Sociologists and other scientists have theorized about the possible evolutionary results of different reproductive strategies. Polygyny is the most common reproductive strategy among human beings and may have some evolutionary value as permitting males with higher dominance (or, depending on the society, with greater wealth and resources) to mate with more than one female, thus ensuring the continuance of genes for large size or greater strength or more aggressiveness.

Most species, including both human and animal species, tend to avoid *incest* or mating with close relatives. The evolutionary reason for this taboo may be that species that avoid mating with kin ensure healthier offspring. In animals, one mechanism for the avoidance of mating with kin is the migration of birds and animals away from their birthplace. In humans, all human cultures have *taboos* or prohibition against incest.

Geneticist *William D. Hamilton* attempted to explain the human (and occasionally, animal) trait of *altruism,* or unselfish concern of one individual for the welfare of another, as favoring *inclusive fitness,* or the reproductive success not only of individuals but also of groups of individuals. Altruism often extends to one's relatives, which Hamilton saw as an example of *kin selection,* or biological favoritism to one's relatives.

While the findings of sociobiology are criticized, particularly for their extension of findings about animal behavior to human beings, sociobiologists feel that their research is important in explaining the evolution and biology of social behavior.

Neurons and the Nervous System

FLASH SUMMARY

The nervous system is made up of the *central nervous system,* which includes the brain and the spinal cord, and the *peripheral nervous system,* or the nerves that are attached to the spinal cord and to the base of the brain. The *spinal cord* is a collection of long, thin nerve fibers running the length of the backbone or spinal column. The central nervous system controls the transmission of information to and from the *nerves* located throughout the body, via the *peripheral nervous system. Neurons* or nerve cells bring information to the brain and, in turn, control the activation of muscles. The neurons are assisted by *glia* (the Greek word for "glue"), or glial cells. The four principal parts of the neuron include:

1. the *soma* or cell body;
2. the *dendrites,* or growths attached to the soma which transmit information;
3. the *axon* or nerve fiber that leads from the soma;
4. the *terminal buttons* at the ends of the axons.

Terminal buttons secrete a *transmitter substance,* also called *neurotransmitters,* that affect the activity of the cells with which the neuron communicates. Many axons are surrounded by a *myelin sheath,* which insulates axons from each other. In the disease *multiple sclerosis,* an individual's own immune system attacks the myelin sheath and strips it away, resulting in sensory and motor impairments, as axons are no longer able to function normally.

Neurons communicate with other cells through the *synapses,* or conjunctions between the terminal button of one neuron and the membrane of another cell. The terminal button sending the message is called the *presynaptic neuron,* while the neuron receiving the message is called the *postsynaptic neuron. A motor neuron* forms synapses with a muscle and controls its contraction. Synapses can be either *excitatory,* in that they excite or stimulate the axon to fire an electrical charge, or *inhibitory,* in that they lower the likelihood that the axons will fire. At most synapses, the effects of excitation or inhibition are short-lived, and are ended by a process called *reuptake,* in which the transmitter substance released by the terminal button is taken back. Some drugs, notably the *SSRI (selective serotonin reuptake inhibitors)* drugs such as Prozac, function by slowing this reuptake process.

A simple reflex such as withdrawing one's hand involves three types of neurons: *sensory neurons* to detect a negative stimulus, *interneurons* in the brain or spinal cord to receive the information and in turn stimulate the *motor neurons* that cause the hand to withdraw. Some chemicals released by the terminal buttons only affect molecules located within a short distance; however, some neurons release chemicals that affect thousands of neurons, some located at a considerable distance. These chemicals are called *neuromodulators.* The best known neuromodulators are called *endorphins* or *opioids,* so called for their drug-like effects. Opioids are triggered while important processes are taking place in the body, such as an animal engaging in a fight; they prevent the individual from feeling pain. Opiates such as opium act on the body in a similar manner, by stimulating special opioid receptor molecules in neurons of the brain.

The Structure of the Brain

FLASH SUMMARY

The human *brain,* which controls our behavior and thought processes, as well as most other bodily systems, contains between 10 billion and 100 billion nerve cells, and approximately the same number of "helper" cells. The human brain has three major parts, the *brain stem,* the *cerebellum,* and the *cerebral hemispheres.* The brain stem is the lowest part of the brain, and controls correspondingly "primitive" brain functions such as physiological activities and automatic behaviors. The cerebellum, attached to the back of the brain stem, controls and coordinates movements. The cerebral hemispheres are the more recently evolved sections of the brain, and control our thoughts, feelings, and behaviors.

The brain and spinal cord are both surrounded by a three-layered set of membranes called *meninges.* Both brain and spinal cord float in a liquid "cushion" called *cerebrospinal fluid (CSF).* The cerebral hemispheres are covered by the *cerebral cortex,* a thin layer of tissue also referred to as "gray matter."

The cerebral cortex is of greatest interest to psychologists, since it controls the functions most important to behavior, including perceiving, learning, planning, and moving. Three areas of the cerebral cortex receive information from the senses: the *primary visual cortex,* which receives visual information; the *primary auditory cortex,* which receives auditory information; and the *primary somatosensory cortex,* which receives information from other bodily senses. The *primary motor cortex* controls bodily movements.

These regions in each hemisphere of the brain receive information from the opposite side of the body; in other words, the right side of the brain receives information from the left side of the body, and vice versa. These connections are termed *contralateral.* While some functions of the hemispheres of the brain are identical; if contralateral, other functions occur primarily in one hemisphere or the other. For example, the left hemisphere participates in the analysis of information, whereas the right hemisphere specializes in synthesis, or perceiving information as a whole. The two hemispheres are connected by the *corpus callosum,* a band of axons or nerves.

The cerebral cortex is also divided into two regions from front to back, divided by a central fissure: the *anterior* or front, which is involved in movement-related activities, and the *posterior* or back, which is involved in perceiving and learning. Scientists also refer to the cerebral cortex in terms of four different *lobes,* or areas of the brain: the *frontal lobe,* the *parietal lobe,* the *temporal lobe,* and the *occipital lobe.* The frontal lobe is not only concerned with motor activity but also with planning, changing strategies, evaluating emotional stimuli, and performing a number of spontaneous behaviors. It also contains the area, called *Broca's area* after physiologist *Paul Broca,* that controls speech.

The parietal lobe is involved in perception of the body; different parts of the left and right parietal lobes are involved with the ability to write clearly, pay attention to stimuli, and draw objects that are seen. The temporal lobe contains both the primary auditory cortex and the auditory association cortex, which can affect hearing and language, or the ability to comprehend language. The occipital lobe, as well as part of the temporal lobe, is involved with vision, in terms of how the person organizes what is perceived by the eyes.

FLASH REVIEW

Complete the map of the brain with the appropriate labels for different areas and functions.

THE STRUCTURE OF THE BRAIN

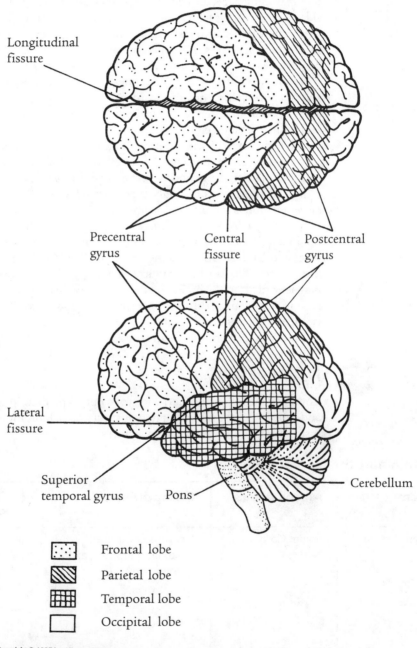

Human Cerebral Hemispheres

Longitudinal fissure

Precentral gyrus   Central fissure   Postcentral gyrus

Lateral fissure

Superior temporal gyrus   Pons   Cerebellum

	Frontal lobe
	Parietal lobe
	Temporal lobe
	Occipital lobe

The Brain and Behavior

....

FLASH SUMMARY

As is evident from the description of brain structure in the figure, many parts of the brain participate in our thoughts, feelings, and behaviors. Several interrelated structures within the brain seem to affect our deepest appetites, emotions, and motives; these structures include the *hypothalamus*, which regulates the autonomic nervous system and has an effect on our internal environment and appetite; the *thalamus*, which receives input from all of the senses and performs some preliminary analyses before passing the information to other parts of the brain; and the *limbic system*, which is involved in aspects of emotional control and behavior.

Studies of various types of brain damage and disorder provide a "window" into brain functioning and the relation of brain activity to behavior. For example, it appears that reasoning is performed in the *prefrontal cortex;* evidence of this connection is provided by individuals who have damaged that area of their brain, and who consequently were unable to perform tasks that required complex reasoning.

Human speech is controlled by several areas in the brain, including Broca's area, described earlier, and another region called *Wernicke's area.* Damage to Wernicke's area creates an inability to recognize spoken words, to understand the meaning of words, and to convert thoughts into words. These symptoms are known as *Wernicke's aphasia,* and can occur in individuals who have suffered a stroke, or damage to a section of the brain due to a blood clot.

In addition to observing either brains that have been damaged or brains of laboratory animals, scientists now have access to brain functioning through many different methods. The first method is *electroencephalography (EEG),* which records the activity of individual neurons through microelectrodes implanted in the brain. A second and newer method is *computerized tomography,* or *CT scans,* in which X-rays scan the patient's head from many different angles, and a computer produces a two-dimensional image of the brain. *Magnetic resonance imaging,* or *MRI,* produces images by means of a strong magnetic field. A fourth imaging device is called *SQUID,* or *superconducting quantum interference device.* The SQUID produces images based on the detection of small changes in magnetic fields in the brain. Finally, *positron emission topography,* or *PET,* measures blood flow in neural areas through absorption of glucose treated with harmless radioactive isotopes. PET scans can reveal the different amounts of activity occurring in the brain as an individual performs a specific task.

FLASH REVIEW

Complete the following chart with your notes and descriptions of the major structures and function of the brain and nervous system. Include any areas or functions that your instructor includes or stresses in lectures.

The Brain and the Nervous System

System	Major Areas	Components	Description of Functions
Nervous System	Spinal Cord Nerves	Neurons composed of soma; dendrites; axon; terminal buttons	Sending and receiving messages from nerve cells throughout the body

Brain	Brain stem Cerebellum Cerebral Hemispheres	Cerebral cortex composed of four lobes: frontal, parietal, temporal, occipital	Frontal Lobe Parietal lobe Temporal lobe Occipital lobe
	Hypothalamus Thalamus Limbic system		
	Broca's area		
	Wernicke's area		

 FLASH TEST

Review the chart of Core Concepts in Chapter 2. Then take the Practice Test on the following pages. Rate your performance according to the Answer Explanations.

PRACTICE TEST

(Chapter 2—Biology and Psychology)

Multiple Choice (3 points each)

1. If identical twins who were separated at birth and raised in different environments show marked similarities in behavior, it is probably because
   a. their adoptive parents are very similar to their birth parents.
   b. their behavior is being affected by their biological, genetic inheritance.
   c. twins have a subconscious telepathic link that makes them similar.
   d. all children are very similar, no matter how they are raised or by whom.

2. Twin studies are useful in disentangling the relative roles of _____ in a given form of behavior.
   a. cognitive and emotional factors
   b. genetic and environmental factors
   c. social and individual factors
   d. cognitive and conative factors

3. A group estimate of how much of a trait comes from genetic contribution is called
   a. chromosomes.
   b. heritability.
   c. genetic predisposition.
   d. behavioral genetics.

4. A female cell contains _____ and a male cell contains _____.
   a. dominant genes; alleles
   b. alleles; dominant genes
   c. two X chromosomes; one X and one Y chromosome.
   d. one X and one Y chromosome; two X chromosomes.

5. If parents contribute different alleles for eye color, the eye color of the child will be determined by
   a. the dominant allele.
   b. the father's eye color.
   c. the mother's eye color.
   d. the recessive allele.

6. Mating patterns identified among both humans and animals include *all except one* of the following: Which one should *not* be included?
   a. polyandry
   b. polygyny
   c. monogamy
   d. polymorphism

7. Geneticist William Hamilton explains the trait of altruism as an example of
   a. inclusive fitness.
   b. taboos.
   c. selection of the fittest.
   d. kin selection.

8. The two main parts or divisions of the nervous system are the central nervous system and the
   a. autonomic nervous system.
   b. sympathetic nervous system.
   c. peripheral nervous system.
   d. spinal cord.

9. The branchlike extensions of neurons that act as the primary receivers of signals from other neurons are the
   a. dendrites.
   b. axons.
   c. glia.
   d. cell bodies.

10. The three basic parts of neuron are
   a. vesicals, gray matter, and synapse.
   b. glial cells, nodes of Ranvier, and synaptic terminals.
   c. cell body, axon, and dendrites.
   d. myelin sheath, cell body, and dendrites.

11. Terminal buttons secrete a(n) _____ that affects the activity of the cells with which the neuron communicates.
   a. glial substance or glue
   b. transmitter substance or neurotransmitters
   c. myelin sheath
   d. interneuron substance

12. The type of neuron found entirely within the brain and spinal cord is called a(n)
   a. sensory neuron.
   b. motor neuron.
   c. interneuron.
   d. afferent neuron.

13. The neuron sending a message is called the _____ neuron, while the neuron receiving a message is called the _____ neuron.
    a. terminal, recipient
    b. presynaptic, postsynaptic
    c. postsynaptic, presynaptic
    d. excitatory, inhibitory

14. Endorphins are chemicals in the brain that produce effects similar to
    a. caffeine.
    b. marijuana.
    c. LSD.
    d. morphine.

15. The three major parts of the brain include *all except one* of the following: Which one should *not* be included?
    a. cerebellum
    b. brain stem
    c. cerebral cortex
    d. cerebral hemispheres

16. The part of the brain of greatest interest to psychologists is the
    a. cerebellum.
    b. cerebral cortex.
    c. brain stem.
    d. somatosensory cortex.

17. The left and right cerebral hemispheres are connected by the
    a. cerebrum.
    b. cerebellum.
    c. midbrain.
    d. corpus callosum.

18. Which association areas are involved in thinking, motivation, planning for the future, impulse control, and emotional responses?
    a. frontal
    b. parietal
    c. temporal
    d. occipital

19. Hearing and language are associated with the _____ lobe.
    a. frontal
    b. parietal
    c. temporal
    d. occipital

20. The _____ lobe enables one to write clearly, pay attention to stimuli, and draw objects that are seen.
    a. frontal
    b. parietal
    c. temporal
    d. occipital

21. The brain structure that regulates our appetite is the
    a. thalamus.
    b. hypothalamus.
    c. limbic system.
    d. thyroid.

22. The area of the brain that controls human speech is the
    a. Broca's area.
    b. Wernicke's area.
    c. prefrontal cortex.
    d. occipital lobe.

23. Which of the following uses X-rays to get a picture of the brain?
   a. the CT scan
   b. the MRI
   c. the PET scan
   d. the EEG

24. The brain imaging method that involves measuring the differences in the brain's magnetic field based upon the electric current produced when neurons fire is called
   a. CT.
   b. SQUID.
   c. MRI
   d. PET.

25. Which procedure would give you a printout of beta, alpha, and delta waves from the brain?
   a. the CT scan
   b. the MRI
   c. the PET scan
   d. the EEG

Essay Questions (5 points each)

1. Describe the study of genetics and how heredity determines our characteristics and behaviors.

2. What is sociobiology, and what types of behaviors are studied?

3. Describe the components of the nervous system, and the actions of the nerves in bringing information to and from the brain.

4. Name the various parts or structures of the brain, and the functions they control.

5. What are some methods of detecting and measuring brain activity?

ANSWER EXPLANATIONS

Multiple-Choice Questions

1. b

Identical twins are the only human beings who share exactly the same genetic makeup; therefore, twin studies are used to try to identify how their behavior is affected by their genetic inheritance versus behavior that is learned in the environment.

2. b

Twin studies are used in an attempt to determine what behaviors may be the result of inherited genetic traits and what behaviors may have developed as a result of environmental factors. Scientific debate about the relative importance of these factors has been called the "nature versus nurture" controversy.

3. b

A group estimate of how much of a given trait comes from genetic contribution is called the heritability of that particular trait.

4. c

The sex chromosomes determine the sex of an individual; a female cell contains two X chromosomes, and a male cell contains one X and one Y chromosome.

5. a

The eye color of a child will be determined by the dominant allele contributed by the parents; the allele for brown eyes is dominant over the allele for blue eyes (which is the recessive allele).

6. d

Types of mating behaviors include monogamy, or one male and one female; polygyny, or one male and several females; polyandry, or one female and several males; and polygyandry, or several females and several males.

7. d

Hamilton views altruism as an example of kin selection, or biological favoritism to one's relatives, which helps the species to survive.

8. c

The nervous system is made up of the central nervous system and the peripheral nervous system.

9. a

The dendrites, or branchlike structures that are attached to the cell body of a neuron, receive impulses from other neurons.

10. c

The neuron is made up of a central cell body, an axon that extends from the cell body and that is primarily responsible for sending messages to other neurons, and dendrites, the branchlike structures that are primarily responsible for receiving messages from other neurons.

11. b

Terminal buttons at the ends of the axons of nerve cells secrete a transmitter substance, or neurotransmitters, that affect the activity of the cells with which the neuron communicates.

12. c

Interneurons are found entirely within the brain and spinal cord; they receive information from sensory neurons and respond via the motor neurons in the peripheral nervous system.

13. b

The neuron sending a message is called a presynaptic neuron; the neuron receiving a message is called a post-synaptic neuron.

14. d

Endorphins, also known as opioids, are chemicals in the brain that are triggered while important processes, such as mating or fighting, are taking place; morphine and opiates act on the body in a similar manner.

15. c

The brain stem, cerebellum, and the cerebral hemispheres are the major parts of the brain; the cerebral cortex is a thin layer of tissue that covers the cerebral hemispheres.

16. b

The cerebral cortex is of greatest interest to psychologists, since it is the area where most of our functions related to behavior, including perceiving, learning, planning, and moving, occur.

17. d

The left and right hemispheres of the brain are connected by the corpus callosum, a band of axons or nerves.

18. a

The frontal lobe is concerned not only with motor activity but also with planning, changing strategies, evaluating emotional stimuli, and performing a number of spontaneous behaviors.

19. c

The temporal lobe contains both the primary auditory cortex and the auditory association cortex, which affect hearing and language.

20. b

The parietal lobe is involved in perception of the body, and includes the abilities to write clearly, pay attention to stimuli, and draw objects that are seen.

21. b

The hypothalamus regulates the autonomic nervous system, and also has effects on our internal environment and appetite.

22. a

The area of the brain that appears to control human speech is Broca's area. Wernicke's area is involved with the translation of thoughts into words and the ability to recognize human words.

23. a

The CT scan, or computerized tomography, is used to get X-ray scans of the brain.

24. b

The SQUID, or superconducting quantum interference device, produces images based on the detection of small changes in the brain's magnetic field.

25. d

An EEG records the activity of individual neurons and the type of electrical brain waves they generate.

Essay Questions

1. Describe the study of genetics and how heredity determines our characteristics and behaviors.

   Genetics is the study of the structure and function of genes and the ways in which genes are passed down through generations. Genes form part of our DNA, which is a "recipe" that determines how our bodies are constructed and, to a certain extent, our capabilities and behaviors. Some people with genetic disorders, for example, are born with mild to severe mental retardation, as in Down syndrome. However, our genes do not entirely determine our capabilities and behaviors, and the controversy about whether heredity or environment is more important has been termed the nature–nurture controversy.

2. What is sociobiology, and what types of behaviors are studied?

   Sociobiology is the study of the genetic bases of social behavior, or behavior that serves an evolutionary purpose. For example, sociobiologists study reproductive strategies, or systems of mating and rearing young, that are used by both animals and humans. Certain types of mating behavior, such as polygyny, may have been helpful in preserving the genetic structure of males with higher dominance. However, the findings of sociobiology are criticized, particularly for their extension of findings about animal behavior to human beings.

3. Describe the components of the nervous system and the actions of the nerves in bringing information to and from the brain.

   The nervous system consists of the brain and spinal cord, which make up the central nervous system, and the nerves in the rest of the body, called the peripheral nervous system. Neurons or nerve cells bring information to the brain and control the actions of muscles. The principal parts of the neuron include the soma, or cell body, the dendrites, or growths attached to the soma, the axon, or nerve fiber that leads from the soma, and the terminal buttons at the ends of the axons. When a transmitter substance, or neurotransmitter, is secreted by the terminal buttons, a message is transmitted from the presynaptic (or sending) neuron to the postsynaptic (receiving) neuron.

   Sensory neurons are those that detect stimuli in the body; interneurons in the brain or spinal cord receive the information, and in turn stimulate the motor neurons that control the muscles.

4. Name the various parts or structures of the brain and the functions they control.

   The brain has three major parts: the brain stem, the cerebellum, and the cerebral hemispheres. The cerebral hemispheres are covered by the cerebral cortex, a thin layer of tissue; the cerebral cortex is of the greatest interest to psychologists, since it controls the functions related to behavior.

   There are four primary lobes or regions of the cerebral cortex: frontal lobe, parietal lobe, temporal lobe, and occipital lobe. Through studies of animals, and also of humans who have experienced some damage to different regions of the brain, scientists have determined that the frontal lobe is concerned not only with motor activity but also with planning, changing strategies, evaluating emotional stimuli, and other behaviors. It also contains Broca's area which controls speech. The parietal lobe is involved with bodily perception, including the ability to write clearly, pay attention to stimuli, and draw objects that are seen. The temporal lobe contains the primary auditory cortex and the auditory association cortex, which affect hearing and language. The occipital lobe is involved with vision and, particularly, how visual information is organized.

5. What are some methods of detecting and measuring brain activity?

   Methods include electroencephalography (EEG), which records the activity of individual neurons through microelectrodes implanted in the brain. Computerized tomography, or CT scans, use X-rays to scan the patients head from different angles, from which a computer creates a two-dimensional image. Magnetic resonance imaging (MRI) produces images by means of a strong magnetic field. SQUID, or superconducting quantum interference device, produces images based on the detection of small changes in magnetic fields in the brain. Positron emission topography (PET) measures blood flow in neural areas through absorption of glucose that has been treated with radioactive isotopes.

UNIT II: BASIC PSYCHOLOGICAL PROCESSES

CHAPTER 3—SENSATION AND PERCEPTION

 FLASH FOCUS

When you complete this chapter, you will be able to:

✓ Define sensation and perception, and describe their evolutionary purpose

✓ Describe the structure of the eye and how vision is processed in the brain

✓ Describe the structure of the ear and how hearing is processed in the brain

✓ Describe the operation of smell, taste, touch, the sense of pain, and the perception of the body in space (kinesthesia)

✓ Discuss the mechanisms that regulate perception, and provide some arguments for or against the possibility of extrasensory perception

Use a highlighter to identify ideas, terms, and people that your instructor refers to in lectures or emphasizes in the course. Add to the chart any other ideas, terms, or people that your instructor discusses.

Core Concepts in Sensation and Perception

Important Ideas	Key Terms	Important People
Sensation	Sensory receptors	Ernst Weber
Perception	Transduction	Gustav Fechner
Psychophysics	Anatomical coding	Christopher Scheiner
Vision	Temporal coding	Thomas Young
Audition	Absolute threshold	I. Biederman
Chemosenses	Difference threshold	Uri Geller
Gustation	Just noticeable difference (jnd)	
Olfaction	Signal detection theory	
Pain	Sensory adaptation	
Touch	Subliminal perception	
Kinesthesis	Psychophysical methods	
Vestibular Sense	Wavelength	
Parapsychology	Electromagnetic spectrum	
Extrasensory perception (ESP)	Visible Spectrum	
	Photoreceptors	
	Ganglion cells	
	Cornea	
	Sclera	
	Iris	
	Aqueous Humor	
	Glaucoma	
	Lens	
	Retina	
	Nearsighted	
	Farsighted	

Optic disk
Optic nerve
Rods
Cones
Fovea
Trichromatic theory
Negative afterimage
Rebound effect
Hertz (Hz)
Pitch
Timbre
Pinna
Ear canal
Eardrum
Ossicles
Hammer
Anvil
Stirrup
Cochlea
Oval Window
Basilar membrane
Round Window
Auditory hair cells
Overtones
Fundamental frequency
Deafness
Postlingually deaf
American Sign Language (ASL)
Oralist approach
Papillae
Taste buds
Olfactory mucosa
Olfactory bulbs
Skin senses
Epidermis
Dermis
Hypodermis
Free nerve endings
Melzack–Wall gate control
Theory
Acupuncture
Endorphins
Proprioceptive cues
Primary visual cortex
Visual association cortex
Templates
Prototypes
Distinctive features
Geons
Precognition
Clairvoyance
Telepathy
Psychokinesis

FLASH SUMMARY

Sensation is defined as the detection of sensory stimuli in the environment, such as light, dark, color, warmth or cold, sweet or sour. *Perception* is defined as the study of the processes through which human beings organize and interpret the experience of the senses. Human beings have a number of different organs to register sensations, but psychologists know that the range of human perception can be considered extensive, when compared to simpler organisms such as amoeba, or limited, when compared to that of other beings. For example, the human sense of smell is much more limited than that of dogs. It is theorized that each species' range of sensation and perception is designed to maximize its survival potential.

Specialized cells called *sensory receptors* receive physical stimuli from the outside; the process of *transduction* converts the physical stimuli into signals that are transmitted to the brain. The brain utilizes a process called *anatomical coding* to interpret the location and type of a particular sensory stimulus; *temporal coding* refers to coding of information over time. For example, a painful or forceful stimulus is transmitted more quickly than a light stimulus.

Psychophysics is the subfield of psychology that studies the relationship between physical stimuli and people's perception of them. Psychologists use the term *absolute threshold* to refer to the smallest amount of a stimulus that can be detected 50 percent of the time. The amount of change that must occur before it can be detected is called the *difference threshold*. The amount of change must be sufficient to produce a *just noticeable difference (jnd)* in sensation, a term coined by German anatomist Ernst Weber. German physiologist Gustav Fechner used Weber's concept of the just noticeable difference to measure the magnitude of sensations in "jnd"s.

A theory called *signal detection theory* posits that every stimulus event requires an individual to discriminate between signal and noise, or background stimuli and random activity. The process of *sensory adaptation* ensures that stimuli do not continue to register as intensely as when first received; for example, entering cold water may be a shock, but an individual adapts quickly to the temperature.

There has been controversy among researchers and the public about the use of *subliminal perception,* or methods of exposing people to messages that, while they did not enter conscious awareness, were registered in the subconscious. While researchers obtained some evidence that messages "embedded" in a movie or television program are registered at some level within the nervous system, subliminal advertising has not been proved effective at actually triggering specific actions, such as purchase of a particular product.

FLASH SUMMARY

The following chart summarizes some of the research methods used by psychologists and other researchers to measure sensory thresholds, termed *psychophysical methods.* Add to the chart any other methods, or any examples or descriptions, provided by your instructor.

A Chart of Psychophysical Methods

Method	Description	Advantages and Disadvantages
Method of limits	Ascending trials increase in intensity until perceived by the subject; descending trials decrease until no longer perceived	Can lead to errors of habituation (participants' tendency to continue to identify a perception after it is no longer perceived) or errors of

		anticipation (tendency of participants to anticipate stimuli before stimulus is actually applied)
Staircase method	Ascending or descending application of stimuli	Can be more efficient, quicker than method of limits
Method of constant stimuli	Stimuli presented in irregular order	Eliminates some of the biases of the method of limits

Vision

FLASH SUMMARY

The eye is designed to detect stimuli that are received through light, or radiant energy that is transmitted in waves. Our eyes can perceive stimuli received through a particular *wavelength*—the distance between the waves—of 380 through 760 nanometers (a nanometer is a billionth of a meter). The entire range of wavelengths is called the *electromagnetic spectrum;* the part that can be perceived by human beings is called the *visible spectrum*.

The eye contains *photoreceptors* that respond to light and pass the information along to *bipolar cells* or neurons. Bipolar cells transmit the information to *ganglion cells,* neurons within the eye, and from the ganglion cells to the brain. The eye includes a *cornea* on the surface of the eyeball, a transparent membrane that admits light; the rest of the eye is covered with a white membrane called the *sclera.* The *iris* of the eye consists of two bands of muscles that control the amount of light that enters the eye. The eyeball is filled with a watery fluid called the *aqueous humor;* if too much liquid is produced, or if it is produced too quickly, it can increase the pressure within the eye, a condition called *glaucoma.*

The *lens* of the eye, located behind the iris, causes images to be focused on the inner surface of the back of the eye, called the *retina.* In 1625, Chrisopher Scheiner, a German astonomer, proved that the lens is simply a focusing device. The lens is flexible, so the eye can receive images of either nearby or distant objects. The change in the shape of the lens to adjust for distance is called *accommodation.* The images produced by the lens are produced upside-down and reversed from left to right, an alteration that is corrected in the brain. The image is supposed to be sharply focused on the retina, but some people have eyes that are too long or too short for proper focus; they are called *nearsighted* (too long, so the image falls short of the retina) or *farsighted* (too short, so the image focuses beyond the retina). These eye conditions can be corrected by lenses that are concave or convex to correctly focus the image.

The retina contains thousands of photoreceptor cells that transmit information to the *optic disk,* where the axons of the photoreceptor cells join the *optic nerve,* which travels to the brain via the bipolar cells and the ganglion cells. The human eye contains both *rods,* photoreceptors that are light-sensitive but cannot detect color, and *cones,* which function to distinguish colors so long as there is a sufficient level of light. The *fovea,* a small structure in the back of the retina, contains only cones. Among mammals, only primates have full color vision. Thomas Young, a British physicist and physician, proposed a *trichromatic theory* of color vision, that the eye contains three types of color receptors which are combined in the brain to produce a spectrum of colors. Another property of eyesight is the *negative afterimage* that is produced by the eye after looking at certain colors for a period of time. This is due to the *rebound effect* of ganglion cells that are firing either faster or slower than normal. Defects in human color vision, which occur more frequently in males, involved *protanopia,* or a lack of photopigment for red cones; *deuteranopia,* or green cones that are filled with red pigment; and *tritanopia,* which affects the yellow/blue system and is much rarer.

Hearing

FLASH SUMMARY

Hearing, or *audition,* is created by the interchanges between sound waves and structures in the ear and brain. Sound waves are measured in cycles per second called *hertz (Hz).* The human ear perceives these vibrations between 30 and 20,000 Hz, and can detect change in the loudness, *pitch* (whether a sound is high or low), and *timbre* (quality) of a sound. Sound waves are received in the ear, an organ made up of a number of parts including the *pinna,* or outer portion, the *ear canal,* or passageway between the outer and the middle and inner ear, and the *eardrum,* a flexible membrane that vibrates in response to sound waves. The eardrum contains three tiny bones; called *ossicles, hammer, anvil,* and *stirrup,* that transmit the vibrations of the eardrum to the liquid-filled *cochlea.*

In the mechanism of hearing, the stirrup presses against a membrane called the *oval window* and transmits sound waves into the liquid in the cochlea. The cochlea is divided into two parts by the *basilar membrane,* a sheet of tissue that contains the auditory receptor cells. Different frequencies of sound cause different parts of the basilar membrane to vibrate. A membrane in the *round window* helps to stabilize the pressure caused by the vibration of the basilar membrane. Neurons located on the basilar membrane, called *auditory hair cells,* translate the mechanical energy of the vibration into neural activity.

Different axons report high-, medium-, and low-frequency sounds, or pitch. By changing the rate of firing, the axons report on the loudness of a sound. Timbre is reported by a combination of sounds, called *overtones,* with the *fundamental frequency,* or pitch, of a sound.

Problems with any of the systems within the ear or auditory nerve can result in partial or total *deafness.* People who are born deaf often become part of a deaf culture that uses sign language to communicate. Others, who become *postlingually deaf* (that is, became deaf after they had learned oral and written language), often never learn sign language and do not become part of the deaf community. There are many debates about the wisdom of either teaching children sign language (*ASL* or *American Sign Language* in the United States) or using an *oralist approach* to their education by putting them into mainstream schools.

Smell and Taste

FLASH SUMMARY

The senses of taste and smell are, together, called the *chemosenses* because they are our means of sensing chemicals in our environment. Taste, or *gustation,* allows us to perceive only four basic tastes: sweet, sour, salty, and bitter. Taste sensations are transmitted to the brain through the *tongue.* The tongue has a number of bumps or *papillae;* each papilla contains as many as 200 taste buds. A *taste bud* is a small organ that contains a number of receptor cells, with hairlike projections called *microvilli.* Chemicals dissolved in the saliva on the tongue interact with special receptors in the microvilli; the receptor cells, in turn, form synapses with the dendrites of neurons that send axons to the brain through three different cranial nerves. The mechanism of taste probably evolved to warn against foods that were poisonous or decomposing.

The sense of smell, or *olfaction,* is the hardest sense to describe, although smells can trigger some of the strongest recollections and associations for humans. In the nose, the receptor cells for smell are located in the *olfactory mucosa,* patches of mucous membrane on the roof of the nasal sinuses, just under the base of the brain. The olfactory mucosa contain receptor cells with axons that pass through small holes in the bone above the mucosa and form synapses with the *olfactory bulbs,* cells at the base of the brain that begin to process olfactory information. Rather than being passed through the thalamus and from there to a specialized region of the cerebral cortex, olfactory information is sent directly to several regions of the limbic system.

The Other Senses

FLASH SUMMARY

Skin is an organ of the body that contains a wide range of *skin senses,* including pain, touch, and temperature. The skin is composed of layers, consisting of the *epidermis,* or outer layer; the *dermis,* which contains nerve endings, blood, and oil-producing glands; and the *hypodermis,* a bottom layer that cushions the body. Receptor cells in the skin respond to different stimuli, and the receptor cells seem to interact with each other; for example, a touch can increase in pressure until it causes pain, at which point the pain receptor cells are activated. The ability to sense pain, as well as touch and temperature, is clearly a sense that is needed for organisms to be able to survive in their environment.

Physiologists believe that pain receptors are located in *free nerve endings,* or the microscopic ends of nerves distributed throughout the body's tissues. Different areas of the body have different pain thresholds, and different individuals also experience pain differently. The *Melzack–Wall gate control theory* attempts to provide an explanation of how pain messages are sent to the brain; it posits that pain messages must go through a number of "gates" which can be open, shut, or partially open; the amount of opening determines how much of the pain message gets transmitted to the brain. A variety of drugs as well as electrical stimulation and *acupuncture* needles are thought to affect the gates, causing the brain to receive fewer pain messages. *Endorphins,* which are natural painkillers produced in the brain, are also thought to prevent pain signals from reaching the brain.

Kinesthesis is the awareness that is created by the movements of muscles, tendons, and joints. Kinesthesia and other internal sensations, such as a stomachache, are called *proprioceptive cues,* since they originate within the body. The *vestibular sense* is the sense of bodily orientation and posture; it enables people to keep their balance and sense of equilibrium. This sense is provided by structures located in or near the cochlea in the ear.

The Process of Perception

FLASH SUMMARY

Perception is the process of selecting and interpreting the sensory information provided by bodily sensations. Physiologists have conducted experiments using isolation tanks, which prevent the individual subject from obtaining any sensory input whatsoever. They have found that the subject frequently experiences dreams, hallucinations, and other altered mental states.

In the process of visual perception, visual information received through the eyes and the optic nerve is sent to the thalamus for initial processing, then passed along to the *primary visual cortex,* which creates a visual map of the neural information. The information is then transmitted to the first level of the *visual association cortex,* which receives visual information in different components, including movement, orientation, widths of lines and edges, and color. The second level of the visual association cortex takes place within different lobes of the brain; for example, the visual association cortex in the temporal lobe combines information about shape, movement, and color to create a perception of three-dimensional form. Damage to specific areas of the brain creates limitations in the ability to perceive information. Damage to the primary visual cortex creates blindness in some portion of the visual field; other kinds of damage can disrupt color vision.

Psychological experiments that ask people to distinguish between figure and ground, or to judge relative distances or groupings of objects, are attempting to determine how the brain makes fine distinctions or perceives a pattern in seemingly disparate objects. Theories of how the brain organizes visual input include the theory that the brain provides *templates,* or memories created by the visual system; the theory that the brain creates *prototypes,* or idealized patterns; and the theory that the brain uses *distinctive features,* or collections of important physical features, to recognize specific items. Another theory, propounded by *I. Beiderman,* suggests that there are thirty-six different basic shapes, called *geons,* that can be combined to produce object recognition.

The brain can be fooled into perceiving patterns or judging distances, as psychologists demonstrate through the use of *illusions,* or incorrect perceptions. The brain can register illusions in size, shape, or distance, because misleading cues lead to assumptions about what is seen. Illusions can also be created for the skin senses; for example, if an individual places one hand in a container of hot water and the other in cold water, then dips both hands into a container of lukewarm water, there will be a dramatic difference in the perceived temperature of the hands placed in lukewarm water; one hand will experience the lukewarm water as hot, and the other hand will experience it as cool.

The Possibility of Extrasensory Perception

FLASH SUMMARY

Psychologists have been involved in the study of *extrasensory perception,* or the idea that there can be perception without sensation, for many years. Those who specialize in this area are called *parapsychologists.* Extrasensory perception includes abilities that have been termed *precognition,* or the ability to foretell future events; *clairvoyance,* or the ability to perceive objects or events that do not affect the senses; *telepathy,* or the ability to "read" another person's thoughts; and *psychokinesis,* the ability to move or affect objects without directly touching them.

In general, researchers have been unable to confirm the existence of any of these extrasensory abilities. And many individuals who have seemed to demonstrate extrasensory abilities, such as *Uri Geller,* who was thought to be able to bend spoons using only his thoughts, have been exposed as having used tricks and deceptions.

FLASH LINK

Go to www.exploratorium.edu/imagery/exhibits.html and explore three different kinds of illusions. Then, answer the following questions:

1. Which of the many types of illusions do you find the most interesting?

2. Which specific illusion was the most interesting? Why?

Now visit www.visionscience.com/VisionScience.html, and answer the following questions:

1. What was your favorite illusion?

2. How is the illusion thought to work?

Adapted from Brian M. Kelley, *Psychology on the Net 2001* (Copyright Allyn and Bacon, Boston, 2001), p. 16.

 FLASH TEST

Review the chart of Core Concepts at the beginning of this chapter. Then take the Practice Test for Chapter 3 on the following pages and rate your performance.

PRACTICE TEST

(Chapter 3—Sensation and Perception)

Multiple Choice (3 points each)

1. Sensation is defined as the
  a. detection of sensory stimuli in the environment.
  b. organization and interpretation of stimuli.
  c. ability to distinguish different tastes.
  d. sense of smell.

2. Perception is defined as the process we use to
  a. organize and interpret stimuli.
  b. detect stimuli.
  c. gather information from the environment.
  d. retrieve information from memory.

3. The process of converting physical stimuli into signals that are received by the brain is called
  a. perception.
  b. transduction.
  c. stimulation.
  d. anatomical coding.

4. The minimum amount of physical stimulation necessary for us to experience a sensation 50 percent of the time is called the
  a. figure-to-ground ratio.
  b. blind spot.
  c. difference threshold.
  d. absolute threshold.

5. The term "just noticeable difference" was coined by
  a. Gustav Fechner.
  b. Sigmund Freud.
  c. Christopher Scheiner.
  d. Ernst Weber.

6. An important principle of signal detection theory is that detection of any stimulus requires that we discriminate between _____ and _____.
  a. signal; response bias
  b. signal; noise
  c. response bias; noise
  d. noise; silence

7. When one gets used to the initial shock of cold water, it is called
  a. signal discrimination.
  b. sensory adaptation.
  c. absolute threshold.
  d. anatomical coding.

8. Research evidence regarding the effects of a subliminal stimulus shows that
   a. it has no effect whatsoever.
   b. the behavioral effects are subtle.
   c. it is a common and robust phenomenon.
   d. its behavioral effects are vicarious in nature.

9. The amount of light that enters the eye is controlled by two bands of muscles called the
   a. retina.
   b. iris.
   c. lens.
   d. pupil.

10. The space immediately behind the _____ is filled with a fluid called _____.
    a. cornea; aqueous humor
    b. sclera; vitreous humor
    c. retina; aqueous humor
    d. optic nerve; vitreous humor

11. Human eyes can perceive stimuli through a wavelength of between
    a. 250 through 550 nanometers.
    b. 850 through 1,200 nanometers.
    c. 380 through 760 nanometers.
    d. 30 and 20,000 Hertz.

12. Blockage of the passage that returns aqueous humor to the blood can result in a condition called
    a. cataracts.
    b. near sightedness.
    c. glaucoma.
    d. protanopia.

13. The negative afterimage produced by the eye is due to the _____ of the ganglion cells.
    a. lasting effect
    b. accommodation
    c. rebound effect
    d. shortening

14. The sensory receptors in the eye are found in the
    a. retina.
    b. cochlea.
    c. ganglion cells.
    d. cornea.

15. The photoreceptors in the eye include
    a. rods and cones.
    b. bipolar cells.
    c. ganglion cells.
    d. bipolar cells.

16. The eardrum transmits vibrations produced by objects in the environment to the receptor cells in the inner ear by means of the
    a. auditory canal.
    b. pinna.
    c. cochlea.
    d. ossicles.

17. A healthy ear can detect frequencies from _____ to _____ Hz.
    a. 10; 10,000
    b. 30; 20,000
    c. 150; 150,000
    d. 15,000; 150,000

18. The characteristic of a sound that is described as high or low is called
  a. pitch.
  b. loudness.
  c. amplitude.
  d. timbre.

19. Gustation is also known as the sense of
  a. taste.
  b. hearing.
  c. smell.
  d. vision,

20. Which of the following is *not* a basic taste for humans?
  a. mint
  b. bitter
  c. salt
  d. sweet

21. In the nose, the receptor cells are located in the
  a. olfactory bulbs.
  b. microvilli.
  c. papillae.
  d. olfactory mucosa.

22. Which of the following situations would best be explained by gate-control theory?
  a. the pain of a pin prick to the skin
  b. the smell of dinner cooking
  c. the taste of your favorite cookie
  d. the sound of paper rustling

23. A small paper cut on the finger can hurt a lot, but when we suffer a major injury like a broken bone, we often feel very little pain at the time of the injury. This is probably because when we suffer a traumatic injury, our brain releases
  a. serotonin.
  b. endorphins.
  c. pheromones.
  d. hormones.

24. Three theories of how the brain processes information include *all except one* of the following. Which one should *not* be included?
  a. template theory
  b. prototype theory
  c. visual association theory
  d. distinctive feature theory

25. If they are shown to exist, telepathy and clairvoyance would be examples of
  a. precognition.
  b. subliminal perception.
  c. extrasensory perception.
  d. Gestalt principles of perception.

Essay Questions (5 points each)

  1. Define and differentiate between the processes of <u>sensation</u> and <u>perception.</u>
  2. Identify the major structures and cells of the eye and describe their functions.
  3. Describe the major features of the inner ear and their functions.
  4. Define <u>illusions</u> as the term is used by psychologists.
  5. Cite evidence for or against extrasensory perception.

Multiple-Choice Questions

1. a

Sensation is defined as the detection of sensory stimuli in the environment, such as light, dark, color, warmth or cold, or sweet or sour.

2. a

Perception is defined as the ability to organize and interpret the stimuli we receive from the environment.

3. b

Transduction refers to the conversion of physical stimuli into signals that are transmitted to the brain.

4. d

The minimum amount of physical stimulation necessary for us to experience a sensation 50 percent of the time is called the absolute threshold.

5. d

Ernst Weber, a German anatomist, coined the term "just noticeable difference" to signify the amount of change necessary before the change is noticeable.

6. b

Signal detection theory posits that every stimulus event requires an individual to discriminate between a signal and a noise.

7. b

Sensory adaptation is the process of getting used to a stimulus; it ensures that a stimulus does not continue to register as intensely as when it is first received.

8. b

Research into subliminal perception, or exposing people to messages that are not perceived by the conscious mind, has shown that, while the signals are received at some level, they do not translate into specific behavioral actions.

9. b

The iris consists of two bands of muscles that control the amount of light that enters the eye.

10. a

The cornea lies on the surface of the eyeball; the eyeball itself, immediately behind, is filled with a fluid called the aqueous humor.

11. c

The human eye can perceive stimuli received through a wavelength of between 380 and 760 nanometers, or the visible spectrum.

12. c

Glaucoma results when the blockage of the passage returning the aqueous humor to the blood, or overproduction of fluid, produces pressure on the inside of the eye.

13. c

The rebound effect is the result of ganglion cells that are firing either more slowly or more rapidly than normal, which produces a negative afterimage of something that we have stared at.

14. a

The sensory receptors in the eye are located in the retina.

15. a

The photoreceptors in the eye contain rods, which are light-sensitive, and cones, which perceive colors.

16. d

The ossicles are the three tiny bones called the hammer, the anvil, and the stirrup. These three bones transmit the vibrations of the eardrum to the liquid-filled cochlea.

17. b

A healthy ear can detect frequencies between 30 and 20,000 Hz.

18. a

Pitch is the characteristic of sound described as being high or low.

19. a

Gustation is the term used for the sense of taste.

20. a

Mint is not a basic taste for humans. The four basic tastes are sweet, sour, bitter, and salty.

21. d

The receptor cells for smells are located in the olfactory mucosa, located at the base of the brain. These receptor cells pass through small holes in the bone above the mucosa and form synapses with olfactory bulbs, which begin to process olfactory information.

22. a

Gate-control theory is a theory to explain the mechanism of pain such as, for example, the pain of a pin prick. Gate-control theory postulates that various gates must be opened or closed to control the amount of the pain message that is transmitted to the brain.

23. b

Endorphins, which are natural substances produced in the brain, are thought to prevent pain signals from reaching the brain. The evolutionary purpose of endorphins is to allow individuals to carry on with essential activities even when painful stimuli are present.

24. c

Theories about how the brain processes visual input include the theory that the brain provides templates or visual memories; that the brain creates prototypes or idealized patterns; that the brain uses distinctive features to recognize specific items.

25. c

Clairvoyance and telepathy are forms of extrasensory perception, or perception that occurs without input from the senses. There is little or no research evidence that any type of extrasensory perception actually exists.

Essay Questions

1. Define and differentiate between the processes of *sensation* and *perception*.

   Sensation is the detection of sensory stimuli in the environment, such as light, dark, or color; warmth or cold; or sweet or sour. Perception is the process of organization and interpretation of the experience of the senses. Sensations are detected in various organs of the body and transmitted through the nervous system to the brain. The brain is the organ that interprets, or perceives, patterns and meaning in the physical stimuli.

2. Identify the major structures and cells of the eye and describe their functions.

   The major features of the eye include the cornea, a transparent membrane to admit light; the iris, two bands of muscles that control the amount of light that enters; the lens of the eye, which focuses images onto the retina, or inner surface of the eye. The eyeball is filled with a watery fluid called the aqueous humor.

   The retina contains thousands of photoreceptor cells that transmit information to the optic disk, where the axons of the photoreceptor cells join the optic nerve, which travels to the brain via the bipolar cells and the ganglion cells. The photoreceptors consist of rods, which perceive light and dark, and cones, which perceive colors. Variations in the shape of the eye can create vision problems, as can too much pressure in the aqueous humor, which produces a condition called glaucoma.

3. Describe the major features of the inner ear and their functions.

   The major features of the inner ear include the eardrum, a flexible membrane that vibrates in response to sound waves; the ossicles (hammer, anvil, and stirrup), tiny bones that transmit the vibrations to the cochlea via the oval window; the basilar membrane, which bisects the cochlea and contains the auditory receptor cells; the round window, which acts to stabilize pressure in the ear; and the auditory hair cells, which translate the mechanical energy of the vibrations in the cochlea into neural activity. Loudness is created by different rates of firing of axons, and pitch is created by the firing of different axons; timbre is a combination of sounds, called overtones, and the fundamental frequency, or pitch, of the sound.

4. Define *illusions* as the term is used by psychologists.

Psychologists use the term *illusions* to refer to incorrect perceptions, or instances in which the brain is tricked into making incorrect assumptions about size, shape, or distance. Illusions can be visual, but they can also be produced by the other senses. As an example, the skin senses can transmit information about the sensations of hot and cold that will trick the brain into believing that lukewarm water is actually warmer or colder than it is.

5. Cite evidence for or against extrasensory perception.

There is actually no compelling scientific evidence of extrasensory perception, whether it be evidence of clairvoyance, precognition, telepathy, or psychokinesis. Most of those who have become known for displaying extrasensory perception, such as Uri Geller, have been found to be using tricks or deception to produce their effects. Evidence of extrasensory perception is still being investigated by parapsychologists, those who specialize in the field.

UNIT II: BASIC PSYCHOLOGICAL PROCESSES

CHAPTER 4—STATES OF CONSCIOUSNESS

 FLASH FOCUS

When you complete this chapter, you will be able to:

✓ Define consciousness and describe the range of variations in the conscious state

✓ Describe the biological changes the occur during the sleep process

✓ Name and describe some common sleep disorders

✓ Differentiate among three therapeutic means of affecting consciousness

✓ Describe the five main categories of psychoactive drugs, including the body systems affected and the physiological effects produced

✓ Discuss what happens in the process of becoming dependent on a drug or alcohol, and in the process of withdrawal

Use a highlighter to identify ideas, terms, and people that your instructor refers to in lectures or emphasizes in the course. Add to the chart any other ideas, terms, or people that your instructor discusses.

Core Concepts in States of Consciousness

Important Ideas	Key Terms	Important People
Consciousness	Circadian rhythms	Wilhelm Wundt
States of consciousness	"Morning person"	John B. Watson
Altered states of consciousness	"Night person"	Robert Ornstein
Biological rhythms	Suprachiasmatic nucleus	David Galin
Selective attention	Pineal gland	Daniel Dennett
Self-awareness	Melatonin	Richard Restak
Sleep	Jet lag	Steven Pinker
Dreams	Materialist perspective	W. Webb
Insomnia	Philosophical perspective	Sigmund Freud
Cognitive perspective	Controlled processing	Carl Jung
Biological perspective	Automatic processing	Allan Hobson
Hypnosis	Short-term (working)	Robert McCarley
Biofeedback	Memory	Franz Anton Mesmer
Meditation	Electroencephalogram (EEG)	K. S. Bowers
Consciousness-altering drugs	Electromyogram (EMG)	Neal E. Miller
Depressants	Electro-oculogram (EOG)	
Barbiturates	Beta waves	
Psychostimulants	Alpha waves	
Narcotics/opiates	Delta activity	
Psychedelics/hallucinogens	REM (rapid eye movement)	
Drug dependence	Sleep	
	Fatal familial insomnia	

	Drug-dependent insomnia Narcolepsy Somnambulism Night terrors Sleep apnea Lucid dream Manifest content Latent content Collective unconscious Mesmerism Posthypnotic suggestion Posthypnotic amnesia Social-cognitive (role-playing) view Neodissociative view Executive/central control Function Monitoring function Theory of dissociated Control Mindful meditation Concentrative meditation Mantra Physiological dependence Psychological dependence Alcoholism Alcoholics Anonymous Opium Morphine Codeine Heroin Withdrawal Amphetamines Cocaine Crack cocaine LSD (lysergic acid Diethylamide)/acid Ecstasy "Designer drugs" Marijuana	

The Definition and Study of Consciousness

FLASH SUMMARY

Consciousness, or the awareness of one's own perceptions, thoughts, feelings, sensations, and external environment, was considered an appropriate subject for study by early psychologists, including *Wilhelm Wundt.* Later, however, behaviorists such as *John B. Watson* argued that consciousness is not an appropriate subject for psychological study, since it is not a physical process that can be studied and measured. During the 1960s and 1970s, however, issues of *altered states of consciousness* due to meditation or drugs, as well as development of information-processing models due to the creation of computers, came to the attention of psychologists, who returned to the study of consciousness.

The term *states of consciousness* refers to the varying degrees of awareness that are experienced by all human beings on a daily basis. *Altered states of consciousness* refers to states of consciousness that have been different states of consciousness that are created either through drugs or through intentional techniques such as meditation or hypnosis.

Consciousness is affected by certain *biological rhythms,* or fluctuations in bodily processes, that occur on a regular basis. The fluctuations of energy that we refer to as being a "morning person" or a "night person" are called the *circadian rhythm.* Other fluctuations, such as the hunger cycle, occur more frequently, and cycles such as mating seasons occur on a longer-term basis. Research has identified the *suprachiasmatic nucleus (SCN),* located within the hypothalamus, as playing an important role in the regulation of internal rhythms; in fact, there is some evidence to suggest that individual cells within the structure may be able to keep track of time.

For longer-term cycles such as the mating cycle, the *pineal gland,* located in the midbrain just in front of the cerebellum, may play an important role. The pineal gland secretes *melatonin,* which has been found to affect many basic physiological processes including sleep or hibernation in some species. Research suggests that taking melatonin may help people to recover from *jet lag,* or the disorientation caused by disruption of one's regular circadian rhythms.

Psychologists have posited a number of theories about the nature of consciousness. In the late 1970s, *Robert Ornstein* proposed that two modes of consciousness are each controlled by one hemisphere of the brain: the active-verbal-rational mode that is dominated by the left hemisphere and the receptive-spatial-intuitive-holistic mode that is dominated by the right hemisphere. Ornstein and collaborator *David Galin* back up their theory with laboratory data on the specialized functions of the left and right hemispheres of the brain. Other models of consciousness have been proposed by *Daniel Dennett* and neurologist *Robert Restak.* In Dennett's book *Consciousness Explained,* Dennett proposed that the brain creates multiple copies of experiences that are continually being updated and analyzed, and this process of analysis creates consciousness. In Restak's book *The Modular Brain,* he suggests that consciousness resides in the many different parts of the brain that control behavior rather than in one centrally organized location. In 1997, *Steven Pinker* maintained that the brain has evolved in order to help humans solve certain problems in their environment in order to survive. In effect, Pinker sees the brain as a computer that happened to evolve reasoning and consciousness. In general today, theories of consciousness reflect either the *materialist perspective,* which relies on studies of physiology, or the *philosophical perspective,* which focuses on the role of subjective experience.

Waking consciousness does not include every single bit of sensory input that we experience, probably because that amount of information would be overwhelming and would have negative effects—we might not be able to pay attention to key information such as an attacking predator. Therefore, the brain utilizes a process called *selective attention* to direct our attention only to selected sensory data. In *controlled processing,* an individual deliberately directs their attention to certain phenomena; for example, when driving, the individual is (hopefully) paying attention to the road and to other cars. In *automatic processing,* several different activities can occur at the same time; for example, the person can drive and also listen to the radio. The process of selective attention also affects memory and the information that is retained by the *short-term (working) memory.*

The process of consciously focusing our mind on ourselves is called *self-awareness.* Some studies suggest that people are more likely to focus on themselves when they are in a negative mood than when they are in a positive mood. While self-awareness is a goal in certain kinds of psychotherapy, it can also have a backlash effect, such as when an individual becomes too self-conscious to perform well.

Sleep and Sleep Disorders

FLASH SUMMARY

Sleep is a process in which the body experiences major physiological changes and the mind experiences changes in consciousness. Scientists can measure changes in brain waves during sleep with an *electroencephalogram (EEG)*, changes in muscle activity with an *electromyogram (EMG)*, and changes in eye movements with an *electro-oculogram (EOG)*. Each of these methods records systematic changes during the process of "falling asleep" and in the various states of sleep. An EEG indicates that brain waves proceed from *beta waves*, which are found in an awake and alert brain, to *alpha waves*, which are of lower frequency, and finally to *delta activity*, which exhibits high-amplitude waves. In the meantime, individuals exhibit changes in eye movements until they enter a state called *REM (rapid eye movement) sleep*. During REM sleep, the brain displays characteristics of beta activity. REM sleep is also associated with the appearance of *dreams*, or images and even stories that occur during sleep.

Scientists have posited several possible purposes of the sleep state: most obviously, that it allows our minds to rest and recover from daily activities. One investigator, *W. Webb*, has posited that sleep developed as an evolutionary response to the increased danger during the night, a period for which human beings do not have adaptive sensory mechanisms. Scientists have also posited that REM sleep, or the state of dreaming, allows humans to consolidate the information and memories acquired during the day. It has been shown that sleep deprivation, and particularly deprivation of the state of REM sleep, adversely affects people and even animals. Studies with animals and human beings deprived of sleep have shown an increasing level of anxiety and irritability, difficulty concentrating, and poor performance on tests; sleep deprivation has even been used as a form of torture to induce pliability in prisoners. A disorder called *fatal familial insomnia* causes individuals to receive less and less sleep, and fewer periods of REM sleep, and is ultimately fatal, although scientists are unsure whether it is either the sleep deprivation itself or other neurological problems that cause death.

Everyone has experienced occasions of *insomnia*, or the inability to fall asleep or to maintain sleep. Instances of insomnia seem to increase with age, and are more common among women than among men. While many people report instances of insomnia, in some instances laboratory studies have shown that they are, in fact, receiving a normal amount of sleep. Taking sleeping pills can even exacerbate insomnia by producing *drug-dependent insomnia*, in which a person needs larger and larger amounts of drugs to combat insomnia. Scientists and physicians recommend the following as tactics to combat insomnia:

1. Read something pleasant or relaxing just before going to sleep.

2. Go to bed at the same time each night.

3. Take a warm bath before going to bed.

4. Avoid coffee, tea, or caffeinated drinks late in the day.

5. Don't smoke, and avoid excessive use of alcohol.

6. Exercise every day, but not just before going to sleep.

7. Don't take naps during the day.

8. Don't be overly concerned about isolated instances of insomnia.

9. If insomnia persists, get up and pursue another activity (reading, working, watching TV) until you become drowsy. Don't focus on the fact that you are not sleeping.

10. Other. (Add your own tactics for combating insomnia to this list.)

Adapted from Robert A. Baron, *Psychology*, Fifth Edition (Allyn and Bacon, Boston, 2001), p. 126.

Other conditions that affect sleep include the condition known as *narcolepsy,* a disorder in which sleep occurs at unexpected, and even inappropriate, times. *Somnambulism,* or sleep walking, is experienced by at least 25 percent of children at some time. A related disorder, *night terrors,* also primarily affects children, who wake up with signs of intense arousal and powerful feelings of fear, but with no particular memories of a dream that induced the feelings. A disorder that more often affects adults is called *sleep apnea,* in which people stop breathing while they are asleep; they then wake up, and when they fall asleep, are awakened again, many times throughout the night.

Dreams are a particularly intriguing state of consciousness that is associated with REM (rapid eye movement) sleep. While people do dream during non-REM sleep, such dreams tend to be less visual, less bizarre, and to contain less action imagery. Researchers estimate that people have around four dreams per night, with each dream lasting between a few seconds to a few minutes. The average person is estimated to have more than 100,000 dreams in a lifetime. In some dreams, individuals become aware that they are dreaming, and can affect events in their dream; this is called a *lucid dream.*

Psychologists have proposed many theories about the nature of dreams. The best known theories are the psychodynamic views of *Sigmund Freud,* who believed that dreams have both a *manifest content,* or obvious story line and characters, and a *latent content,* or hidden meaning and symbolism. Freud used dreams extensively in the process of psychoanalysis. *Carl Jung,* a student of Freud who developed his own theoretical school, believed that dreams were an expression of the *collective unconscious,* a storehouse of primitive ideas and imagery. More contemporary schools of *cognitive thought* posit that dreams express current wishes and desires, and issues with which a person is currently struggling. In the *biological perspective,* individuals are simply experiencing attempts by the cortex to coordinate haphazard, incoherent images arising from the two hemispheres of the brain. Two researchers from Harvard Medical School, *Allan Hobson* and *Robert McCarley,* theorize that, during REM sleep, some parts of the brain that contain memories, vision, audition, and even emotion, are activated by cells in the hindbrain, particularly the pons. The cortex attempts to synthesize these messages, but produces only a fragmented message. This theory is supported by other researchers who contend that the brain is simply undertaking "housecleaning" activities to clear away images and memories that are no longer needed in conscious thought.

Altered Consciousness as a Therapeutic Technique

FLASH SUMMARY

Hypnosis is an altered state of consciousness in which one person (the hypnotist) apparently controls the thoughts and behaviors of another (the subject). The process was first introduced to the public by *Franz Anton Mesmer,* an Austrian physician, in the eighteenth century. Mesmer believed that the process, which came to be known as *mesmerism,* could be used to treat disease. Hypnotists have used both *posthypnotic suggestion,* in which a subject is influenced to do something after the process of hypnosis has been completed, in response to a cue or stimulus, and *posthypnotic amnesia,* in which the subject does not recall having been hypnotized.

Some people who are the subjects of hypnosis appear to enter into an altered state of consciousness that resembles sleep, and they become highly susceptible to the suggestions of the hypnotist. It is estimated that about 15 percent of people are highly susceptible to hypnosis, 10 percent are highly resistant, and the remainder fall somewhere in between. It has also been found that people who are more susceptible to hypnosis have high levels of visual imagery, vivid fantasies, and expect to be influenced by hypnotic suggestions. Thus, scientists have theorized that hypnosis may involve the individual's expectations about the outcome of hypnosis and on their attempts to conform to what they feel is expected of them. This view, called the *social–cognitive* or *role-playing view*, holds that the effects of hypnosis are the result of the relationship between the hypnotist and the subject, and the subject's tendency to play the "social role" of obeying the hypnotist's suggestions.

The *neodissociative view* of hypnosis contends that the process of hypnosis produces a split between the *executive* or *central control function*, which regulates our behavior, and the *monitoring function*, through which we observe our own behavior. Hypnosis then creates a barrier or dissociation that prevents hypnotic experiences or suggestions from entering into consciousness. *K. S. Bowers* has also suggested, in the *theory of dissociated control*, that hypnotism reflects a weakening of the central control function rather than a total dissociation. There seems to be some evidence for both dissociative and social-cognitive theories, although the weight of evidence supports the social-cognitive view.

Hypnosis has been used to control pain, to break habits such as smoking, and even to assist individuals in bringing unconscious memories to conscious recollection. Both the American Medical Association and the American Psychological Association have opposed the use of hypnosis in criminal proceedings, since the process is not entirely understood. However, therapists have made use of hypnosis to bring traumatic events to conscious recollection and, in some cases, to aid in the treatment of phobias.

Another process that has been used to alter consciousness is *biofeedback*. Psychologist *Neal E. Miller* had trained rats to control certain glandular processes thought to be involuntary, and he believed that humans could also benefit from the same techniques. In biofeedback, people learn to monitor and control some of their bodily functions, such as relaxing the heart and lowering the blood pressure through relaxation techniques. People usually learn biofeedback techniques with the aid of electrodes that monitor and display brain waves. While there is some skepticism about the use of biofeedback to improve health or regulate pain, research indicates that it can actually be helpful in some instances.

Another technique that is used to alter consciousness is *meditation*, or the use of a variety of techniques, including relaxation and concentration, to produce an altered state of consciousness. People who practice meditation claim that it can be used to increase self-awareness, produce feelings of inner peace or detachment, reduce anxiety and a variety of physical symptoms like headaches, asthma, and other illnesses. In *mindful meditation*, individuals attempt to empty the mind and remain still; in *concentrative meditation*, individuals concentrate on a visual image or a word called a *mantra* that is repeated over and over. Some studies have shown that people practicing meditation are actually able to change physiological responses such as oxygen intake, brain-wave activity, and sleep patterns. However, more research needs to be done in order to understand exactly how the process of meditation affects the brain.

Altered Consciousness as a Result of Drugs

FLASH SUMMARY

Consciousness-altering drugs are drugs, or biological agents, that produce changes in conscious awareness. These drugs fall into a number of categories, including *depressants* such as alcohol; *barbiturates,* contained in sleeping pills and relaxants; *stimulants* such as amphetamines; *opiates,* or painkilling drugs; and *psychedelic* or *hallucinogenic* drugs, which cause hallucinations.

Drugs, including alcohol, are powerful substances, because they can produce *dependence*. The dependence on drugs can be either *physiological,* in which dependence is based on biological changes in the body, or *psychological,* in which individuals experience a strong desire to continue using the drug. Drug use, of both legal and illegally obtained drugs, is prevalent in the United States, as is drug dependence.

Alcohol is called a depressant, since it acts on the central nervous system to decrease arousal and diminish inhibitions. Alcohol is also referred to as a *sedative– hypnotic* drug, since it relaxes, calms, and eventually produces sleep in the user. Alcohol is the most prevalent drug in the United States. The U.S. Department of Health and Human Services estimates that about 80 percent of urban adults have used alcohol at some time, and some 10 million people in the United States are thought to be either problem drinkers or alcoholics. *Alcoholism* is a physiological and psychological dependence on alcohol that may have some genetic component. Chronic excessive use of alcohol is associated with loss of brain tissue, liver malfunctions, and impaired cognitive and motor abilities. There are many different kinds of treatment programs that assist people with alcohol problems in reducing their dependence on alcohol; some of the best known programs, such as *Alcoholics Anonymous,* which is a free, voluntary program, have a goal of abstinence from alcohol. Other programs aim to help the problem drinker to understand the root causes of his or her dependence and to minimize the effects of alcohol consumption.

Barbiturates and tranquilizers are also classed as sedative–hypnotic drugs. Barbiturates act by decreasing the excitability of neurons throughout the nervous system. They are also depressants that calm the body by depressing the central nervous system. Today, however, barbiturates have mostly been replaced by *tranquilizers,* which sedate and calm people; Valium and Xanax are examples of tranquilizers. Both barbiturates and tranquilizers can be psychologically and physiologically addictive.

Narcotic drugs, or *opiates,* are drugs that are derived from the opium poppy, including *opium, morphine, codeine,* and *heroin.* Both morphine and codeine are prescribed for pain relief and, in the case of codeine, for cough suppression. Heroin is a highly addictive drug that causes a rush of pleasurable sensations, followed by drowsiness and impaired concentration; the drug must be taken every 6 hours or so, or the heroin addict will go into *withdrawal,* a physiological process characterized by nausea, stomach cramps, depression, insomnia, and pain. There are an estimated 850,000 heroin addicts in the United States.

Amphetamines and *cocaine* are called *psychostimulants,* since they increase alertness, reduce fatigue, and elevate the mood. They act on the central nervous system and increase blood pressure and heart rate. The drugs produce psychological dependence, as well as states of exhaustion, lethargy, and depression in the absence of the drug. Processed cocaine that is smoked is called *crack cocaine;* it is highly addictive, probably because inhaling the drug causes large amounts to be absorbed into the body. Consistent use of cocaine produces sleep disorders, irritability, panic attacks, and even mental disorders such as paranoia, agitation, and suicidal behavior. Overdosing on cocaine can cause heart attacks, hemorrhages, and stroke. About 43 percent of admissions to drug treatment centers are for addiction to cocaine.

Psychedelic drugs, also called *hallucinogens,* can range from *LSD (lysergic acid diethylamide or "acid")* to *Ecstasy.* Drugs such as Ecstasy are called *"designer drugs,"* because they were deliberately manufactured in a chemical lab to induce certain states of consciousness. Hallucinogenic drugs usually create mind-altering and vivid imagery, as well as changes in perception of time and distance. Ecstasy is known to produce physiological changes, since it acts by destroying cells that enable dopamine to be reabsorbed into the body. Ecstasy and LSD can both produce psychological difficulties, sometimes weeks after the drugs are taken (called "flashbacks"), that can include confusion, depression, and paranoia. Since Ecstasy is manufactured by many different people under different conditions, other substances may inadvertently be created that can have lethal effects.

Marijuana, or the leaves of the cannabis plant, is also a psychedelic drug, which is usually smoked. The effects of marijuana are experienced immediately and disappear completely after 3–5 hours; marijuana interferes with attention and memory, as well as creates slowed reaction times and impaired performance of motor tasks. Long-term use may produce lasting changes in the chemistry of the brain, including problems with attention, memory, and learning. Marijuana is not physiologically addictive, but it can produce psychological dependence. Anecdotal evidence suggests that marijuana is helpful to some individuals who suffer from AIDS or who are undergoing chemotherapy for cancer, by suppressing nausea and increasing appetite. However, efforts to decriminalize marijuana have been unsuccessful, and even medical use of the drug has been banned by recent court decisions.

 FLASH REVIEW

Complete the following table of consciousness-altering drugs and their effects. Include any other types of drugs, or any additional information, which is provided by your instructor in your class.

Drugs and Their Effects

Classification	Type of Drug	Body Systems Affected	Psychologically Addictive?	Physiologically Addictive?
Depressants	Alcohol	Depress central nervous system, dampen arousal systems	Yes	Yes
Barbiturates	Barbiturates Tranquilizers	Decrease excitability of neurons, depress central nervous system		
Narcotics				
Psychostimulants				
Psychedelics				

 **FLASH TEST**

Review the table of Core Concepts at the beginning of this chapter. Then take the Practice Exam on the following pages, and rate your performance.

PRACTICE TEST

(Chapter 4—States of Consciousness)

Multiple Choice (3 points each)

1. Our awareness of our abilities to perceive, to remember, and to think is called
   a. cognition.
   b. information processing.
   c. consciousness.
   d. metaperception.

2. The events of which we become conscious are determined by
   a. perception.
   b. cognition.
   c. consciousness.
   d. selective attention.

3. Fluctuations in bodily processes and in consciousness over the course of a single day are known as
   a. biological rhythms.
   b. circadian rhythms.
   c. recurring rhythms.
   d. reverberating rhythms.

4. Alcohol, drugs, meditation, and hypnosis can induce
   a. regular states of consciousness.
   b. circadian states of consciousness.
   c. unconscious consciousness.
   d. altered states of consciousness.

5. In the attentional state labeled _____, we choose to pay attention to only certain sensory data.
   a. automatic processing
   b. limited attention
   c. attention deficit
   d. controlled processing

6. If you think of yourself as a "night" person, when will you be best able to pay attention in the classroom?
   a. morning classes
   b. afternoon classes
   c. all day Saturday classes
   d. it really does not matter

7. What type of processing is being demonstrated when you are watching a basketball game on television and listening to your favorite song on the stereo?
   a. controlled
   b. latent
   c. automatic
   d. manifest

8. Assuming you are fully awake and alert, your EEG pattern would probably contain many
   a. delta waves.
   b. alpha waves.
   c. beta waves.
   d. theta waves.

9. During REM sleep, the brain displays characteristics of
   a. alpha activity.
   b. beta activity.
   c. delta activity.
   d. little or no activity.

10. The evolutionary or circadian theory of why we need sleep can be summarized as follows.
   a. I've been up for 16 hours and I'm tired, worn out, and sleepy.
   b. It will be dark soon, and it's safer to be in bed than out and about.
   c. I learned a lot today, so I need sleep to properly process and store my new knowledge.
   d. A lot happened today, so I need sleep to purge my brain of the trivia and clean out my overloaded brain circuits.

11. Sleepwalking is called
   a. narcolepsy.
   b. sleep apnea.
   c. somniloquy.
   d. somnambulism.

12. Excessive daytime sleepiness and sudden, uncontrollable attacks of REM sleep are symptoms of
   a. narcolepsy.
   b. sleep apnea.
   c. somniloquy.
   d. somnambulism.

13. Which of the following factors are *not* correlated with increased levels of insomnia?
   a. sex
   b. age
   c. daily exercise
   d. stress

14. Which of the following recommendations should *not* be used to combat insomnia?
   a. Remain in bed, and focus on the passage of time.
   b. Take daily exercise, but not just before going to bed.
   c. Don't take naps during the day.
   d. Avoid coffee, tea, or caffeinated drinks late in the day.

15. Sigmund Freud believed that dreams function to
   a. replenish our physical and mental energy.
   b. cleanse the unconscious of unnecessary mental images.
   c. help us solve daily problems or rehearse stressful events.
   d. satisfy our unconscious sexual and aggressive wishes.

16. Researchers Hobson and McCarley theorize that dreams are a result of
   a. a need to rehearse daily hassles and stressful events.
   b. the desire to satisfy unconscious sexual and aggressive urges.
   c. the need to clean overloaded mental circuits.
   d. the random firing of cells in parts of the brain that contain memories, vision, audition, and emotion.

17. The process of hypnosis was first utilized by_____.
   a. Freud.
   b. Breuer.
   c. Hilgard.
   d. Mesmer.

18. Two contrasting views about the process of hypnosis are the _____ view and the _____ view.
   a. neoclassic; perpetual
   b. social–cognitive; neodissociation
   c. cognitive; dissociation
   d. classic; sensational

19. A technique in which people use information about their bodies' involuntary responses in order to control those responses is called
    a. meditation.
    b. biofeedback.
    c. hypnosis.
    d. synthesis.

20. A person who meditates daily by focusing on a short prayer or one word is using which kind of meditation?
    a. mindful
    b. concentrative
    c. hypnotic
    d. induced

21. Alcohol is classified as a(n)
    a. depressant.
    b. stimulant.
    c. amphetamine.
    d. hallucinogen.

22. Barbiturates take effect in the body by
    a. decreasing the excitability of neurons throughout the nervous system.
    b. increasing the heart rate and mental alertness.
    d. destroying cells that allow dopamine to be reabsorbed into the body.
    d. create vivid imagery without sensory input.

23. Drugs that generate sensory perceptions for which there are no external stimuli are
    a. stimulants.
    b. depressants.
    c. hallucinogens.
    d. endorphins.

24. Cocaine and Ecstasy both put users at greater risk for
    a. liver disease.
    b. heart attacks.
    c. depression.
    d. anemia.

25. According to the American Psychological Association, continued drug use that interferes with one's major life roles at home, school, and work, and contributes to legal or psychological problems is called
    a. illicit drug use.
    b. drug affliction.
    c. substance abuse.
    d. depressive abuse.

Essay Questions (5 points each)

1. What are the key characteristics of consciousness?
2. Describe the process of falling asleep and some common sleep disorders.
3. Name some therapeutic means of controlling consciousness, and discuss their effectiveness.
4. List and describe the major categories of consciousness-altering drugs.
5. Differentiate between physiological and psychological drug dependence, and give examples of each.

ANSWER EXPLANATIONS

Multiple-Choice Questions

1. **c**

    Consciousness is the awareness of one's own perceptions, thoughts, feelings, sensations, and external environment.

2. d

Selective attention is the process of directing the attention only to selected sensory data; for example, when driving a car, a person chooses to pay close attention to traffic signals, other cars, and pedestrians.

3. b

Circadian rhythms is a term meaning the daily fluctuations of energy and other bodily processes experienced by human beings.

4. d

Altered states of consciousness can be produced either by the intake of various drugs or by voluntary means such as meditation, hypnosis, or biofeedback.

5. d

In the state called controlled processing, we limit the amount of sensory input to which we pay attention.

6. b

Someone whose circadian rhythm makes them more alert and responsive during the later part of the day (a "night" person) should take classes during the afternoon.

7. c

When you are taking in sensory input from two different activities at the same time, you are utilizing automatic processing.

8. c

Beta waves are generated by the brain and measured by an EEG, when an individual is fully awake and alert.

9. b

Brain waves during REM sleep have characteristics of beta activity, or the activity that one would expect from a person who is awake and alert.

10. b

According to the evolutionary or circadian theory posited by W. Webb and others, sleep is an evolutionary response that is intended to protect us during our most vulnerable hours.

11. d

The correct term for sleepwalking is somnambulism.

12. a

Narcolepsy is a disorder that causes the sufferer to fall asleep suddenly and unexpectedly, and often at inappropriate times.

13. c

Daily exercise can actually help to prevent insomnia. Insomnia is more prevalent among women than men, and increases as people age; stress also increases the likelihood of insomnia.

14. a

Focusing on the fact that one is not asleep is not an effective treatment for insomnia; it is more effective to get up and pursue some quiet activity such as reading, television, or even work, until one feels drowsy.

15. d

Freud believed that dreams are an expression of our latent desires, which have to do with sexuality (and often with forbidden expressions of sexuality) and aggression.

16. d

Hobson and McCarley posit that dreams are simply the cortex's attempt to synthesize the random and meaningless firing of cells in the brain.

17. d

Franz Mesmer first used the process of hypnosis, termed "mesmerism," for the treatment of disease in eighteenth-century Austria.

18. b

The social-cognitive view sees hypnosis as a process of social role-playing, in which the subject attempts to meet the expectations of the hypnotist; the neodissociative view contends that hypnosis actually produces a split or dissociation between the control function and the monitoring function of the brain.

19. b

Biofeedback is a technique in which individuals use feedback such as brain waves to help control those responses, usually with relaxation messages.

20. b

Focusing on one word, often called a mantra, or on a short prayer or phrase, is an example of concentrative meditation. In mindful meditation, individuals simply try to empty their minds and remain still.

21. a

Alcohol is classified as a depressant, since one of its effects is the depression, or decrease in arousal, of the central nervous system.

22. a

Barbiturates act to decrease the excitability of neurons throughout the nervous system, thus causing sensations of calmness and drowsiness.

23. c

Hallucinogens are a class of drugs that create visual imagery without corresponding visual sensory input; they may also create changes in perception of time and distance.

24. b

Cocaine and Ecstasy both have an effect on the heart through stimulation of the body's systems, and overuse can lead to heart attacks.

25. c

The American Psychological Association uses the term "substance abuse" to indicate any dependence, either physiological or psychological, on either drugs or alcohol; such dependence eventually leads to negative consequences including disruption of one's life roles.

Essay Questions

1. What are the key characteristics of consciousness?

Key characteristics of consciousness include awareness of and response to one's environment. Consciousness may include self-awareness, or being aware of one's own thoughts, feelings, and responses. States of consciousness may range from full alertness during the day to states of sleep and dreaming at night, and can include altered states of consciousness such as hypnosis or drug-induced states. Altered states of consciousness are generally very different from ordinary awareness and responsiveness.

2. Describe the process of falling asleep, and name some common sleep disorders.

The process of falling asleep involves changes in brain waves, measured by electroencephalograms, from beta waves, or a normal state of waking consciousness, through alpha waves, a lower-frequency wave, to delta activity, which are high-amplitude waves. At the same time, the movement of the eyes proceeds from non-REM (nonrapid eye movement) to REM (rapid eye movement), at which point the individual is asleep. REM sleep is associated with dreaming; and periods of REM sleep alternate with non-REM sleep throughout the night. People or animals deprived of REM sleep display poorer performance on tests, and it is theorized that REM sleep may play a part in learning.

Sleep disorders include insomnia, or inability (or seeming inability) to sleep; narcolepsy, a disorder in which one falls asleep suddenly and unexpectedly; somnambulism, or sleep-walking; and (usually in children) night terrors, or an experience of arousal and fear.

3. Name some therapeutic means of controlling consciousness, and discuss their effectiveness.

Therapeutic means of controlling consciousness include hypnosis, a process in which the hypnotist is seemingly in control of the subject's thoughts and behavior; biofeedback, in which an individual learns to control processes such as brain-wave activity and heart rate through learned relaxation techniques; and meditation, in which an individual learns to focus attention inward, through either emptying the mind or focusing on a word or symbol, and which also results in a feeling of relaxation and clearer thinking.

There are different theories regarding the activity of hypnosis, with one school, the social-cognitive theorists, contending that the subject is playing a social role and conforming to the expectations of the hypnotist. Another school believes that the control mechanism of the mind is actually diverted or dissociated during the process of hypnosis, so that there is a "disconnect" between sensation and conscious thought. There is some research to support both of these theories, although somewhat more research that supports the view that hypnotism is a social construct.

There is also some physiological evidence of changes in bodily states produced by both biofeedback and meditation, in terms of lowered blood pressure and slowed heart rates; however, more needs to be learned about exactly how these processes work.

4. List and describe the major categories of consciousness-altering drugs.

Major categories of psychoactive, or consciousness-altering, drugs include depressants, including alcohol; barbiturates, including tranquilizers; stimulants, including caffeine and amphetamines; opiates, including opium, morphine, and heroin; and psychedelics or hallucinogens, including marijuana, LSD, and "designer drugs" such as Ecstasy. All of the psychoactive drugs have some effect upon the central nervous system and/or functions of the brain. The depressants "depress" the activity of the central nervous system and dull the senses; they also inhibit coordination and normal functioning of the senses.

The barbiturate drugs may suppress the release of excitatory neurotransmitters, and cause feelings of relaxation, as well as confusion, memory lapses, and inability to concentrate. Stimulants inhibit the reuptake of neurotransmitters, dopamine and norepinephrine, which produces increases in blood pressure, heart rate, and respiration; when the drugs wear off, they can cause depression, anxiety, and fatigue. Opiates, which are derived from opium, produce substances that are thought to mimic substances in the brain (opioid peptides or endorphins) and are extremely pleasurable. However, opiates are both psychologically and physiologically addictive, and produce pain and nausea upon withdrawal from the drugs. Finally, psychedelics or hallucinogens are drugs that are manufactured in chemical laboratories to create certain effects in the brain, including visual hallucinations. Marijuana, derived from the cannabis plant, is also classified as a psychedelic drug. The psychedelic drugs also interfere with normal performance and may produce long-term effects such as depression and apathy.

5. Differentiate between physiological and psychological drug dependence, and give examples of each.

Physiological drug dependence means that the body requires continued doses of the drug, such as heroin, in order to function. Withdrawal from the drug will cause both mental states such as irritability and paranoia and physical symptoms such as nausea and pain.

Psychological dependence indicates that a person has a strong desire to continue using the drug, despite any possible negative impact on health or life. For example, hallucinogenic drugs do not create physiological dependence, but withdrawal may involve psychological effects including confusion, depression, and paranoia.

Many drugs, including alcohol, have a negative effect on the body's systems, and may make the user more vulnerable to heart attack, liver disease, hemorrhage, and stroke.

UNIT II: BASIC PSYCHOLOGICAL PROCESSES

CHAPTER 5—LEARNING AND MEMORY

 FLASH FOCUS

When you complete this chapter, you will be able to:

✓ Define learning and describe and differentiate classical and operant conditioning

✓ Discuss the various types of cognitive learning

✓ Explain the process of memory creation

✓ Discuss memory retrieval and the different causes and types of forgetting

✓ Describe some of the findings on the connection between the memory and the brain and hormonal systems

Use a highlighter to identify ideas, terms, and people that your instructor refers to in lectures or emphasizes in the course. Add to the chart any other ideas, terms, or people that your instructor discusses.

Core Concepts in Learning and Memory

Important Ideas	Key Terms	Important People
Learning	Unconditioned stimulus	Ivan Pavlov
Classical (Pavlovian)	Unconditioned response	Edward L. Thorndike
Conditioning	Conditioned stimulus	B. F. Skinner
Operant (instrumental)	Conditioned response	Wolfgang Kohler
Conditioning	Higher-order conditioning	Edward Tolman
Reinforcement	Strength	Albert Bandura
Punishment	Timing	Allan Baddeley
Schedules of reinforcement	Frequency	Hermann Ebbinghaus
Cognitive learning	Predictability	Wilder Penfield
Insight	Extinction	Elizabeth Loftus
Latent learning	Skinner box	Sir Frederick Bartlett
Cognitive map	Shaping	
Observational learning/	Positive reinforcement	
Modeling	Negative reinforcement	
Memory	Adversive stimulus	
Information-processing	Escape conditioning	
Approach	Avoidance conditioning	
Atkinson–Shiffrin model	Primary reinforcer	
Sensory memory	Secondary reinforcer	
Short–term/working memory	Primary punisher	
Long-term memory	Secondary punisher	
Craik–Lockhart/levels-of-	Learned helplessness	
processing model	Continuous reinforcement	
repressed memory	Fixed-interval schedule of	
"Flashbulb" memory	Reinforcement	

Eidetic imagery	Variable-interval schedule of reinforcement	
	Fixed-ratio schedule of reinforcement	
	Variable-ratio schedule of reinforcement	
	Modeling	
	Encoding	
	Storage	
	Consolidation	
	Retrieval	
	Displacement	
	Declarative/explicit memory	
	Episodic memory	
	Semantic memory	
	Nondeclarative/implicit Memory	
	Priming	
	Recall	
	Retrieval cues	
	Recognition	
	Relearning/savings method	
	Savings score	
	Nonsense syllables	
	Serial position effect	
	Primacy effect	
	Recency effect	
	State-dependent memory Effect	
	Encoding failure	
	Consolidation failure	
	Retrograde amnesia	
	Decay	
	Interference	
	Motivated forgetting	
	Amnesia	
	Retrieval failure	
	Tip-of-the-tongue (TOT) Phenomenon	
	Prospective forgetting	
	Reconstruction	
	Schemas	
	Anterograde amnesia	

Learning and Learning Theory: Classical Conditioning

FLASH SUMMARY

Learning can be defined as a relatively permanent change in behavior that occurs as a result of experiences in the environment. Psychologists have identified several different ways in which learning occurs, including *classical conditioning*, *operant conditioning*, and *cognitive learning*.

The first type of learning, classical conditioning, is associated with the Russian physiologist *Ivan Pavlov*. While studying the digestive system of dogs, Pavlov noticed that the dogs began to salivate before their food was actually brought to them, when they saw their trainers coming toward them. Pavlov abandoned his study of the digestive processes in order to investigate this phenomenon. In a now-famous experiment, he trained the dogs to associate the ringing of a bell with the introduction of their food, and found that, after a short time, the dogs salivated at the sound of the bell. This process has been called *classical*, or *Pavlovian, conditioning*.

Pavlov termed the stimulus that normally produces a reflexive response the *unconditioned stimulus* (in this case the presentation of the food itself), and the normal response (salivation) the *unconditioned response*. He called the bell the *conditioned stimulus*, since through repetition it creates a *conditioned response*, in this case the salivation.

Other psychologists proved that classical conditioning also applies to human beings. One psychologist conducted experiments with infants, in which sounds or lights were linked to the stimulus of a nipple, and the infants soon began to react with sucking motions to only the sounds or lights.

Classical conditioning can be used in conjunction with both positive and negative stimuli (such as loud noises). Advertising makes use of the principles of classical conditioning to attach pleasant associations, such as the sight of beautiful places or pleasant activities, to a neutral stimulus such as a can of beer.

Later psychologists determined that other stimuli may take on the positive or negative associations of the original conditioned stimulus, in a process called *higher-order conditioning*. For example, a negative stimulus like an electric shock can be associated with a bell; the bell can then be associated with a light and with the presence of a specific individual, and the successive stimuli of the light and the individual will stimulate the same negative reaction as the original stimulus, the bell.

Scientists also determined that key factors, including the *strength, timing,* and *frequency* of the unconditioned stimulus affected whether conditioning always occurred. The predictability of the pairing of the unconditioned and conditioned stimuli also affected conditioning. They also determined that the process of conditioning could be reversed through *extinction,* in which the unconditioned stimulus is withheld, which gradually reduces the probability of the conditioned response.

FLASH LINKS TO CLASSICAL CONDITIONING

The following websites provide descriptions and illustrations of classical or Pavlovian conditioning.

1. www.brembs.net/classical/classical.html
2. www.Indiana.edu/~iuepsyc/P103/lear/lear.html

Learning and Learning Theory: Operant Conditioning

FLASH SUMMARY

Several psychologists, including *Edward L. Thorndike,* in the late 1800s, and *B. F. Skinner,* in the 1930s, focused on the process of instilling behavior after the fact by providing rewards or punishments for specific behaviors. This kind of conditioning came to be called *operant or instrumental conditioning*. Differences between classical and operant conditioning include that the behaviors influenced in operant conditioning are usually voluntary, as opposed to involuntary, and that a consequence follows, rather than coexists with, the behavior.

Skinner frequently worked with a mechanism that came to be called the *Skinner box,* a box that contains a mechanism that can be operated by the subject of the experiment and a mechanism for delivery of the consequence, which is either positive (such as food) or negative (such as an electric shock). For example, a hungry rat is placed into the Skinner box, and eventually comes into contact with a lever that, when it is pressed, delivers a measure of food. After hitting the lever by accident, the rat gradually learns to press the lever intentionally to receive more food. This gradual process of reinforcing selected behaviors is called *shaping*.

A *reinforcer* is any event that increases the probability of a recurrence of the response that preceded it; reinforcers can be *positive*, such as food, or *negative*, such as electric shocks. Negative reinforcement increases the probability of a response through removal of an *adversive stimulus;* for example, a rat may learn to avoid an electric shock by going in a particular direction in a maze. In *escape conditioning,* the subject of the experiment learns to end an adversive stimulus by taking some action, such as pressing a bar in order to end an electric shock. In *avoidance conditioning,* the animal learns that taking the action can avoid the adversive stimulus, so the negative stimulus is never applied. Reinforcers are also termed *primary* reinforcers, such as food or water needed for survival, or *secondary* reinforcers, such as good grades or salary increases. Secondary reinforcers have value only when linked with primary reinforcers.

Punishment is the presentation of an unpleasant stimulus, or removal of a pleasant stimulus, in order to decrease the probability of a particular behavior. A *primary punisher* is a stimulus that is inherently painful or unpleasant, such as an electric shock or a spanking. A *secondary punisher* is a stimulus that is relatively neutral but acquires punishing qualities when linked with the primary punisher. Psychologists have learned that punishment by itself is often not sufficient to extinguish behaviors, and that punishment combined with reinforcement is more effective. Punishment can be used to extinguish unwanted behaviors, but it cannot be used to establish new, desired behaviors. The process of exposing subjects to repeated punishment can also lead to *learned helplessness,* in which subjects stop making any response at all to negative stimuli.

As with classical conditioning, psychologists have discovered that the strength, timing, and frequency of reinforcements affect the speed of learning and the amount of work that an individual will undertake in order to obtain a reward or avoid punishment. Psychologists worked with different *schedules of reinforcement* and found that, while *continuous reinforcement* is the simplest reinforcement pattern, *interval schedules* based on time periods and *ratio schedules* based on output can also be effective. A *fixed-interval schedule* of reinforcement provides a reward (or punishment) within a fixed-time period; a *variable-interval schedule* provides reinforcement after varying amounts of time after the appropriate response is made. A *fixed-ratio schedule* provides reinforcement after a given amount of work (such as pressing a bar a certain number of times), whereas a *variable-ratio schedule* provides reinforcement after a predetermined but variable number of responses. A variable-ratio schedule of reinforcement has been found to produce the highest productivity rates, and this information has been used in work settings, such as setting compensation schedules for sales people, and in other settings, such as gambling at slot machines.

FLASH LINKS TO OPERANT CONDITIONING

The following web sites on operant conditioning provide overviews and descriptions of operant conditioning.

1. www.brembs.net/operant/
2. http://epsych.msstate.edu/adaptive/Fuzz/index.html

Cognitive Learning

FLASH SUMMARY

Today, many psychologists take a more comprehensive view of the learning process than of the methods of conditioned learning pioneered by Pavlov and Skinner. The study of *cognitive learning* includes cognitive processes such as thinking, knowing, problem solving, remembering, and creating mental representations. *Wolfgang Kohler,* a German psychologist, studied the behavior of apes and chimpanzees, and realized that they were capable of creative problem-solving behaviors using elements that were outside of their normal experience, such as wooden poles or chairs. Sometimes, the chimpanzees seemed to experience a sudden *insight,* or realization of a relationship between seemingly disparate elements in a problem situation, that enabled them to solve the problem.

Edward Tolman came to believe that learning could take place without reinforcement, which he called *latent learning.* Tolman experimented with rats in a maze and showed that rats that only received a reward after they had been placed in a maze and allowed to wander for a number of days outperformed rats that were rewarded every day for negotiating the maze. Tolman concluded that the rats had formed a *cognitive map,* or mental representation, of the maze, but did not demonstrate their learning until they received reinforcement.

Another type of learning, called *observational learning* or *modeling,* was pointed out by *Albert Bandura,* who believed that learning can result when people observe the behavior of others and note the consequences of that behavior. Parents, movie stars, or athletes can be powerful models for behavior. Bandura also came to believe that aggressive behavior was particularly subject to observational learning, which he demonstrated in experiments in which children imitated adults' aggressive behaviors toward a clown doll. His research originally stimulated some of the debate over the influence of television and movie violence on children's behavior.

Memory Processing and Retrieval

FLASH SUMMARY

Most of the current efforts to understand the process of human memory have been made within the context of the *information-processing approach.* This approach consists of *encoding* information that is to be stored within the memory; *storage* of the information in the brain, which involves the process of *consolidation;* and *retrieval,* or bringing the information into consciousness.

According to the *Atkinson–Shiffrin model,* there are three different interacting memory systems called *sensory, short-term,* and *long-term memory.* Sensory memory refers to information that is taken in by the senses and retained for only a very brief time (only a fraction of a second in the case of visual images, and several seconds in the case of sounds). Short-term memory enables us to retain only limited amounts of information (unlike sensory memory, which can contain vast amounts of information) for less than 30 seconds. Short-term memory has only a limited capacity, and when it is filled to capacity, *displacement* can occur, in which each new, incoming item pushes out an existing item which is then forgotten. Short-term memory can hold only about seven to nine "bits" of information such as a phone number; a nine-digit zip code, for example, is difficult or impossible for most people to remember. The process of *rehearsal,* or repeating the information over and over, can help to retain it in short-term memory, but it can easily be lost when the individual is interrupted or distracted.

Psychologist *Allan Baddeley* suggests that a more appropriate term for short-term memory is *working memory,* since it provides a kind of "mental workstation" where information can be manipulated. Research has determined that the prefrontal cortex is the primary area of the brain responsible for short-term or working memory.

Long-term memory is the storehouse of permanent or relatively permanent memories. *Declarative* or *explicit memory* stores facts, information, and personal life events that can be brought to mind either verbally or in the form of images; declarative memory includes *episodic memory,* or the memory of events; *semantic memory,* or memory of general knowledge, includes objective facts and information; *nondeclarative* or *implicit memory* includes motor skills, habits, and conditioned responses, such as eating with a fork or driving a car. *Priming* is a process by which an earlier encounter with a stimulus can increase the speed or accuracy of naming the stimulus.

Psychologists *Craik* and *Lockhart* have proposed an alternative model to the three-system model of memory; they propose a *levels of processing model.* This model presumes that individuals progress from shallow levels of processing, in which information simply creates awareness to a deeper level of processing that takes place when the person interacts with the information, such as making an association with a previous memory.

Psychologists have used three methods to measure memory: *recall,* which is producing information without *retrieval cues; recognition,* which only requires the recognition of previously acquired memories; and *relearning,* or the *savings method,* which compares the amount of time required to relearn information with the time required to learn it originally. The percentage of time saved in relearning material, called the *savings score,* indicates how much material was stored in long-term memory.

Remembering and Forgetting

FLASH SUMMARY

Hermann Ebbinghaus, a late-nineteenth-century psychologist, conducted the first experimental studies on learning and memory. He created *nonsense syllables* to measure the length of time required to learn a list of syllables and then the time that elapsed before they were forgotten. He then compiled a "curve of forgetting" that indicates that the largest amount of information is forgotten very quickly, then gradually tapers off.

The *serial position effect,* or remembering items in a sequence, indicates that information that is taken in at the beginning of a sequence is more likely to be remembered (the *primacy effect*), as is information at the end of the sequence (the *recency effect*); whereas information in the middle of the sequence is more likely to be forgotten. There is also evidence that location, or environmental context, affects memory; for example, people may remember things by going to stand where they were when they initially thought of the item. Also, memory can be affected by alcohol and other drugs; people have been found to be better able to remember when they are in the same state as when they originally learned the information, called the *state-dependent memory effect.* Stress and anxiety also affect the ability to retain information.

Psychologists since then have studied the processes of why we remember certain information and why we forget other information. They have identified many possible causes of forgetting, including *encoding failure,* in which memories fail to be encoded into the long-term memory, and *consolidation failure,* or the failure to create a permanent long-term memory, which can occur due to an accident or illness that causes a loss of consciousness, such as a seizure. *Retrograde amnesia* is a term for the process of losing the memories that occurred shortly before the loss of consciousness.

Other causes of forgetting include *decay,* or memory that fades over time; *interference,* or information or associations stored just before or just after a particular memory that can interfere with the ability to recall the information; *motivated forgetting,* which helps to protect people from memories that are unpleasant or frightening; and *retrieval failure,* or the inability to locate information at the time it is required. The *tip-of-the-tongue (TOT) phenomenon* is a common retrieval failure experience. Another type of forgetting is *prospective forgetting,* or forgetting to carry out some action, such as stopping by the drugstore to pick up a prescription.

Wilder Penfield, a Canadian neurosurgeon, believes that memory is permanently recorded in the brain, like a tape recorder, and only needs the appropriate stimulation in order to be retrieved. *Elizabeth Loftus,* a leading memory researcher, believes that memory is a *reconstruction* that may or may not be entirely accurate. *Sir Frederick Bartlett,* like Elizabeth Loftus, believed that people systematically distort facts and experiences. He felt that memories that conflicted with people's *schemas,* or representations of reality, were altered by distortion or selective retention in order to fit into these frameworks.

Controversial areas in the field of memory include the accuracy of eyewitness testimony, which studies have shown can be very variable and often inaccurate; the influence of hypnosis on eyewitness testimony; and whether *repressed memories* can be "recovered" through therapy.

Other unusual types of memories include *flashbulb memory,* which is an unusually vivid recollection of the time and place of receiving some extremely shocking information, such as learning of an assassination; and *eidetic imagery,* also called "photographic" memory, or the ability to retain the image of a visual stimulus for several minutes and to answer questions based on this retained image. Eidetic imagery is most often found in children, and the ability is lost before adulthood, although there are a few people who retain the ability into adulthood. Cultural factors can also influence memory, such as cultures that are based in oral tradition, in which elders may have many facts and relationships committed to memory.

Memory and the Brain

FLASH SUMMARY

Research into individuals who have suffered brain damage or disease has helped to shed some new light on the process of memory (and forgetting). One famous case, of a man called H.M. whose hippocampal area was surgically removed, resulted in *anterograde amnesia,* in which H.M. could remember nothing that occurred to him after the surgery. He retained only the memories of his first 27 years, and nothing of the remainder of his life. Another individual who sustained massive trauma to the brain in a motorcycle accident was unable to recall any personal memories, although his semantic memory of information about places and things, such as geography and politics, was unharmed. This indicated that the frontal lobe plays a crucial part in episodic memory.

Some hormones, such as estrogen in women, may be involved in the process of memory; estrogen has been shown to have an effect in improving memory in women with Alzheimer's disease. Other memories may be intensified by the action of hormones such as adrenaline (epinephrine) or noradrenaline (norepinephrine).

FLASH LINKS TO MEMORY AND THE BRAIN

The following websites explore the structures of memory and provide an article about the working memory and the brain from *Scientific American.*

1. www.mines.u-nancy.fr/~gueniffe/CoursEMN/I31/ILS/e_for_e/nodes/NODE-8-pg.html

2. www.sciam.com/0897trends.html

FLASH REVIEW

The following chart lists some techniques that can be used to improve memory. For more information on each of these techniques, you can consult a number of "self-help" books on memory improvement. For information on research results into practical methods to improve memory, go to www.mentalmuscles.com/about.html.

Techniques To Improve Memory

Mnemonic Device	Description	Example
Rhyme	Used to remember a sequence of items	The alphabet (ABCs)
First-letter technique	Form a word, phrase, or sentence with the first letter of each word to be remembered	The color spectrum (ROY G. BIV)
Method of loci ("in the first place")	Link familiar locations with objects to be recalled	Grocery list (e.g., bread = garage, apples = basement, napkins = front door)
Pegword system	Rhyming words linked with words on a list to be remembered	One = bun; two = shoe; three = tree; then, link number rhymes to an image of what is to be remembered, e.g., one/bun linked to an image of milk pouring onto a bun will cause you to remember that the first item is milk
Other:		

 FLASH TEST

Review the chart of Core Concepts for this chapter. Then take the Practice Test for Chapter 5 on the following pages and rate your performance.

PRACTICE TEST

(Chapter 5—Learning and Memory)

Multiple Choice (3 points each)

1. The physiologist who accidentally discovered classical conditioning while studying the digestive system in dogs was

    a. Ivan Pavlov.
    b. B. F. Skinner.
    c. John B. Watson.
    d. Robert Rescorla.

2. The process by which a response normally elicited by one stimulus comes to be controlled by another stimulus is called
    a. operant conditioning.
    b. habituation.
    c. classical conditioning.
    d. vicarious learning

3. In classical conditioning, the stimulus that naturally elicits the reflexive behavior is called the _____ stimulus.
    a. unconditioned
    b. conditioned
    c. discriminative
    d. signaling

4. Any neutral stimulus paired with a stimulus such as food that elicits a response is called a(n) _____ stimulus.
    a. unconditioned
    b. discriminative
    c. orienting
    d. conditioned

5. Lisa was stung by a bee when she reached for a flower. She then became very afraid of flowers. One day, her boyfriend handed her a flower. After that, she felt a small degree of fear whenever she saw her boyfriend. The transfer of her fear from the stimulus of the flower to her boyfriend is an example of
    a. spontaneous recovery.
    b. response generalization.
    c. higher-order conditioning.
    d. imitation learning.

6. The name of the procedure in which the unconditioned stimulus no longer follows the conditioned stimulus is
    a. punishment.
    b. negative reinforcement.
    c. discrimination.
    d. extinction.

7. An example of a stimulus that acquires its desirable properties because of its association with other desirable stimuli is
    a. money.
    b. food.
    c. water.
    d. electrical shocks.

8. Learning an association between particular behaviors and their consequences occurs in
    a. classical conditioning.
    b. operant conditioning.
    c. conditioned taste aversion.
    d. blocking.

9. In operant conditioning, procedures that strengthen behaviors are termed
    a. reinforcements.
    b. consequences.
    c. shaping.
    d. chaining.

10. The psychologist who is formally credited with discovering what is now known as operant conditioning is
    a. Ivan Pavlov.

    b. B. F. Skinner.

    c. Edward Thorndike.

    d. John Garcia.

11. The device invented by B. F. Skinner to control the subject's reactions to particular stimuli is known as the
    a. puzzle box.
    b. maze.
    c. control chamber.
    d. Skinner box.

12. Any stimulus that follows a response and decreases the frequency of that response over time is called a
    a. positive reinforcer.
    b. negative reinforcer.
    c. punisher.
    d. discriminative stimulus.

13. The most effective type of reinforcement schedule has been found to be the
    a. variable-interval schedule.
    b. fixed-ratio schedule.
    c. variable-ratio schedule.
    d. fixed-interval schedule.

14. Learning that is based on thinking, problem solving, and remembering is called
    a. cognitive learning.
    b. Pavlovian conditioning.
    c. operant learning.
    d. classical conditioning.

15. In a set of famous experiments, Edward Tolman showed that rats can learn their way around in a maze even without reinforcement. Tolman concluded that the rats
    a. were distracted by the food reward.
    b. learned to ignore the food reward.
    c. learned cognitive maps of the maze.
    d. showed insight learning in the maze.

16. Albert Bandura's experiments showed that children who watched an adult attack a doll were more likely to attack the doll later on. This is evidence for the importance of
    a. classical conditioning.
    b. maturational development.
    c. stimulus generalization.
    d. observational learning.

17. The three tasks of memory are
    a. receiving, processing, storage.
    b. encoding, storage, retrieval.
    c. limiting, compression, processing.
    d. decoding, compression, retrieval.

18. According to the Atkinson–Shiffrin model, the three interacting memory systems are called
    a. receiving, processing, storage.
    b. encoding, storage, retrieval.
    c. sensory, short-term, and long-term.
    d. explicit, episolic, and semantic.

19. Ralph has looked up a phone number to dial, but before he can dial the number, someone asks him the time. He has now forgotten the phone number, which he had stored in
    a. sensory memory.
    b. short-term memory.
    c. explicit memory.
    d. semantic memory.

20. Memory that can hold large quantities of information for a very short period of time is the
    a. sensory memory.

    b. short-term memory.

    c. explicit memory.

    d. semantic memory.

21. Declarative or explicit memory stores
    a. motor skills and habits.
    b. information to be manipulated.
    c. conditioned responses.
    d. facts, information, and personal life events.

22. If a person had damage to his nondeclarative or implicit memory, he would no longer remember
    a. specific life events.
    b. skills such as how to drive a car.
    c. facts and information.
    d. phone numbers.

23. Three methods used to measure memory include *all except one* of the following; which one should *not* be included?
    a. recall
    b. recognition
    c. retrieval cues
    d. relearning

24. All except one of the following is a cause of forgetting; which one of the following is *not* a cause of forgetting?
    a. encoding failure
    b. serial position effect
    c. consolidation failure
    d. decay

25. "Flashbulb memory" is an unusual type of memory that involves
    a. the ability to retain visual information, such as a page of text, for several minutes.
    b. the ability to recall only personal memories and no information about places and things.
    c. an unusually vivid recollection of the time and place where one received shocking information.
    d. the ability to accurately identify a crime suspect's facial features.

Essay Questions (5 points each)

1. Define learning and describe and distinguish between classical conditioning and operant conditioning.

2. Define cognitive learning and describe the contributions of Wolfgang Kohler, Edward Tolman, and Albert Bandura to different aspects of cognitive learning.

3. Describe the functions of sensory, short-term, and long-term memory.

4. List and differentiate among at least five different types of forgetting.

5. Select and defend the position of Penfield, that all memories are permanently recorded in the brain, or that of Bartlett and Loftus, that memories are only a reconstruction that may or may not be accurate.

ANSWER EXPLANATIONS

Multiple-Choice Questions

1. **a**

Ivan Pavlov was the Russian physiologist who, while studying the digestive systems of dogs, realized that conditioning (now called classical or Pavlovian conditioning) was taking place.

2. **c**

Classical conditioning is the process by which a response normally elicited by one stimulus comes to be controlled by another stimulus.

3. **a**

The unconditioned stimulus is the stimulus that naturally elicits a reflexive behavior, such as the presence of food causing salivation in dogs.

4. d

The conditioned stimulus is one that has been paired with the unconditioned stimulus until it elicits the reflexive behavior.

5. c

Lisa's association of fear with the flower and then with the sight of her boyfriend is an example of higher-order conditioning.

6. d

The process by which the unconditioned stimulus no longer follows the conditioned stimulus is called extinction.

7. a

Money is an example of a stimulus, or reinforcer, that acquires its value through association with other stimuli.

8. b

In operant conditioning, subjects learn to associate certain behaviors with either positive or negative consequences; for example, an animal learns that pressing a lever causes food to drop into a dish.

9. a

In operant conditioning, the positive or negative consequences of certain behaviors are called reinforcers.

10. c

Edward Thorndike is credited with discovering the principles of operant conditioning. Later, B. F. Skinner came to be associated with these principles.

11. d

The device used by Skinner to control the input of stimulus to a subject is today known as the Skinner box.

12. c

A stimulus that follows a response and decreases the frequency of the response is called a punisher.

13. c

Scientists have found that the variable-ratio schedule is most effective in producing higher rates of productivity and in stimulating certain behaviors such as continual operation of slot machines.

14. a

Cognitive learning is learning that is associated with thinking, problem solving, and remembering.

15. c

Tolman's experiments showed him that the rats were performing latent learning, and that they had formed cognitive maps of the maze that were not demonstrated until they received reinforcement.

16. d

Bandura's experiments emphasized the importance of observational learning or modeling, which occurs when people observe the behavior of others and note the consequences of that behavior.

17. b

The three tasks of memory are encoding, storage, and retrieval. (Storage involves the process of consolidation of material to be stored.)

18. c

The Atkinson–Shiffrin model posits three different, interacting memory systems, called sensory, short-term, and long-term.

19. b

Ralph had stored the phone number in his short-term memory, but it was displaced by the new question about the time.

20. a

The sensory memory can hold a large amount of information for a very short period of time, only a fraction of a second for visual images and several seconds for sounds.

21. d

Declarative or explicit memory stores facts, information, and personal life events; it includes episodic memory, the memory of events, and semantic memory, or memory of general knowledge.

22. b

Nondeclarative or implicit memory includes motor skills and conditioned responses, such as eating with a fork or driving a car.

23. c

The three methods used to measure memory include recall, recognition, and relearning or the savings method. Recall involves producing information without retrieval cues or hints.

24. b

Psychologists have identified a number of causes for forgetting information, including encoding failure, consolidation failure, and decay. The serial position effect refers to factors that influence the ability to remember items in a sequence.

25. c

"Flashbulb memory" refers to the ability to vividly recall and time and place in which one received shocking information, such as news of a sudden death. This type of memory is particularly associated with tragic news events such as learning of the assassination of John F. Kennedy or the death of Princess Diana.

Essay Questions

1. Define learning, and describe and distinguish between classical conditioning and operant conditioning.

Learning can be defined as a relatively permanent change in behavior that occurs as a result of experiences in the environment. Classical conditioning, which was discovered by Russian physiologist Ivan Pavlov, involves the process of associating an unconditioned stimulus, such as food, with a conditioned stimulus, such as the ringing of a bell. This conditioning is affected by the strength, timing, and frequency as well as by the predictability of the unconditioned stimulus.

Operant conditioning, which is associated with the works of Edward L. Thorndike and B. F. Skinner, involved instilling certain behaviors in subjects by providing either positive or negative reinforcement for certain behaviors. Behaviors involved in operant conditioning are usually voluntary as opposed to involuntary, and the consequence follows, rather than coexists with, the behavior.

2. Define cognitive learning, and describe the contributions of Wolfgang Kohler, Edward Tolman, and Albert Bandura to different aspects of cognitive learning.

Cognitive learning includes cognitive processes such as thinking, knowing, problem solving, remembering, and creating mental representations. Kohler studied the behavior of apes and chimpanzees and realized that they are capable of creative thought and demonstrate insight, or the realization of a relationship between disparate elements in a problem that enabled them to solve the problem. Tolman realized that learning could be latent, in other words, not displayed until reinforcement was received. He believed that rats in a maze, who were not motivated to learn the maze, were nonetheless creating cognitive maps, or mental representations, of the maze. Albert Bandura studied observational learning or modeling, in which individuals learn by observing the behavior of others as well as the consequences of that behavior. The theory of observational learning took on particular importance in the debates over whether the influence of media violence on children's behavior.

3. Describe the functions of sensory, short-term, and long-term memory.

Sensory memory involves very short-term storage of a (potentially) large amount of information received by the senses. Short-term memory, also called working memory, enables us to retain only limited amounts (around seven to nine bits) of information for a bit longer than sensory memory. Interruptions and distractions can often cause short-term memory to be lost. Long-term memory is the storehouse of relatively permanent memories, consisting of personal memories and facts and information. It is also where skills, such as driving or using a fork, are retained.

4. List and differentiate among several different causes and types of forgetting.

Scientists believe that forgetting may be caused by an encoding failure, in which memories are never stored in long-term memory; consolidation failure, or the failure to create a permanent long-term memory; decay, or a memory that has faded over time; interference, in which information or associations stored around the desired information interfere with the ability to recall; and retrieval failure, or the inability to locate information at the time it is required. Some other types of forgetting include motivated forgetting, in which a person forgets things that are unpleasant or frightening; and prospective forgetting, in which one forgets to carry out some action.

5. Select and defend the position of Penfield, that all memories are permanently recorded in the brain, or that of Bartlett and Loftus, that memories are only a reconstruction that may or may not be accurate.

Penfield's work as a neurosurgeon convinced him that people have all of their memories intact, like a tape recorder that has complete storage of information, and need only the appropriate stimulation in order to retrieve a particular memory. His evidence for this belief was his work in stimulating the brains of patients who were then able to experience vivid memories.

Both Bartlett and Loftus believed that people distort facts and experiences, so that memories are reconstructions that may not be entirely accurate. Their beliefs seem to be supported by the variability of eyewitness testimony, which tends to be unreliable and to be influenced by many factors, such as their surroundings or preexisting beliefs or prejudices.

UNIT II: BASIC PSYCHOLOGICAL PROCESSES

CHAPTER 6—LANGUAGE AND THOUGHT

 FLASH FOCUS

When you complete this chapter, you will be able to:

✓ Define cognition and thought, and name the basic components of thought

✓ Describe some decision-making strategies and the factors that can affect decision making

✓ Describe several approaches to problem solving and the factors that can cause difficulty in solving problems

✓ Define linguistics, psycholinguistics, and language, and discuss the basic components of language

✓ List several of the phases of language development from infancy to age four

✓ Identify theories of language acquisition and explain the focus of each

Use a highlighter to identify ideas, terms, and people that your instructor refers to in lectures or emphasizes in the course. Add to the charts any other ideas, terms, or people that your instructor discusses.

Core Concepts in Language and Thought

Important Ideas	Key Terms	Important People
Cognition	Formal concept	George Miller
Thought	Natural concept	Noam Chomsky
Concept	Prototypes	Eric Lenneberg
Proposition	Exemplars	Benjamin Whorf
Image	Visual images	Eleanor Heider Rosch
Mental model	Schemas	
Reasoning	Formal reasoning	
Decision making	Everyday reasoning	
Heuristics	Confirmation bias	
Framing	Hindsight effect	
Problem solving	Additive strategy	
Metacognitive processing	Elimination by aspects	
Mental set	Availability heuristic	
Linguistics	Representativeness heuristic	
Language	Anchoring-and-adjustment heuristic	
Psycholinguistics	Escalation of commitment	
Phonology	Trial and error	
Semantics	Algorithms	
Syntax	Analogy	
Language acquisition device	Functional fixedness	
Transformational grammar	Symbols	

Theory	Phonemes	
Theory of learning readiness	Morphemes	
Whorf's linguistic relativity hypothesis	Cooing	
	Babbling	
	Telegraphic speech	
	Surface structure	
	Deep structure	

Thinking

FLASH SUMMARY

Cognition describes thinking and other higher mental processes such as problem solving and reason. *Thought,* or how we represent the world with our mental processes, is made up of *concepts, propositions,* and *images.* A *concept,* a basic unit of thought, is a mental classification system we use to group ideas, objects, or experiences that have similarities. A *formal concept* is defined by rules and helps us determine whether an object fits into a group. A *natural concept* doesn't have rules that tell us whether an object belongs to a group and is less definitive than a logical concept. Natural concepts often are derived from examples, or *prototypes.*

It is not known exactly how our minds represent concepts. It may be that we store the characteristics of natural concepts in our memory; these characteristics, or *exemplars,* give us a base line for comparing the characteristics of other objects to determine whether they fit into the same group. Another idea is that *visual images,* or mental pictures of objects or experiences, represent concepts. A third point of view proposes a relationship between *schemas*—representations of our knowledge and assumptions about the world—and concepts. Regardless of how concepts are represented, they help us think and communicate quickly and spare us the need to assess every object or experience in great detail.

The representations our minds form are manipulated by our thought processes, which often need to relate concepts. Thanks to our sophisticated language skills, our mental manipulations form sentences called *propositions* that relate concepts to one another or relate one characteristic of a concept to the overall concept. A *mental model,* which can represent a group of propositions, helps us in the external world as we interact with objects and experiences.

Reasoning lets us draw conclusions based on information. In solving a problem that has only one right answer, assuming we all have the information and the problem is clear-cut, we can use *formal reasoning.* Most of the time, though, our thinking deals with problems that can be solved by any of several outcomes, and we may not have all the information; in these cases, we use *everyday reasoning.* A negative mood can cause anxiety or distraction, while a positive mood may prompt many varied memories—and either can adversely affect our powers of reasoning.

Reasoning can be affected by thinking that causes us to become entrenched in our opinions. This thinking, called *confirmation bias,* considers only information that supports conclusions or opinions we've already formulated. Another factor that can affect reasoning is the *hindsight effect*: after learning of an outcome or event, people believe they could have predicted it. When the outcome results in something positive, such people want to be credited for it. When the outcome is negative, people may reduce the effect of hindsight by trying to avoid any role in what occurred.

 **FLASH LINK**

Visit these websites to learn more about cognition, thinking, problem solving, and related topics. Add your own findings to this table.

Websites on Cognition, Thinking, Problem Solving, and Related Topics

URL, Name, Owner	Description of Content

http://serendip.brynmawr.edu/bb/pd.html
   Serendip
   Bryn Mawr College
	This site provides links to articles on brain and behavior, including interactive exhibits.

http://psych.hanover.edu/APS/exponnet.html
   Psychological Research on the Net
   American Psychological Society
	Visit this site for links to research on topics that include cognition.

www.brainconnection.com Brain Connection	At this site, you'll find articles on learning, thinking, learning solutions, and thinking and problem solving.
Others	

Decision Making

 FLASH SUMMARY

In the course of each day, we encounter opportunities for *decision making*, the process by which we evaluate alternatives and select from among them. In making decisions, people can at times consider very calmly the advantages or disadvantages of a given choice. But it's not always easy to approach decision making calmly, and so the process can be affected by other factors, such as opinions that others may offer, or intuition. We arrive at a decision by using any of several methods or approaches.

When you use the *additive strategy* to make a decision, you evaluate the available option relative to each factor that's important to the decision. Adjusting for factors that are more important than others, you choose the option that you rate the highest.

In using the *elimination by aspects* method, you determine criteria for rating the options, arrange them by importance (starting with the most important), and rule out options that don't meet the most important criterion. You continue to rule out options as you evaluate them for each criterion; your choice is the option that's left.

Heuristics, or rules of thumb derived from experience that are used in decision making and problem solving, can't guarantee a correct decision, but they help us make decisions quickly. We use the *availability heuristic* when we need to determine, for example, the importance or frequency of something. The occurrences that are most available in memory tend to be those that are the most important or frequent. Using the *representativeness heuristic*, we base a decision on the degree to which something resembles a prototype; a greater resemblance increases the chances that the object belongs with the prototype. The *anchoring-and-adjustment heuristic*, which works from a reference point such as an asking price, allows people to arrive at a decision by adjusting available information.

Decision making can be influenced by *framing*, or how information about possible outcomes of a decision is presented. Research has found that people tend to avoid risks when an outcome focuses on gains, such as saving lives, and to take risks when an outcome focuses on losses, such as losing lives. The effect of framing is also influenced by whether the information about the outcomes is complete; providing the most complete information possible can reduce its effect.

Continuing to support a failed decision despite evidence of a poor outcome is known as *escalation of commitment*. Suppose you've made a decision, and the early results of it don't measure up. Because you want to give your decision a chance, you continue as planned. But as the poor results continue, do you own up to your mistake and try something else? If you're like many people, you'll be motivated to support your decision. As the worsening situation affects others, you may feel pressure to continue; by now, more people are committed to supporting you. One way to avoid this trap is by limiting the resources that can be invested in carrying out a decision. In addition, performing decision making as a group, so that no one person is responsible for the decision, prevents people from feeling compelled to support it if it fails. Accountability for decisions and results may also help avoid escalation of commitment.

FLASH REVIEW

Approaches to Decision Making

Briefly describe a scenario in which you might apply each decision-making approach shown in the following table.

Approach	When You Might Use It
Availability heuristic	To determine the importance or frequency of something
Elimination by aspects	
Representativeness heuristic	
Additive strategy	
Anchoring-and-adjustment heuristic	

Solving Problems

FLASH SUMMARY

The process by which we find ways to achieve goals is *problem solving*. A simple problem-solving method is *trial and error*, in which you try different approaches and hope one will work. Because there's no guarantee of achieving the outcome you want, trial and error has limited effectiveness. Another problem-solving technique uses *algorithms*, whose rules you follow to arrive at a solution. Using *heuristics*—rules of thumb—is effective for problem solving because heuristics rely on strategies derived from our experience. When we apply methods that have been effective in similar circumstances, we use *analogy*.

Sometimes as people solve a problem, they talk themselves through to a solution. Talking helps them focus on what's important to solving the problem and keeps them away from what's unimportant. Research indicates that the talking brings about heightened awareness called *metacognitive processing* that may let us see our own participation in solving the problem.

When we can't solve a problem, it can mean we don't have what we need to do so; for example, information may be missing. But sometimes, the inability to solve a problem comes from our thinking. For example, if our thinking about using an object allows us to consider using it only as we have previously, rather than to visualize novel ways, we are affected by *functional fixedness*. When we fall back on known ways of solving a problem simply because they have worked in the past, instead of trying other methods, we get into a rut known as *mental set*.

 FLASH REVIEW

Decision-Making Strategies

Provide the name of each decision-making strategy.

Definition	Strategy
Talking through a problem to find a solution	
Relying on past experience	
Applying methods that have been effective in similar circumstances	
Trying different approaches, hoping one will work	
Drawing from past experiences	
Following a set of rules to arrive at a solution	

The Structure of Language

 FLASH SUMMARY

Linguistics is the study of language. *Language* uses a set of *symbols* that must meet specific criteria to be viewed as a language. Specifically, the set of symbols must convey meaning, have structured rules that define how the symbols can be combined, and through those combinations, allow those who use it to create sentences and understand vast numbers of meanings. *Psycholinguistics* is concerned with the study of how we acquire, understand, and produce language, and with the structure of language and the rules for its use. Phonology, semantics, and syntax, or sounds, meaning, and organization, form the basis of all languages.

The study of patterns of speech, the arrangement of speech sounds, and the rules that govern pronunciation are the focus of *phonology*. The basic units of sound that make up a spoken language are *phonemes*. In the English language, a phoneme sounds like an individual letter or combination of letters; for example, the sounds of *d, m,* and *sh. Morphemes*, which are made up of two or more phonemes, are the basic units of meaning in a language. Used individually or in combinations, morphemes make up words.

To provide the rules that determine the ways in which sounds and words can be combined, *syntax* is required. Syntax is what structures a language and arranges it, giving it order. *Semantics* examines the meaning conveyed by words and the relationships among the words that form a sentence. In addition, because a word can have different meanings based on the sentences in which it is used, semantics helps us understand the meaning of a word in a particular context.

FLASH LINK

Visit these websites to learn more about linguistics, psycholinguistics, and related topics. Add your own findings to this table.

Websites on Linguistics, Psycholinguistics, Language, and Related Topics

URL, Name, Owner	Description of Contents
www.parentingme.com/language.htm Language Development	This site is dedicated to the understanding of language development.
http://cogprints.soton.ac.uk/view-psyc.html CogPrints	CogPrints is an electronic archive for papers in any area of psychology including linguistics.
www.isca-speech.org International Speech Communication Association (formerly called European Speech Communication Association)	This organization promotes international speech communication, science, and technology.
www.lsadc.org Linguistics Society of America	This website provides links to topics such as language and brain, meaning and semantics, and language and thought.
Others:	

Language Development

FLASH SUMMARY

The first form of communication observed in babies is crying, which progresses to *cooing* at around 6 weeks. Between 3 and 6 months, babies start *babbling;* as they move toward 12 months and begin to understand some words, the babbling gradually changes into relatively recognizable words that refer to a person or object. After the first few words, babies experience significant vocabulary growth, somewhere between ages 1 and 2. A 2-year-old toddler in our culture may have a vocabulary of about 200 words, most of them nouns.

Initially, toddlers use the words singly, sometimes accompanying them with gestures. At this age, they may not be able to pronounce words clearly, so gesturing becomes a way to help them communicate. By age 2 or 3, toddlers progress to 2-word sentences and use *telegraphic speech*, which includes only essential content words, and have a 200-word vocabulary.

As young children start to understand the meaning of the speech they hear around them, their semantic abilities begin to develop. At this point, adjectives come into their vocabulary, allowing them to describe their thoughts and feelings. They learn to communicate wants and needs by expanding their two-word sentences to include other words, beginning simply and becoming more complex, and by using inflection. They then begin to use prepositions, which lets them use more specific language and form questions.

In addition to learning and using sounds and words, young children need to develop syntax capabilities, which help them express meaning. The length of the sentences young children form increases regularly as they grow older and need to communicate more complex ideas. From this point, children begin to put more than one idea in a sentence and demonstrate increased awareness of syntax. Moving toward age 4, a child may have a vocabulary of 900 words.

 FLASH REVIEW

Milestones of Language Development

Arrange these key milestones of children's language development in the correct order, starting with the one that occurs first.

Use of adjectives	
A vocabulary of 900 words	
Babbling	
Use of prepositions	
Cooing	
A vocabulary of 200 words	
Putting more than one idea in a sentence	
Use of single words accompanied by gestures	
Development of syntax capabilities	
Use of telegraphic speech	

Theories of Language Acquisition

FLASH SUMMARY

In trying to understand language and how humans acquire it, researchers have identified critical factors and formulated theories over the decades. Varying amounts of evidence have substantiated each theory, but researchers haven't identified all the factors that contribute to the development of language.

Some theorists and researchers believe biological factors are the basis of language acquisition and development. They believe that the number of meaningful and correctly formed sentences we can create exceeds what we could learn or imitate.

George Miller, a psychologist, theorized that language acquisition stems from an inborn capability that predisposes us to learn and use language. Both Miller and *Noam Chomsky* believed that we are equipped with a *language acquisition device* that facilitates learning language. Chomsky additionally developed the *transformational grammar theory*, which forwards the notion of two types of structures in sentences that are stored differently in the brain: the *surface structure* deals with the words, and the *deep structure deals* with the underlying meaning. *Eric Lenneberg's* theory of *learning readiness* claimed that when we are born, we are equipped with both the capacity for language and the preparedness to learn it.

Other researchers focused on the relationship between language and thought. According to *Benjamin Whorf's linguistic relativity hypothesis*, language determines thought; thus, the language we speak gives us a perception of the world that differs from those who speak other languages. Whorf used as evidence the number of words for snow in two different languages: one with many descriptive words and another with one. The group that used many words for talking about snow, Whorf claimed, thought about snow differently from the group that used a few words for it.

The work of *Eleanor Heider Rosch* disproved Whorf's idea. Working with English-speaking Americans, whose language has many color names, and Dani tribe members from New Guinea, whose language has two color names, Rosch determined that both groups were equally capable of thinking about and discriminating among colors.

FLASH REVIEW

Theories of Language Development

Complete this table by identifying the proponents of each theory of language development, and write a sentence or two that characterize each perspective. Include any additional information or perspectives that your instructor emphasizes in your class.

Theory	Proponent(s)	Key Features
Linguistic relativity hypothesis	Benjamin Whorf Eleanor Heider Rosch	The language we speak influences or determines our thoughts. Because the way we think is shaped by the words that are available to us, people who speak different languages may have different perceptions of the world.
Transformational grammar theory		

Language acquisition device (LAD)		
Learning readiness		
Other		

 FLASH TEST

Review the information in the Core Concepts chart for this chapter. Then take the Practice Test on the next pages, and rate your performance.

PRACTICE TEST

(Chapter 6—Language and Thought)

Multiple Choice (3 points each)

1. Cognition is described as
   a. rules that help us determine whether an object belongs to a group.
   b. a mental classification system we use to group together ideas, objects, or experiences that have similarities.
   c. thinking and other higher mental processes such as problem solving and reason.
   d. sentences that relate concepts to one another or one characteristic of a concept to the overall concept.

2. Which of these terms is not a component of thought?
   a. concepts
   b. propositions
   c. visual images
   d. prototypes

3. _____ let/lets us draw conclusions based on information.
   a. Reasoning
   b. Thought
   c. Thinking
   d. Exemplars

4. An error in thinking that considers only information that supports conclusions or opinions we've already formulated is _____
   a. the hindsight effect.
   b. confirmation bias.
   c. everyday reasoning.
   d. a mental model.

5. Decision making is the process of
    a. evaluating alternatives and selecting from among them.
    b. evaluating the available options relative to each factor that's important to the decision.
    c. determining the importance or frequency of something.
    d. drawing conclusions based on information.

6. When you use the representativeness heuristic, you
    a. rate options relative to each factor that's important to the decision.
    b. work from a reference point and arrive at a decision by adjusting available information.
    c. rule out options according to whether they meet established criteria.
    d. base a decision on the degree to which something resembles a prototype.

7. Framing can
    a. help us adjust for factors that are more important than others.
    b. influence a decision depending on how the information about outcomes is presented.
    c. help us evaluate alternatives and select from among them.
    d. lead us to overestimate how frequently something occurs.

8. Continuing to support a failed decision despite evidence of a poor outcome is known as
    a. trial and error.
    b. risk tasking.
    c. the availability heuristic.
    d. escalation of commitment.

9. Thanks to our sophisticated language skills, our mental manipulations form sentences called _____ that relate concepts to one another or relate one characteristic of a concept to the overall concept.
    a. mental models
    b. exemplars
    c. propositions
    d. cognition

10. When we fall back on known ways of solving a problem simply because they have worked in the past, instead of trying other methods, we get into a rut known as
    a. mental set.
    b. functional fixedness.
    c. confirmation bias.
    d. heuristics.

11. _____ , which occurs when you talk yourself through to the solution of a problem, results in heightened awareness that may let you observe your own participation in solving the problem.
    a. Reasoning
    b. Trial and error
    c. Metacognitive processing
    d. Framing

12. When you are dealing with a problem that can be solved by any of several outcomes, and you don't necessarily have all the information, you are using _____
    a. a mental model.
    b. everyday reasoning.
    c. formal concepts.
    d. formal reasoning.

13. Function fixedness occurs when
    a. your thinking allows you to consider using an object only as you have previously rather than to visualize novel ways.
    b. you follow a set of rules to arrive at a conclusion.
    c. you rule out options that don't meet the most important criterion.
    d. you try different approaches and hope one will work.

14. Which of these is not a basic component of language development?
    a. semantic development
    b. the acquisition of grammar

    c. linguistic relativity hypothesis

    d. phonological development

15. The smallest units of sound in spoken language are
    a. morphemes.
    b. linguistics.
    c. underextensions.
    d. phonemes.

16. _____ is the study of how we acquire, perceive, understand, and produce language.
    a. Psychology
    b. Psycholinguistics
    c. Phrenology
    d. Phonics

17. According to researcher Eric Lenneberg, learning readiness is an example of
    a. a learning theory.
    b. semantics.
    c. a biological theory.
    d. the linguistic relativity hypothesis.

18. _____ proposed the theory that humans have an inborn biological capacity for acquiring and using language.
    a. Benjamin Whorf.
    b. George Miller.
    c. Eric Lenneberg
    d. Beatrix Gardner and Allen Gardner

19. The study of language, including speech sounds, meaning, and grammar, is
    a. linguistics.
    b. psycholinguistics.
    c. neurolinguistics.
    d. phonemes.

20. What is transformational grammar?
    a. the idea that specific functions of the brain are located in one hemisphere
    b. Noam Chomsky's theory that every sentence has both a surface structure and a deep structure, each dealing with specific aspects of the sentence
    c. Benjamin Whorf's theory that our thoughts—and our views of the world—are determined by the language we speak, because the words that are available to us determine our thinking
    d. The notion that language and cultural values are so strongly tied together as to influence how people respond when they take the same test in both their native language and another language they speak

21. Which of these is not a criterion that must be met before a system of symbols is considered a language?
    a. It must have structured rules that define how the symbols can be used.
    b. The symbols must convey meaning.
    c. Combinations of the symbols may be used, allowing for the creation of a virtually unlimited number of sentences.
    d. It must use symbols that are easily understood.

22. The research of _____ disproved Benjamin Whorf's linguistic relativity hypothesis.
    a. Eric Lenneberg
    b. David Premack
    c. Eleanor Heider Rosch
    d. Noam Chomsky

23. Both _____ and _____ believed that we are equipped with a language acquisition device that facilitates learning language.
    a. Eleanor Heider Rosch; Benjamin Whorf
    b. George Miller; Noam Chomsky
    c. Eric Lenneberg; Noam Chomsky
    d. George Miller; Eleanor Heider Rosch

24. A _____ is the smallest unit of meaning in a language.
    a. morpheme
    b. phoneme
    c. genome
    d. surface structure

25. Telegraphic speech refers to
    a. the cooing sounds made by infants at about six months.
    b. the one-word sentences young children as they begin talking.
    c. the tendency of parents to adjust how they speak when they talk to a baby or toddler.
    d. the spoken language used by young children in which words are left out.

Essay Questions (5 points each)

1. How do our minds represent concepts?

2. Discuss three factors that can reduce a person's ability to reason.

3. Describe escalation of commitment and discuss some ways of reducing the likelihood that it will occur.

4. Identify and describe the three basic components of language.

5. Describe Benjamin Whorf's linguistic relativity hypothesis and the proof he offered for his hypothesis. Then describe how Whorf's theory was disproved.

ANSWER EXPLANATIONS

Multiple-Choice Questions

1. **c**
   Cognition describes thinking and other higher mental processes such as problem solving and reason.

2. **d**
   Prototypes are not components of thought.

3. **a**
   Reasoning lets us draw conclusions based on information.

4. **b**
   An error in thinking that considers only information that supports conclusions or opinions we've already formulated is the hindsight effect.

5. **a**
   Decision making is the process of evaluating alternatives and selecting from among them.

6. **d**
   When you use the representativeness heuristic, you base a decision on the degree to which something resembles a prototype.

7. **b**
   Framing can influence a decision depending on how the information about outcomes is presented.

8. **d**
   Continuing to support a failed decision despite evidence of a poor outcome is known as escalation of commitment.

9. **c**
   Thanks to our sophisticated language skills, our mental manipulations form sentences called propositions that relate concepts to one another or relate one characteristic of a concept to the overall concept.

10. **a**
    When we fall back on known ways of solving a problem simply because they have worked in the past, instead of trying other methods, we get into a rut known as mental set.

11. **c**
    Metacognitive processing, which occurs when you talk yourself through to the solution of a problem, results in heightened awareness that may let you observe your own participation in solving the problem.

12. b

When you are dealing with a problem that can be solved by any of several outcomes, and you don't necessarily have all the information you need, you are using everyday reasoning.

13. a

Functional fixedness occurs when your thinking allows you to consider using an object only as you have previously rather than to visualize novel ways.

14. c

The linguistic relativity hypothesis is not a basic component of language development.

15. d

The smallest units of sound in spoken language are phonemes.

16. b

Psycholinguistics is the study of how we acquire, perceive, understand, and produce language.

17. c

According to researcher Eric Lenneberg, learning readiness is an example of a biological theory.

18. b

George Miller proposed the theory that humans have an inborn biological capacity for acquiring and using language.

19. a

The study of language, including speech sounds, meaning, and grammar, is linguistics.

20. b

Transformational grammar is Noam Chomsky's theory that every sentence has two types of structure: a surface structure, which is the words that make up the sentence, and a deep structure, which is the meaning that underlies the words.

21. d

The symbols are not required to be easily understood for a set of symbols to be considered a language.

22. c

The research of Eleanor Heider Rosch disproved Benjamin Whorf's linguistic relativity hypothesis.

23. b

George Miller and Noam Chomsky believed that we are equipped with a language acquisition device that facilitates learning language.

24. a

A morpheme is the smallest unit of meaning in a language.

25. d

Telegraphic speech refers to the spoken language used by young children in which words are left out.

Essay Question Answers

1. How do our minds represent concepts?

   It's not known exactly how our minds represent concepts. It may be that we store the characteristics of natural concepts in our memory; these characteristics, or exemplars, give us a base line for comparing the characteristics of other objects to determine whether they fit into the same group. Another idea is that visual images, or mental pictures, of objects or experiences represent concepts. A third point of view proposes a relationship between schemas—representations of our knowledge and assumptions about the world—and concepts. Regardless of how concepts are represented, they help us to think and communicate quickly, and spare us the overhead of assessing every object or experience in great detail.

2. Discuss three factors that can reduce a person's ability to reason.

   Three factors that can affect our ability to reason are mood states, confirmation bias, and the hindsight effect.
   It's easy to understand how a negative mood, which can make a person feel anxious, inattentive, angry, distracted, or discouraged, can undermine reasoning. But a positive mood can also get in the way of reasoning. In a positive mood state, we tend to have not only more memories but also memories that are scattered

or dispersed. In a more creative situation, such as a brainstorming exercise, these memories can be helpful, but in a situation that requires reasoning, the memories get in our way.

Reasoning also can be affected by a factor that causes us to become entrenched in our opinions. This thinking, called *confirmation bias,* considers only information that supports conclusions or opinions we've already formulated.

A third factor that can affect reasoning is the *hindsight effect:* after learning of an outcome or event, people believe they could have predicted it. When the outcome results in something positive, such people want to be credited for it. When the outcome is negative, people may reduce the effect of hindsight by trying to avoid any role in what occurred.

3. Describe escalation of commitment, and discuss some ways of reducing the likelihood that it will occur.

Escalation of commitment occurs when we feel compelled to continue to support a decision even when it's a bad one. As a situation worsens, we tend to invest more time and resources, hoping the situation will turn around. We may be unable to figure a way out of the bad decision, and to make matters worse, others who have become committed to the idea may resist a change.

We can avoid the trap of escalation of commitment in several ways. One way is to limit the resources that are available for implementing a decision or plan. Another way is to have a group handle decision making, rather than make one person responsible for it. A third technique is accountability: when we know that we will be held accountable for our decisions and outcomes, we are less likely to continue to support a failed decision

4. Identify and describe the three basic components of language.

Phonology, semantics, and syntax are the three basic components of language. The study of patterns of speech, the arrangement of speech sounds, and the rules that govern pronunciation are the focuses of phonology. Syntax is required to provide the rules that determine the ways in which sounds and words can be combined. Syntax is what structures a language, arranges it, and gives it order. Semantics examines the meaning conveyed by words and the relationships among the words that form a sentence. In addition, because a word can have different meanings based on the sentences in which it is used, semantics helps us understand the meaning of a word in a particular context.

5. Describe Benjamin Whorf's linguistic relativity hypothesis and the proof he offered for his hypothesis. Then describe how Whorf's theory was disproved.

According to Benjamin Whorf's linguistic relativity hypothesis, language determines thought, so the language we speak give us a perception of the world that differs from those who speak other languages. Whorf used as evidence the number of words for snow in two different languages: one with many descriptive words and another with one. The group that used many words for talking about snow, Whorf claimed, thought about snow differently from the group that used few words for it.

Eleanor Heider Rosch worked with two groups: English-speaking Americans, whose language has many color names, and Dani tribe members from New Guinea, whose language has two color names. Members of both groups briefly viewed color chips of 11 colors, and after 30 seconds, were asked to choose the 11 colors from a selection of 40 color chips. Rosch determined that both groups were equally capable of thinking about, remembering, and discriminating among colors, which meant that the language the groups spoke did not determine their abilities to perceive color.

UNIT II: BASIC PSYCHOLOGICAL PROCESSES

CHAPTER 7—MOTIVATION AND EMOTION

 FLASH FOCUS

When you complete this chapter, you will be able to:

✓ Describe and differentiate among six different theories of motivation

✓ Discuss the primary human motivators, and some disorders that can affect those motivators

✓ Define emotion and some of the physiological and cognitive theories explaining emotion

✓ Discuss some of the gender and cultural differences that may affect the perception and display of emotions

Use a highlighter to identify ideas, terms, and people that your instructor refers to in lectures or emphasizes in the course. Add to the chart any other ideas, terms, or people that your instructor discusses.

Core Concepts in Motivation and Emotion

Important Ideas	Key Terms	Important People
Motivation	Drive	Konrad Lorenz
Evolutionary theory	Need	Clark Hull
Drive theory	Arousal	R. M. Yerkes
Homeostasis	Motives	J. D. Dodson
Arousal theory	Incentives	David McClelland
Yerkes–Dodson law	Extrinsic motivation	Donald Hebb
Expectancy theory	Intrinsic motivation	Edward Deci
Cognitive theory	Overjustification effect	Abraham Maslow
Humanistic theory	Physiological needs	Alfred Kinsey
Maslow's hierarchy of needs	Safety needs	William Masters
Eating disorders	Belongingness needs	Virginia Johnson
Heterosexual	Esteem needs	Philip Shaver
Bisexual	Cognitive needs	William James
Homosexual	Aesthetic needs	Carl Lange
Emotion	Self-actualization needs	Walter Cannon
Physiological theories of emotion	Hypothalamus	Philip Bard
Cognitive theories of emotion	Anorexia nervosa	James LeDoux
James–Lange theory of emotion	Bulimia	Stanley Schachter
Facial feedback hypothesis	Aggression	Jerome Singer
Cannon–Bard theory of emotion	Achievement	
Schachter–Singer approach	Limbic system	
Display rules	Amygdala	

Theories of Motivation

FLASH SUMMARY

Motivation can be defined as internal processes that activate, guide, and maintain behavior. Psychologists and other scientists have set out a number of theories to explain how and why living creatures, including human beings, are motivated to undertake certain activities. Early theorists, including *Konrad Lorenz,* posited theories that are now called *evolutionary theories,* which seek to explain human behaviors in terms of natural selection. These theories are all based on the premise that organisms that are more successful in basic processes, such as eating, drinking, and reproduction, are better able to adapt and survive.

Another approach to motivation is termed *drive theory.* Drive theory also assumes that organisms are motivated by the need to attain or maintain some goal that helps the species to survive. A *drive* is a condition of internal arousal that directs an organism to satisfy an internal *need,* such as the need to satisfy hunger or reduce pain. Psychologists such as *Clark Hull* asserted that an organism had to be motivated in order to take action. These theories posited the desired state or ultimate goal of the organism to be *homeostasis,* or maintenance of a constant state of inner stability or balance. However, many psychologists today believe that drive theory by itself does not adequately explain some human activities that seem contrary to basic physiological needs, such as the motivation to diet, or the choice to abstain from sexual activity.

An alternative theory of motivation, called *arousal theory,* posits that organisms seek to maintain optimal levels of *arousal* by varying their exposure to surrounding stimuli. Psychologists *R. M. Yerkes* and *J. D. Dodson* first explored the link between performance and arousal in what is now known as the *Yerkes–Dodson law,* which sets out a relationship between arousal and level of task difficulty. The law posits that performance is at its peak when arousal is at moderate levels; too much or too little arousal can result in poor performance. For example, someone who does not care very much about a particular school exam is unlikely to do very well on it.

Expectancy theory is another major theory of motivation that focuses on individuals' expectations about reaching a goal. Achievement researcher *David McClelland* conducted work in this area. Expectancy theory assumes that individuals have different *motives,* or internal conditions that impel them toward a particular goal, which may or may not be related to a physiological need. Such *incentives* can consist of anything that has value to the individual.

Cognitive theory asserts that people actively and regularly determine their own goals and the means of achieving those goals. Cognitive theory differs from expectancy theory in that cognitive theory emphasizes the importance of conscious decision making. *Donald Hebb,* an early researcher who anticipated the development of cognitive theory, was one of the psychologists who sought to move beyond simple descriptions of satisfaction of physiological needs.

Cognitive theorists distinguish between *extrinsic motivation,* which is motivation supplied in the form of rewards from the external environment, and *intrinsic motivation,* or motivation that has no apparent reward apart from the pleasure and satisfaction of the activity itself. Researcher *Edward Deci* and others studied the relationship between extrinsic and intrinsic rewards and found, among other things, that after a task has been extrinsically rewarded, it is unlikely that it will be performed solely for intrinsic motivation; they called this the *overjustification effect.*

Humanistic theory emphasizes the entirety of life rather than the individual components of behavior. *Abraham Maslow,* one of the founders of the humanistic approach in psychology, created a *hierarchy of needs,* which explains that people are motivated by physiological needs; however, once those needs are satisfied, people strive to attain higher needs such as the need for belonging, esteem, and self-actualization.

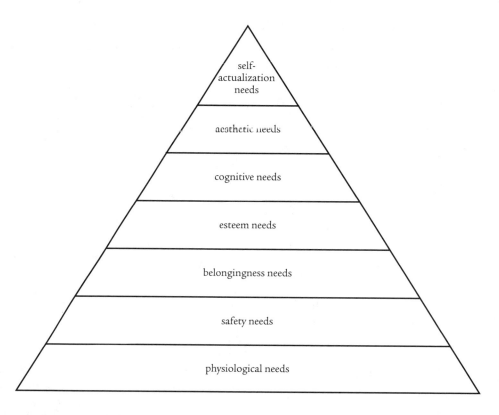

 FLASH REVIEW

The following chart summarizes some of the main theories of motivation. Add any information that your instructor chooses to discuss or emphasizes in the course.

A Chart of Theories of Motivation

Theory	Key Theorists	Key Ideas	Examples
Evolutionary	Konrad Lorenz	Natural selection influences motivation	Explains reproductive behavior, pain avoidance, etc.
Drive	Clark Hull	Individuals are motivated by drives, with the goal of homeostasis.	Explains basic needs such as needs for food, water
Arousal	R. M. Yerkes J. D. Dodson	Organisms seek optimal arousal.	There is a level of arousal that stimulates peak performance.
Expectancy	David McClelland	Expectations and need for achievement motivate behavior	Achievement is a learned behavior, such as the motivation to be slender and fit.

| Cognitive | Edward Deci | Individuals are motivated by both extrinsic and intrinsic factors. | Motivation is inborn, but can be affected by extrinsic rewards. |
| Humanistic | Abraham Maslow | Once physiological needs are met, individuals go on to meet higher needs. | Needs range from basic physiological needs, to cognitive, aesthetic, and self-actualization needs. |

Primary Physiological Motivators

FLASH SUMMARY

Primary physiological motivators include hunger, thirst, and the need to reproduce. Other needs for human beings include needs to achieve, which may involve aggressive behavior. Thirst is an obvious motivator, but hunger is more complex. Feelings of hunger are controlled by several different mechanisms in the body, including the *hypothalamus,* as well as the liver and other bodily organs. In these various systems, there are detectors that respond to such factors as the amount of glucose or blood sugar in the body. However, hunger is also strongly affected by the sight, smell, and taste of food.

Obesity is a problem experienced by almost one-third of Americans today, and it appears that several factors are responsible. One is the effect of habit; Americans have gotten into the habit of overeating, with meals that are high in calories and (sometimes) low in nutritional value. However, there are also other factors at work, including genetic factors. Since gaining weight during times of plenty could be a positive factor in evolutionary development, certain populations, such as the Native American Pima of Arizona, have a genetic predisposition for weight gain. The Pima currently suffer from diabetes, a disease associated with being overweight, at a rate that is eight times the national average for the disease.

Human beings have also developed *eating disorders* that include *anorexia nervosa* and *bulimia.* These disorders primarily affect young women, and have developed as the gap between the actual weight of most women and the "ideal" weight exhibited by models and media stars has increased. Anorexia nervosa is characterized by an irrational fear of gaining weight that causes compulsive dieting to the point of starvation. Adolescents with anorexia occasionally lose as much as 20–25 percent of their body weight, and some die from the disease. Anorexic individuals do experience hunger, are preoccupied with food, and may exercise relentlessly. Their self-perception about their body size is grossly distorted. Anorexic individuals may suffer from low blood pressure, impaired heart function, dehydration, electrolyte disturbance, and sterility, as well as possible decreases in the amount of brain matter. Some psychologists believe that the central issue in anorexia is control, and that the people (primarily young women) who suffer from the disease are attempting to assert control over a portion of their lives. Treatment of anorexia is difficult, since individuals suffer from delusional thinking and a false self-perception, and hospitalization is often required.

Up to 50 percent of anorexics also develop bulimia, which is a disorder characterized by secretive episodes of binge eating followed by purging, or self-induced vomiting. Sufferers may also use large quantities of laxatives or diuretics. Bulimia also causes a number of physical problems, including damage to the teeth caused by stomach acid, dehydration, swelling of the salivary glands, kidney damage, and hair loss.

Bulimics often experience emotions of depression, shame, and guilt due to their inability to control their binges. Bulimia is most common among adolescent girls, although 10–15 percent of all bulimics are males. Bulimia is also difficult to treat, with cognitive-behavioral therapy and antidepressant drugs being the most effective treatments to date.

The motivation to engage in sexual behavior is also a powerful force. In human beings, sexual behavior is not necessarily linked to hormonal cycles, as it is in many other species. Researchers studying human sexual behavior included *Kinsey,* who initiated surveys of sexual behavior in America in the 1950s, and physicians *Masters* and *Johnson* in the 1960s, who observed and recorded incidents of sexual behavior.

Scientists and others have encountered different attitudes toward sexual behavior between men and women, and evolutionary theorists have posited that men are motivated to have sexual relations with as many women as possible, whereas women are more interested in lasting relationships. However, the wide variety of attitudes and behaviors exhibited by human beings makes it difficult to generalize. Also, whereas most men and women are *heterosexual,* or attracted to the opposite sex, a number of human beings are *bisexual*—attracted to members of both sexes—or *homosexual,* seeking partners of their own sex. Genetic and biological factors may influence sexual preference, but much research remains to be done to analyze the roles of both heredity and environment on sexual preference.

Other powerful primary motivations include *aggression,* which is the desire to dominate or inflict harm upon others, and *achievement,* or the desire to excel or accomplish something. Psychologists have debated whether aggression is an inborn or a learned characteristic, and most now agree that aggression seems to be elicited by external events and stimuli. There is evidence that exposure to extreme levels of violence in the media affects aggression levels. McClelland and other researchers ranked and studied individuals and their need for achievement. They found that high achievers set goals of moderate difficulty that could be achieved through hard work and determination. Low achievers, on the other hand, were motivated more by fear of failure than by the expectation of success.

FLASH LINK TO EATING DISORDERS

The following site provides information on eating disorders.

http://site.health-center.com/brain/eatingdisorder/default.htm

Emotion
....

FLASH SUMMARY

Emotion is a term that refers to a wide variety of subjective states, such as happiness, sadness, fear, and anger. An emotion is a subjective response, often including physiological changes, which is interpreted in a particular way by the individual and which often leads to a change in behavior. While human beings usually experience the same kinds of emotions, the intensity of those emotions may vary widely. Researchers cannot even agree on a list of "basic" emotions. *Philip Shaver* created a list of six basic categories of emotions, but found that the basic categories can overlap, and that many other emotional states can be grouped under them.

Theories of emotions include *physiological theories* and *cognitive theories.* One of the first physiological theories is called the *James–Lange theory,* after *William James* and *Carl Lange,* who separately took very similar approaches to the study of emotion. This theory posits that individuals experience certain physiological changes which they then interpret as emotional states. In other words, people only experience emotion after their body has become aroused and, in response, has produced certain physiological changes. (A related but more modern physiological approach, called the *facial feedback hypothesis*, posits that sensations from the face provide cues or signals to the brain that act as feedback to help a person determine an emotional response.)

Another approach, called the *Cannon–Bard theory* after physiologists *Walter Cannon* and *Philip Bard*, attempted to explain how people distinguished among emotions that may provide the same physiological cues. They posited that both the cerebral cortex and the thalamus are stimulated simultaneously, so that one area (the cortex) produces the emotional component of the experience, while the thalamus produces the physiological changes. This theory has been discredited due to further brain research that showed that the limbic system is involved in emotional responses, but it did lead to more modern theories of emotions.

A modern theorist, *Joseph LeDoux*, discovered the central role of the *amygdala*, a structure within the limbic system, in the creation of emotions. LeDoux posits that emotional responses, such as fear, are evolutionary strategies to produce appropriate physical responses, such as an increase in heart rate and muscle tension. These responses are "hard-wired" into the brain, and subjective emotions follow similar and closely related pathways.

Cognitive theories of emotion include the *Schachter–Singer approach*, developed by *Stanley Schachter* and *Jerome Singer,* which incorporate elements of the Cannon–Bard and the James-Lange theories. The Schachter-Singer approach posits that people interpret physical sensations within a specific context. In experiments, they injected individuals with epinephrine, a stimulant that creates physiological changes such as increased heart rate and energy levels. These individuals were then placed among others who had been instructed to behave in certain ways to demonstrate happiness, sadness, or some other emotional state. The individuals who were experiencing the physiological changes did indeed interpret their physical symptoms according to the emotions being displayed by the actors. However, other researchers have challenged the Schachter-Singer approach in experiments showing that cognitive processes alone can produce feelings of emotion.

Another controversial area involving emotion is the issue of gender differences in experiencing emotions. Some researchers have found that women reported more intense and more frequent emotions than did men, with the exception of anger. Further research also found that women experienced more intense physiological reactions than men. Thus, while women report greater happiness and life satisfaction in surveys than do men, they also report more sadness and are twice as likely to report being depressed; they also admit to greater fear than do men.

Different cultures also have different "rules" about the expression of emotion, which are called *display rules*. Certain cultures may suppress the expression of certain types of emotion; for example, the Japanese culture discourages the display of negative emotions when other people are present. In East Africa, young males from Masai society are expected to look stern and unemotional and to exchange long, unbroken stares.

FLASH LINK

Visit the following sites on motivation and emotion; summarize the contents of the sites, and add your own findings to the list.

Web Sites on Motivation and Emotion

URL, Name, Owner	Description of Contents
www.nimh.nih.gov/publicat/baschap1.cfm The National Institute of Mental Health	Introduction to the study of motivation and emotion from the NIMH

http://choo.fis.utoronto.ca/FIS/Courses/ LIS1230sharma/motive4.htm	A discussion of several theories of motivation
http://eqi.org	A resource for measuring so-called "emotional intelligence"
http://sol.brunel.ac.uk/~jarvis/bola/ motivation/masmodel.html	A discussion of Maslow's hierarchy of needs model of motivation
Other:	

FLASH REVIEW

Conduct a Study of Jealousy

1. Visit the web site www.psychtests.com/jealousy.html, and take the Jealousy Self-Assessment.

2. Select a sample of your classmates of both genders and ask them to take the same Self-Assessment.

3. Compare the results of the survey. How do results vary by gender? What conclusions can you draw from these results? What cautions should you exercise before generalizing from these results?

FLASH TEST

Review the chart of Core Concepts for this chapter. Then take the Practice Test for Chapter 7, and rate your performance.

PRACTICE TEST

(Chapter 7—Motivation and Emotion)

Multiple Choice (3 points each)

1. Internal processes that activate, guide, and maintain behavior over time are called
   a. reinforcement.
   b. motivation.
   c. instincts.
   d. emotions.

2. Evolutionary theories of motivation are associated with
   a. Konrad Lorenz.
   b. Clark Hull.
   c. R. M. Yerkes
   d. Alfred Kinsey

3. Drive theory posits that organisms take action in order to
   a. increase their level of arousal.
   b. satisfy basic instincts.
   c. satisfy an internal need.
   d. obtain incentives.

4. Drive theory states that the ultimate goal of the organism is
   a. achievement.
   b. homeostasis.
   c. arousal.
   d. satisfaction of needs.

5. Which of the following suggests that performance on tasks is best when arousal level is appropriate to the difficulty of the task?
   a. instinctual theory of motivation
   b. James–Lange theory
   c. Maslow's hierarchy of needs
   d. the Yerkes–Dodson law

6. Arousal theories of motivation focus on an organism's efforts to
   a. maintain their basic biological systems so they can survive.
   b. reach a goal it believes to be reasonable and important.
   c. achieve an optimum level of nervous system activation.
   d. establish a sense of self-worth and personal growth.

7. In expectancy theory, McClelland and others assume that individuals are impelled toward particular goals by rewards called
   a. expectations.
   b. motivators.
   c. drives.
   d. incentives.

8. The cognitive theory of motivation differs from expectancy theory in its emphasis on
   a. conscious decision making.
   b. instincts.
   c. a hierarchy of needs.
   d. incentives as motivators.

9. One theory of motivation that involves an arrangement of needs from the most basic to the highest level is called
   a. drive theory.
   b. arousal theory.
   c. expectancy theory.
   d. humanistic theory.

10. Since Ralph plays the piano because he enjoys doing so, he can be called high in _____ motivation.
   a. altruistic
   b. extrinsic
   c. intrinsic
   d. musical

11. The highest needs in Abraham Maslow's hierarchy of needs pyramid are
   a. self-actualization needs.
   b. aesthetic needs.
   c. cognitive needs.
   d. physiological needs.

12. Feelings of hunger are controlled by
   a. the stomach.
   b. the senses of sight, smell, and taste.
   c. the hypothalamus, the liver, and other bodily organs.
   d. the brain.

13. The Pima of Arizona are a good example of the role of _____ in the determination of one's weight.
   a. environmental factors
   b. cognitive factors

    c. social factors

    d. genetic factors

14. Anorexia and bulimia are two eating disorders that are
    a. easily cured with antidepressant drugs.
    b. easily treated with cognitive-behavioral therapy.
    c. relatively easy to treat if the whole family participates in therapy.
    d. very difficult to treat effectively.

15. People with anorexia nervosa
    a. have an intense fear of becoming obese.
    b. lose their appetites.
    c. avoid situations related to food or to eating.
    d. tend to binge and then purge what they have eaten.

16. Bulimia is characterized by
    a. loss of appetite.
    b. overeating and then purging of the food.
    c. bizarre food rituals.
    d. a refusal to eat.

17. The researcher who studied American sexual behavior in the 1950s by means of a survey was
    a. William Masters.
    b. Elizabeth Johnson.
    c. Alfred Kinsey.
    d. Alfred Adler.

18. Research indicates that _____ provides an answer as to why the short-term sexual strategies of males and females are different.
    a. operant conditioning
    b. evolutionary psychology
    c. goal-setting theory
    d. Maslow's hierarchy

19. The desire to harm or injure someone else is called
    a. aggressive motivation.
    b. hurtful aggression.
    c. injurious aggression.
    d. aggression compulsion.

20. When psychologists define emotion, they include
    a. only our internal, subjective feelings.
    b. only our physiological responses.
    c. only our external, observable behaviors.
    d. internal states, biological responses, and behaviors.

21. Which theory of emotion suggests that you become happy as a result of noticing that you are smiling and laughing?
    a. James–Lange
    b. Cannon–Bard
    c. Schachter–Singer
    d. Opponent-process

22. The region of the brain that has been shown to play a significant role in conditioned emotional responses is the
    a. hippocampus.
    b. amygdala.
    c. hypothalamus.
    d. corpus callosum.

23. The Schachter–Singer approach views emotions as a
    a. release from social conventions.

b. perception of events in the external environment.

c. cognitive assessment of environmental stimulation.

d. combination of both cognitive processes and autonomic processes.

24. Gender differences in the experience and expression of emotions are

   a. based on biological differences between men and women.

   b. strongly influenced by cultural factors.

   c. so minor as to be insignificant.

   d. not worthy of further research.

25. Cultural "rules" about the appropriate expression of emotions are called

   a. cultural norms.

   b. display rules.

   c. cultural standards.

   d. taboos.

Essay Questions (5 points each)

1. Name and describe six different theories of motivation.

2. Discuss some of the disorders associated with the primary motivator of hunger.

3. Describe some factors that have been found to influence the motivators of aggression and achievement.

4. Compare and contrast the physiological and cognitive theories of emotion.

5. Describe some of the cultural and gender differences in the experience and display of emotions.

ANSWER EXPLANATIONS

Multiple-Choice Questions

1. **b**

   Motivation is defined as internal processes that activate, guide, and maintain behavior over time.

2. **a**

   Evolutionary theories of motivation are associated with theorist Konrad Lorenz; however, his theories, which were based on studies of instinctual behavior in animals, gave way to a more contemporary evolutionary perspective.

3. **c**

   Drive theory states that organisms undertake actions in order to satisfy internal needs.

4. **b**

   Drive theory states that the ultimate goal of the organism is homeostasis, or maintenance of a constant state of inner stability or balance. While the satisfaction of needs is necessary to maintain homeostasis, it is not the ultimate goal.

5. **d**

   The Yerkes-Dodson law posits that performance is at its peak when arousal is at moderate levels; too much or too little arousal can result in poor performance.

6. **c**

   Arousal theories focus on the organism's attempts to achieve an optimum level of nervous system activation.

7. **d**

   Expectancy theory posits that individuals are motivated toward a particular goal, which may or may not be related to a physiological need, by rewards called incentives.

8. **a**

   The cognitive theory of motivation differs from expectancy theory in its emphasis on conscious decision making.

9. d

Humanistic theory emphasizes the entirety of life and includes Maslow's hierarchy of needs, an ascending order of needs from basic physiological needs to needs such as aesthetic satisfaction and self-actualization.

10. c

In cognitive theory, an individual who performs an activity simply for enjoyment is satisfying an intrinsic motivation, with no apparent reward apart from the pleasure and satisfaction of the activity itself.

11. a

According to Maslow's hierarchy of needs, the highest need is for self-actualization, which can be sought after other, more basic needs have been satisfied.

12. c

Feelings of hunger are controlled by several different mechanisms in the body, including the hypothalamus as well as the liver and other bodily organs, where detectors respond to factors such as the amount of glucose in the body.

13. d

The Pima of Arizona demonstrate a genetic predisposition for weight gain, which has led to high rates of obesity and diseases such as diabetes among the tribe.

14. d

Anorexia and bulimia are very difficult to treat effectively, partly due to the delusional thinking and false self-perception that accompany the diseases.

15. a

People with anorexia nervosa have an intense fear of becoming obese.

16. b

Bulimia is characterized by binge eating, followed by purging, through either vomiting or excessive use of laxatives and diuretics.

17. c

The Kinsey Report, a groundbreaking report on American sexual habits and behavior, was produced by Dr. Alfred Kinsey in the 1950s.

18. b

Evolutionary psychology posits that men and women differ in their short-term sexual strategies according to the principles of natural selection and preservation of the species.

19. a

The aggression motivation is the desire to harm or injure someone else.

20. d

The psychological study of emotion includes the study of not only physiological responses but also of internal states and behaviors.

21. a

The James–Lange theory of emotion posits that individuals experience physiological changes which they then interpret as emotional states. A related modern theory called the facial feedback hypothesis similarly posits that feedback from the face provides cues or signals that help determine an emotional response.

22. b

Modern researchers, including Joseph LeDoux, have discovered the central role of the amygdala, a structure within the limbic system, in the creation of emotions.

23. d

The Schachter–Singer approach views emotions as a combination of both cognitive processes and autonomic processes.

24. b

Gender differences in experiencing and expressing emotions are strongly influenced by social factors; women are generally allowed more leeway than men in experiencing and reporting their emotions.

25. b

Cultural rules about the expression of emotions are called display rules.

Essay Questions

1. Name and describe six different theories of motivation.

   Theories of motivation include the evolutionary theory, which developed from the work of Konrad Lorenz and others; drive theory, propounded by Clark Hull; arousal theory, associated with R. M. Yerkes and J. D. Dodson, among others; expectancy theory, propounded by David McClelland and others; cognitive theory, developed by Edward Deci; and humanistic theory, epitomized by Abraham Maslow. The evolutionary and drive theories posit that organisms are motivated by internal needs that help the individual organism, as well as the species, to survive. The drive theory asserts that the ultimate goal of an organism is homeostasis, or a constant state of inner stability and balance.

   In contrast to the drive theory, the arousal theory posits that organisms seek to maintain optimal levels of arousal. Expectancy theory assumes that individuals are motivated by incentives, or rewards, that can consist of anything that has value to the individual. Cognitive theory places more emphasis on conscious decision making, and differentiates between intrinsic and extrinsic motivation. Finally, humanistic theory looks at the entirety of life and posits that, once basic physiological needs are met, an individual attempts to satisfy "higher" needs, culminating in the need for self-actualization.

2. Discuss some of the disorders associated with the primary motivator of hunger.

   Hunger is a primary motivator that has resulted in some disorders that are based on the facts of modern life. Overweight is a problem experienced by many Americans who are no longer in danger of starvation, but who suffer from an oversupply of foods that are high in calories and (at times) low in nutritive value. Overweight is a difficult problem that is influenced by both genetic and environmental factors.

   Anorexia nervosa and bulimia, related disorders that occur mostly in young or adolescent women, are caused by social pressures to be thin. In anorexia, an individual has a distorted self-perception and an irrational fear of gaining weight, which leads the person to become obsessed with food and to severely limit their intake of food, to the point of starvation. Bulimia is characterized by "binging" on foods, followed by either vomiting or using laxatives or diuretics to rid the body of food. Both disorders cause severe health problems and are very difficult to treat.

3. Describe some factors that have been found to influence the motivators of aggression and achievement.

   While there has been debate about whether aggression is inborn or learned, it is now generally believed to be a response elicited by external events and stimuli, possibly including the prevalence of violence in the media. Psychologists have found that the rates of violence vary widely among different cultures. There are also some studies that have linked rates of violence to the levels of the hormone testosterone in males.

   The achievement motivation is the desire to excel or to accomplish something. Achievement levels of individuals have been measured by tests, including the Thematic Apperception Test (TAT). Individuals with high levels of achievement motivation have been found to be more successful in various measures (such as grades in school, promotions on the job, salaries) than those with low achievement levels. Among other things, researchers have found that high achievers tend to set moderately difficult goals that could be achieved through hard work and determination rather than unrealistically difficult goals.

4. Compare and contrast the physiological and cognitive theories of emotion.

   Physiological theories of emotion include the James–Lange theory and the Cannon–Bard theory. Both of these theories, as well as the more recent facial feedback hypothesis, posit that individuals experience changes in physiological states which they then interpret as emotional states. Cognitive theories, such as the

Schachter–Singer approach, also posit that individuals experience and interpret physiological reactions, but additional research has shown that individuals can experience emotions through cognitive processes alone, without a corresponding physiological change.

5. Describe some of the cultural and gender differences in the experience and display of emotions.

While different cultures are similar with regard to the basic emotions that are identified and how they are displayed through facial expressions, cultures also differ widely in their display rules, or the cultural rules that dictate how emotions should be expressed. For example, in Japanese society, it is not appropriate to display negative emotions in public. Another researcher found that even 3-year-old girls, when given an unattractive gift, reacted by smiling; in other words, they had learned to mask disappointment and to display an "appropriate" reaction.

Research has also encountered gender differences in the reported experiencing and display of emotions. Research indicates that women tend to experience greater intensity of emotions; culturally, women are also permitted more leeway to express their emotions (with the exception of anger).

UNIT III: HUMAN DEVELOPMENT

CHAPTER 8—HUMAN DEVELOPMENT

 FLASH FOCUS

When you complete this chapter, you will be able to:

✓ Describe prenatal and infant development

✓ Discuss the cognitive, social, moral, and gender role aspects of child development

✓ Discuss physical, social, and identity development in adolescence

✓ Discuss physical, cognitive, and social changes that take place in adulthood and later life

Use a highlighter to identify ideas, terms, and people that your instructor refers to in lectures or emphasizes in the course. Add to the chart any other ideas, terms, or people that your instructor discusses.

Core Concepts in Human Development

Important Ideas	Key Terms	Important People
Developmental psychology	Birth defects	Jean Piaget
Zygote	Fetal alcohol syndrome (FAS)	Lawrence Kohlberg
Embryo	Reflexes	Carol Gilligan
Fetus	Attachment	Harry Harlow
Piaget's stages of cognitive	Assimilation	Erik Erikson
Development	Accommodation	Daniel Levinson
Kohlberg's stages of moral	Sensorimotor stage	B. J. Reinke
understanding	Object permanence	Elisabeth Kübler-Ross
Gilligan's morality of caring	Preoperational stage	
Temperament	Symbolic play	
Gender identity	Conservation	
Gender stability	Concrete operations stage	
Gender consistency	Logical thought	
Social learning theory	Formal operations stage	
Cognitive development	Interpropositional thinking	
Theory	Preconventional level of	
Gender schema theory	morality	
Adolescence	Conventional level of morality	
Puberty	Postconventional level of	
Secondary sex	morality	
Characteristics	Social smiling	
Parental responsiveness	Empathy	
Parental demandingness	Attachment	
Peer group	Crystallized intelligence	
Personal identity	Fluid intelligence	
Identity crisis	Senile dementia	

Erikson's stages of Psychosocial development Gender intensification Gender role stereotypes Menopause Midlife crisis Empty nest syndrome	Alzheimer's disease Denial Anger Bargaining Depression Acceptance	

Prenatal Development and Development in Infancy

FLASH SUMMARY

Developmental psychology is the branch of psychology that studies changes that occur throughout the human life cycle. These changes begin even before birth, and as soon as the sperm and ovum have combined to create a new organism containing a combination of genes from both sets of parents. For the first 2 weeks, the fertilized ovum, called a *zygote*, consists of not much more than a mass of rapidly dividing cells. From 2 weeks until 6 weeks, the organism is called an *embryo*, and begins to develop a head, limbs, and most of its internal organs, including sex organs and glands. After the first 6 weeks, the developing organism is called a *fetus*; ideally, it will remain in the womb for more than 7 additional months.

Many external factors can affect the development of the embryo and fetus, including alcohol, drugs, and infections such as German measles. Any of these factors can severely impact the development of the fetus, causing *birth defects*. Rubella (German measles) can cause blindness, deafness, or heart disease; other diseases, such as AIDS, can be passed on to the developing infant. Drugs such as caffeine have been shown to slow fetal development; smoking causes risks of decreased birth weight and size and increases the chances of miscarriage or stillbirth. Exposure to cocaine can cause premature birth, brain lesions, heart deformities, and other effects. Excessive use of alcohol by the birth mother can cause a combination of symptoms known as *fetal alcohol syndrome (FAS)*.

Once the infant is safely delivered, growth continues to be rapid; during the first year, infants triple in weight, to about 20 pounds, and increase in body length by about one-third. Since their stomachs have only a limited capacity, they need to be fed frequently, every 2-1/2 to 4 hours. They also have difficulty maintaining their body temperature, therefore, they must be kept warm. Infants possess simple *reflexes* or responses to stimulation in certain areas of the body, such as a sucking reflex and a gripping reflex. Within a few months, infants are capable of locomotion, first by means of crawling along the ground and eventually around the end of their first year by standing alone and even walking.

At this early stage, infants can respond to classical conditioning in learning to associate a bell, a light, or a stroking touch, with the imminent appearance of food; these conditioned stimuli will cause a sucking reflex. Newborns also respond to operant conditioning; within 2 months, they can learn to turn their heads in response to stroking, for the reward of a bottle of milk. Research indicates that newborns can also distinguish between different colors, odors, and sounds. They can also recognize forms or patterns. The abilities to recognize faces—particularly the face of the mother or primary caregiver—and to perceive depth are also acquired very early. They also display *attachment*, or bonding, with their caregiver.

In terms of the development of cognitive abilities, the work of *Jean Piaget*, a Swiss psychologist, is still considered to be of great importance. Piaget observed a number of children and identified a series of *stages of cognitive development*. Piaget identified two processes at work in the incorporation of new information: *assimilation,* or incorporation of new information into existing frameworks or *schemas;* and *accommodation,* or the modification of existing schemas as the result of new information or experiences. Piaget's stages of development are summarized in the following chart.

 FLASH SUMMARY

The following chart summarizes the stages of development identified by Piaget in his research with children. Add to the chart any ideas or additional information that is provided either by your instructor in class or by your text or readings.

Piaget's Stages of Cognitive Development

Stage	Age	Description
Sensorimotor stage	Birth to 18 to 24 months	Basic cause-and-effect relationships *Object permanence* (realization that an object out of sight continues to exist)
Preoperational stage	Between 18 and 24 months to 7 years	*Symbolic play* *Conservation* (knowledge that physical attributes remain the same even though outward appearance is altered)
Stage of concrete operations	7 to 11 years	Understanding of relationships, series, reversibility; beginning of *logical thought*
Stage of formal operations	12 years to adulthood	Capable of hypothetical and deductive reasoning; *interpropositional thinking* (testing the validity of alternative propositions)

Building on Piaget's work, yet focusing on the development of *moral understanding,* *Lawrence Kohlberg* examined how children develop a sense of right and wrong. Kohlberg posited development that occurs in three stages: the *preconventional level,* or an understanding of morality based on the consequences of one's actions; the *conventional level,* or morality that is based upon rules and laws; and the *postconventional level,* which is based on abstract principles and values. Kohlberg felt that children operated at the preconventional level but were capable of progressing to the conventional level. In adolescence or early adulthood, individuals are capable of attaining the postconventional level. However, many people do not attain this level and operate throughout their lives on a conventional level of morality.

One researcher, *Carol Gilligan,* noted that Kohlberg had based his studies exclusively on the observation of boys. Gilligan conducted her own studies, and reported a difference between a male sense of morality based upon principles of justice and a female sense of morality based upon *caring*. While several studies have not corroborated the gender differences reported by Gilligan, there is no doubt that boys and girls are socialized differently and respond to different pressures from a very early age.

Researchers studying emotional development noticed that emotional and cognitive development occur simultaneously, and that there are many connections between the two types of development. Infants as young as 2 months old exhibit *social smiling* in response to others' smiles, and exhibit angry emotions within the first year. Infants also develop a capacity to "read" the emotions of others at a very early age. By the time they are 10 years old, children have learned to express sadness and to either express or withhold expressions of anger. Children also develop a stable *temperament*, or characteristic mood level and emotional reactivity, that is viewed as part of their personality. Children also appear to develop *empathy*, or the ability to recognize and share the feelings of others, relatively early, before the age of 2 years. Children also demonstrate *attachment* to their caregivers as infants. Psychologist *Harry Harlow's* famous (or infamous) studies of baby monkeys that were deprived of their mothers demonstrated that contact comfort—hugging, cuddling, and caresses—is essential to normal growth and development in primates, as well as in humans.

Children—and even infants—begin the process of developing *gender identity* early in life. Gender identity refers to the understanding of whether one is male or female. *Gender stability* is the assurance that one's gender identity will not change; however, *gender consistency*, the understanding that sex identity remains the same no matter if one engages in dress or behavior of the opposite sex, develops at around 6 or 7 years of age. A number of different theories exist to explain gender development: *social learning theory*, which posits that children learn gender roles by modeling behavior and by being rewarded for so-called "appropriate" behavior; *cognitive development theory*, which posits that gender identity is simply an outgrowth of increasing cognitive understanding; and *gender schema theory*, which posits the development of gender schemas that include social beliefs about the abilities and characteristics of the sexes.

Development in Adolescence

FLASH SUMMARY

Adolescence is now formally acknowledged as a stage of development that occurs after the onset of *puberty*, or sexual maturation, and before full adult development. Adolescence is a relatively modern development that is recognized in Western society; many other cultures do not acknowledge such a separate developmental stage. Between ages 10 and 12 for girls and 12 or 13 for boys, children experience a sudden growth spurt that is one aspect of puberty. Other aspects include increasing levels of sex hormones and the development of *secondary sex characteristics*, including a lower voice and the development of facial hair in boys, and the onset of menstruation and the development of breasts in girls.

In Western society, adolescents experience many social and emotional changes that accompany the physical process of maturation. Adolescents have been shown to be subject to wider and more intense mood swings than older people; however, contrary to popular belief, most adolescents reported feeling happy and self-confident rather than stressed and unhappy. Differences in parenting styles also influence adolescent development; scales of *parental responsiveness* and *parental demandingness* have indicated that whether parents are warm and responsive or cold and neglectful, and whether parents are controlling or permissive, have strong and lasting effects on children and adolescents.

Adolescents are also extremely involved in developing friendships and social networks, and the importance of the *peer group* illustrates that adolescents have a strong need to belong to a group at this time. There is intense pressure to conform to the values and behaviors of the peer group with regard to dress, food, music, entertainment, and even political orientation. The development of friendships and the presence or absence of social success are important in the development of a *personal identity* during adolescence. However, researchers have found evidence that children who are troubled develop into troubled adolescents, whereas children who are generally happy and welladjusted are more likely to stay well adjusted. For both boys and girls, time spent in playing sports seems to be an effective counter to negative feelings about body image that can arise during adolescence. Physical activity is associated with higher achievement, weight reduction, improved muscle tone, and stress reduction.

Psychoanalyst *Erik Erikson* coined the term *identity crisis* to refer to the stage of psychosocial development encountered during adolescence. He believed that individuals must meet and resolve different developmental issues during the life cycle. Erikson's *eight stages of psychosocial development* are set out in the following table. Erikson felt that, during adolescence, young people who are able to develop plans to achieve career and personal goals and who decide which social groups they belong to will be able to form an effective personal identity. Those who are unable to cope with the formation of a personal identity will remain confused about their lives

 FLASH SUMMARY

The following chart summarizes the eight stages of psychosocial development posited by Erik Erikson. Add to the chart any additional information or examples provided by your instructor or encountered in your reading.

Erikson's Eight Stages of Psychosocial Development

Period	Conflict(s)	Positive Resolution	Negative Resolution
Childhood	Trust vs. mistrust Autonomy vs. self-doubt Initiative vs. guilt Competence vs. inferiority	Trust, security, confidence, independence, curiosity, competence, industry	Insecurity, doubt, guilt, low self-esteem, sense of failure
Adolescence	Identity vs. role confusion	Strong sense of self-identity	Weak sense of self
Adulthood	Intimacy vs. isolation Generativity vs. stagnation Integrity vs. despair	Capacity to develop deep and meaningful relationships and care for others; consideration for future generations; personal sense of worth and satisfaction	Isolation, unhappiness, selfishness, stagnancy, sense of failure and regret

One of the most important developments at this time is the continuing development of a gender identity. Boys and girls are likely to experiment with various types of behaviors, including those related to male–female relationships and dating. Some adolescents become extreme in their orientation to either their male or their female identities; this *gender intensification* may be short-lived. In general, girls have been found to suffer a loss of self-esteem during adolescence, whereas boys often experience increased self-esteem. In the course of establishing a gender identity, either boys or girls may adopt *gender role stereotypes,* such as the belief that "boys don't cry" or that girls are submissive.

Experimentation with sexual behavior, including sexual intimacy, is increasingly common in adolescence. About 60 percent of white male teenagers have intercourse by age 18, and about 60 percent of white female adolescents have done so by age 19. Reasons for the earlier age of sexual experimentation include changes in attitudes toward sexual behavior, increased availability of contraceptives, and earlier sexual maturity. The rate of teenage pregnancy is higher in the United States than in any other developed country. The consequences of a teenage pregnancy are serious for the mother, who tends to bear a lower-birth-weight infant, is less likely to receive prenatal care, and is more likely to drop out of school.

Development in Adulthood and Beyond

FLASH SUMMARY

Physical, cognitive, and even social development takes place much more slowly in adults and older persons. Muscular strength peaks during the late twenties or early 30s and then begins to slowly decline; by age 70, muscle strength has decreased by about 30 percent in both men and women. However, regular physical exercise can slow down or even reverse some of these losses, including physical endurance. Sensory systems, such as vision and hearing, also decline, but can also be compensated for by external aids and behavior compensations, such as compensating for hearing loss by attending more carefully to other people's gestures and lip movements. Highly developed sensory and motor skills, such as the ability to type quickly, have been shown to suffer only minimal decline with age. Women also experience *menopause,* which is the cessation of menstruation and fertility, between ages 45 and 55. While some women experience symptoms such as mood swings or irritability, most women do not experience psychological problems at menopause. Also, the experience of menopause varies widely with different cultures. In some cultures, where menopause marks an increase in women's status, there are few if any negative symptoms reported.

Tests of intellectual ability have shown that scores on ability tests increase until the late 30s and early 40s, then enter a period of stability until the mid-50s or early 60s, followed by a gradual decline. Investigators have identified two types of intelligence, called *crystallized intelligence,* the ability that depends on skill and knowledge (such as vocabulary and general information), and *fluid intelligence,* the capacity for abstract reasoning. Tests have indicated that crystallized intelligence is often maintained until late in life, as long as the individual is in good health. Fluid intelligence appears to decline with age. The ability to perform cognitive tasks quickly also appears to decline with age, which could be due to decreases in sensory function, or a general increase in caution.

In their social development, there is varied evidence for the existence of a *midlife crisis* for either men or women. *Daniel Levinson* conducted interviews with a number of men and claimed to have encountered in most of his subjects a midlife crisis characterized by transition, anxiety, and turmoil. Other investigators, however, have found no evidence of such a midlife crisis. *B. J. Reinke* and colleagues interviewed a number of women between the ages of 30 and 60, and found a number of transitional periods in the women's lives that were mainly related to the raising of children and, finally, to the departure of children from the family. Researchers have also found little or no evidence to support the so-called *empty nest syndrome,* in which women were supposed to be grieving the absence of children. Instead, research has shown that most women reported increased life satisfaction at that time.

The age of 65 to 70 is generally considered to be the beginning of old age. In older age, the brain does tend to slow down due to the breakdown of the myelin that covers the axons in the cortex. The brain takes longer to process information, and reaction time is slower. Sensory capacity also decreases, with some loss of sight, including impaired night vision, and hearing loss, particularly in the higher frequencies. Stamina and energy tend to decline, along with some decline in heart, lung, kidney, and muscle function. About 80 percent of Americans over age 65 have one or more chronic conditions such as arthritis, rheumatism, heart problems, or high blood pressure. The leading causes of death among older Americans, both male and female, are heart disease, cancer, and stroke.

Other illnesses that affect older Americans include *senile dementia,* or senility, a state of severe mental deterioration that affects about 5–8 percent of those age 65 or older, about 15–20 percent of those over 75, and about 25–50 percent of those over 85. About 50-60 percent of all cases of senility are caused by *Alzheimer's disease,* a progressive degeneration of brain cells that results in impaired memory, intellect, and personality. Heredity appears to be a major factor in development of Alzheimer's disease. Much work is now being done to produce drugs that can delay the deterioration associated with Alzheimer's.

The very oldest Americans, those over 95 years, often exhibit better mental and physical condition than people 20 years younger. They appear to have a genetic predisposition that enables them to resist disease and to remain active and involved longer than most people. Losses suffered in later life, including the loss of a spouse, tend to create a greater risk for health problems and produce a higher mortality rate among survivors. *Elisabeth Kübler-Ross* is known for her studies of attitudes toward death and dying; she identified five stages people go through in coming to terms with impending death, including *denial, anger, bargaining, depression,* and *acceptance.*

FLASH LINKS FOR HUMAN DEVELOPMENT

The following websites provide information on the various stages of development.

1. Prenatal, infancy, and childhood:
   www.visembryo.com/
   www.w-cpc.org/fetal.html
   www.earlychildhood.com/
   http://idealist.com/children/

2. Adolescence:
   www.yale.edu/ynhti/curriculum/units/
   1991/ 5/91.05.07.x.html
   http://education.Indiana.edu/cas/adol/adol.html
   www.personal.psu.edu/faculty/n/x/nxd10/
   adolesce.htm

3. Adulthood and beyond:
   www.css.edu/depts./grad/nia/index.htm
   www.Norwich.edu/srad/index.html
   www.hcoa.org/
   www.buckinstitute.org/
   www.nih.gov/nia/

FLASH REVIEW

Visit the website of the National Institute on Aging at www.nih.gov/nia/, and review some of the recent studies of aging. Write a brief report on methods that have been discovered that promote healthy aging.

 **FLASH TEST**

Review the chart of Core Concepts for this chapter. Then take the Practice Test for Chapter 8 on the following pages and rate your performance.

PRACTICE TEST

(Chapter 8—Human Development)

Multiple Choice (3 points each)

1. Which series below shows the proper order of prenatal development?
   a. embryo, zygote, fetus
   b. fetus, zygote, embryo
   c. zygote, fetus, embryo
   d. zygote, embryo, fetus

2. Research into the visual preference of infants has shown that they prefer to look at
   a. sharp angles.
   b. human faces.
   c. bright colors.
   d. funny pictures.

3. Developmental psychology is the study of
   a. changes throughout the human life cycle.
   b. cognitive changes that occur through the life cycle.
   c. physical changes that occur through the life cycle.
   d. various developmental crises that occur throughout the life cycle.

4. External factors that can affect the development of the embryo and fetus include *all except one* of the following. Which one should *not* be included?
   a. drugs and alcohol
   b. smoking
   c. watching television
   d. certain contagious diseases

5. Infants must be fed every
   a. 8 hours.
   b. 6 hours.
   c. 2-1/2 to 4 hours.
   d. 1/2 hour.

6. Infants can respond to _____ types of learning.
   a. classical and operant conditioning
   b. cognitive
   c. hypothetical reasoning
   d. symbolic

7. In developmental psychology, another word for "bonding" is
   a. caregiving.
   b. temperament.
   c. attachment.
   d. mutualism.

8. Harlow's experiments with infant monkeys showed that the basis for the infant's attachment to its mother is
   a. nourishment.
   b. fear.
   c. contact comfort.
   d. sounds the mother makes.

9. A theory that presupposes that all human beings go through an orderly and predictable series of changes is known as

    a. a synchronous theory.
    b. a successive theory.
    c. an asynchronous theory.
    d. a stage theory.

10. The phase of the life span that is characterized by an increasing ability to think logically and reason abstractly is the _____ phase.
    a. childhood
    b. adolescent
    c. preadult
    d. adulthood

11. In Piaget's theory of cognitive development, children in the sensorimotor stage
    a. know the world only through muscle activities and sensory impressions.
    b. are struggling with the basic concepts of logic and conservation.
    c. are focused inward on their growing mental abilities, not on their environment.
    d. are particularly in need of warm, loving support from their parents.

12. In Piaget's theory, infants and children use accommodation to
    a. compensate for their lack of experience in communicating their ideas to others.
    b. modify existing schemas to fit new information.
    c. transform new knowledge to fit existing schemata.
    d. apply existing information to new information.

13. According to Piaget, the process by which new information is modified to fit existing schemas is called
    a. accommodation.
    b. assimilation.
    c. adaptation.
    d. adjustment.

14. The idea that things do not disappear when they are moved out of sight is called _____, and it is acquired during the _____ stage of cognitive development.
    a. accommodation; preoperational
    b. egocentrism; sensorimotor
    c. concrete operational thinking; concrete operational
    d. object permanence; sensorimotor

15. The _____ period of cognitive development is marked by rapid development of language usage and of the ability to represent objects symbolically.
    a. sensorimotor
    b. preoperational
    c. concrete operational
    d. formal operational

16. According to Kohlberg, the order of levels of moral development is preconventional, conventional, and
    a. postconventional reasoning.
    b. formal conventional reasoning.
    c. ultraconventional reasoning.
    d. nonconventional reasoning.

17. At the _____ level of moral development, we tend to judge morality in terms of what supports and preserves the social order.
    a. preconventional
    b. conventional
    c. postconventional
    d. abstract

18. Our ability to recognize the emotions of others, to understand these emotions, and to share them ourselves is called
    a. caregiving.
    b. compassion.
    c. emotionality.
    d. empathy.

19. Secondary sex characteristics include *all except one* of the following. Which one should *not* be included?
    a. appearance of facial hair in adolescent boys.
    b. onset of menstruation in adolescent girls.
    c. development of external genitalia.
    d. development of breasts in adolescent girls.

20. Which of the developmental crises posited by Erik Erikson is displayed in adolescence?
    a. identity versus role confusion
    b. intimacy versus isolation
    c. autonomy versus shame and doubt
    d. integrity versus despair

21. A culture's expectations of the attitudes and behaviors that are appropriate for men and women is called
    a. gender.
    b. gender role.
    c. gender identity.
    d. gender type.

22. Pregnant teenagers face which of the following increased risks?
    a. risk of death in childbirth
    b. risk of low-birth-weight infants
    c. risk of losing their boyfriend's support
    d. risk of birth defects

23. As older people experience decline in their sensory systems, they
    a. learn to adjust and use additional cues to decode sensory information.
    b. make more frequent visits to medical professionals.
    c. begin to feel depressed and useless to society.
    d. retire from their jobs due to a decline in higher-level skills.

24. Elisabeth Kübler-Ross proposed that the typical reaction to learning of a terminal illness is to go from denial and anger to
    a. acceptance and then depression.
    b. depression and death.
    c. bargaining, depression, and then perhaps acceptance.
    d. fear, despair, and avoidance.

25. A study of the "oldest old" found that the elderly who lived healthy and productive lives past the age of 95 did so because of
    a. positive attitude and motivation.
    b. good diet and exercise.
    c. support from family and friends.
    d. a genetic advantage that made them more resistant to disease.

Essay Questions (5 points each)

1. Name some possible negative influences on prenatal development.

2. List Piaget's stages of cognitive development and some of the types of thinking that are associated with each stage.

3. Describe the crisis faced in adolescence, according to Erikson's psychosocial stages of development.

4. What are some of the physical and mental changes that occur in mid- to late adulthood?

5. According to Elisabeth Kübler-Ross, what are the stages experienced by people when death is imminent?

ANSWER EXPLANATIONS

Multiple-Choice Questions

1. **d**
   The order of prenatal development is zygote, embryo, and finally the fetus.

2. b

Research with infants indicates that they prefer to view pictures of human faces; they particularly respond to the features of their primary caregiver.

3. a

Developmental psychology studies all of the changes, including cognitive, physical, and social, that take place throughout the human life cycle.

4. c

Watching television has not been shown to have an adverse effect on the embryo or fetus (although it could decrease the IQ of the mother).

5. c

Infants, whose stomach has only a limited capacity but who are growing very rapidly, must be fed every 2-1/2 to 4 hours.

6. a

Infants can respond to both classical and operant conditioning, in which they are either conditioned to respond to a stimulus such as a bell or light or rewarded for response to a particular stimulus such as stroking.

7. c

"Attachment" is the term used in developmental psychology to refer to the bonding that develops initially between the infant and its primary caregiver.

8. c

Harlow's experiments with infant monkeys demonstrated that the monkeys' attachment to their caregiver is based on contact comfort.

9. d

Stage theory is a theory that presupposes that all human beings go through a similar series of changes.

10. a

During childhood, children are increasingly able to think logically and reason abstractly.

11. a

According to Piaget's theory of cognitive development, children in the sensorimotor stage primarily experience the world through muscle activities and sensory impressions.

12. b

In Piaget's view, infants and children use accommodation to modify existing schemas to incorporate new information or experiences.

13. b

According to Piaget, new information is modified to fit existing schemas by the process of assimilation.

14. d

The idea that things do not disappear when they are out of sight is called object permanence, and it is acquired during the sensorimotor stage of cognitive development.

15. b

The preoperational period of cognitive development is marked by rapid development of language usage and by the ability to represent objects symbolically.

16. a

According to Kohlberg's stages of moral reasoning, following the preconventional and conventional stages of reasoning is the postconventional stage.

17. b

At the conventional level of moral reasoning, we tend to judge morality in terms of what supports and preserves the moral order.

18. d

Empathy is the quality of recognizing, understanding, and to a degree, sharing the emotions of others.

19. c

The development of external genitalia occurs very early in fetal development; the appearance of facial hair, breasts, and the onset of menstruation are all secondary sex characteristics that occur in adolescence.

20. a

According to Erikson, adolescents face the developmental crisis of identity versus role confusion.

21. b

A gender role is a socially defined set of expectations of the attitudes and behaviors that are appropriate for men and women.

22. b

Pregnant teenagers face an increased risk of delivering a low-birth-weight infant; there are also other substantial risks, including the lower likelihood of prenatal care and the increased rate of dropping out of school, associated with teen pregnancies

23. a

Studies have shown that as people age and their sensory systems decline, they compensate by using other cues to decipher sensory information.

24. c

The stages proposed by Elisabeth Kübler-Ross include denial, anger, bargaining, depression, and finally, perhaps, acceptance of impending death.

25. d

One study of the very elderly (over 95 years old) concluded that the determining factor in their longevity was the genetically inherited ability to resist disease.

Essay Questions

1. Name some possible negative influences on prenatal development.

   Negative influences on prenatal development can include environmental effects introduced by the mother, such as poor diet, smoking, or use of alcohol or drugs. Smoking can produce low-birth-weight babies, which are more at risk for developmental difficulty; and excessive alcohol consumption can cause fetal alcohol syndrome (FAS), a combination of symptoms including learning difficulties. Other negative influences include exposure of the fetus to diseases such as German measles, which can cause birth defects, and the AIDS virus, which can be passed on to the developing infant.

2. List Piaget's stages of cognitive development and some of the types of thinking that are associated with each stage.

   Piaget's stages of cognitive development include the sensorimotor stage, from birth to 18 and 24 months; the preoperational stage, from 18 to 24 months and 7 years; the stage of concrete operations, from 7 to 11 years of age; and the stage of formal operations, from 12 years to adulthood. In the sensorimotor stage, the child learns basic cause-and-effect relationships and concepts such as object permanence. In the preoperational stage the child learns to represent people and ideas through symbolic play and principles of conservation. At the stage of concrete operations, children begin to understand relationships and series, the concept of reversibility, and to exhibit logical thought. At the stage of formal operations, adolescents and adults are capable of hypothetical and deductive reasoning and interpropositional thinking.

3. Describe the crisis faced in adolescence according to Erikson's psychosocial stages of development.

   According to Erikson's stages of development, adolescents must face and resolve a conflict between identity and role confusion. This led to the use of the term "identity crisis" to describe the period of adolescence. According to Erikson, an adolescent, who resolves this crisis will be able to plan for his or her future career, and lifestyle and will develop a strong sense of self-identity. The adolescent who does not successfully meet this stage of development will have a weak sense of self.

4. What are some of the physical and mental changes that occur in mid- to late adulthood?

   Changes experienced in mid- to late adulthood include deterioration of sensory systems, decline of muscular strength (but little decline in endurance), and the decline of certain types of cognitive abilities. For example, fluid intelligence, which is often used by mathematicians, declines in later life, whereas crystallized intelligence, or skill and knowledge, is maintained until late in life. Some abilities such as highly developed sensory and motor skills decline only minimally.

   There is conflicting evidence of a "midlife crisis" experienced by either men or women. Women do experience menopause, or the cessation of periods, and some women in Western society experience psychological symptoms related to menopause; however, in other societies in which women achieve greater social status as they age, such symptoms are almost nonexistent. It has also been found that the so-called empty nest syndrome, which was supposed to affect women after the children left home, is nonexistent; instead, the departure of children from the family has been found to have a positive effect on both parents.

5. According to Elisabeth Kübler-Ross, what are the stages experienced by people when death is imminent?

Elisabeth Kübler-Ross identified five stages that people go through in anticipation of impending death: denial, anger, bargaining, depression, and acceptance. While other researchers have challenged the exact order or experience of all of these stages, Kübler-Ross' research continues to have importance because it addressed a "taboo" subject in America: the end of life.

UNIT III: HUMAN DEVELOPMENT

CHAPTER 9—PERSONALITY

 FLASH FOCUS

When you complete this chapter, you will be able to:

✓ Define personality, and describe what is meant by "personality types"

✓ Describe and differentiate among the main schools of personality development, including the psychoanalytic, trait, learning theory, and humanistic theories of personality

✓ Describe some of the psychobiological studies of personality

✓ Name and describe the major types of personality assessment tools, and assess their effectiveness

Use a highlighter to identify ideas, terms, and people that your instructor refers to in lectures or emphasizes in the course. Add to the chart any other ideas, terms, or people that your instructor discusses.

Core Concepts in Personality

Important Ideas	Key Terms	Important People
Personality	Situational/external factors	Sigmund Freud
Personality types	Unconscious	Carl Jung
Psychoanalytic theories	Conscious	Alfred Adler
Psychosexual stages of	Preconscious	Karen Horney
development	Id	Carl Rogers
Neo-Freudian	Ego	Abraham Maslow
Jungian/analytic approach	Superego	Gordon Allport
Humanistic theories	Pleasure principle	Raymond Cattell
Client-centered therapy	Reality principle	Hans Eysenck
Trait theories	Freudian slips	Albert Bandura
Type theory	Fixation	Julian Rotter
"Big five" traits:	Oral stage	M. Zuckerman
Extraversion/introversion	Anal stage	Hathaway and McKinley
Agreeableness/antagonism	Phallic stage	Hermann Rorschach
Conscientiousness/	Latency stage	Henry Murray
undirectedness	Genital stage	C. D. Morgan
Neuroticism/emotional	Oedipus complex	Peter Myers
Stability	Penis envy	Isabel Briggs
Openness to experience	Collective unconscious	
Learning approaches	Archetypes	
Social-cognitive theory	Birth order	
Social learning theory	Basic anxiety	
Personality assessment	Fully functioning persons	

Objective personality tests	Self-concept	
Projective personality tests	Unconditional positive regard	
	Hierarchy of needs	
	Self-actualization	
	Peak experiences	
	Central traits	
	Secondary traits	
	Cardinal trait	
	Functional autonomy	
	Source traits	
	Surface traits	
	Self-system	
	Self-efficacy	
	Self-reinforcement	
	Observational learning	
	Internals	
	Externals	
	Minnesota Multiphasic Personality Inventory(MMPI)	
	Validity scale	
	Rorschach Inkblot Test	
	Thematic Apperception Test (TAT)	
	Neuroticism, Extraversion, and Openness Personality Inventory (NEO-PI)	
	Myers–Briggs Type Indicator (MBTI)	

Personality Defined

FLASH SUMMARY

Personality is defined in psychology as the particular pattern of thinking and behavior that differentiates one person from another, and that persists over time. Psychologists study personality and personality development in order to learn what causes individual differences in behavior. Psychological studies to date have led to the creation of a number of different theories of personality development and methods by which personality differences can be studied and classified. Research on human personality includes identification of distinctive personality characteristics and determining the variables that produced and control them.

Many systems of personality classification involve the creation of *personality types,* or different categories into which personality characteristics can be assigned. While the concept of personality types is useful in creating hypotheses about personality development, many psychologists today believe that individuals cannot be assigned to discrete categories, but instead exhibit differences in the degree to which they exhibit certain characteristics.

Early theorists such as Freud believed that personality was a stable and constant factor; later theorists, however, began to stress the importance of environmental factors on personality development. There has also been considerable debate about whether personality is really a stable enough factor to be measured or whether there is so much variability among individuals that scientists can't make any useful predictions. Today, most psychologists agree that people do exhibit a considerable degree of consistency in their behavior, but their behavior is also strongly influenced by *situational/external factors.*

Theories of Personality Development
....

FLASH SUMMARY

Psychoanalytic theories of personality development began with *Sigmund Freud,* who developed his theories about personality and mental illness out of his experiences in his own clinical practice and his observations of practitioners who were using hypnosis to treat various mental disorders. Freud's basic, and groundbreaking, observation was that most of the mental processes that take place in human beings do so at the *unconscious* level. Freud identified three different levels of activity and corresponding aspects of personality, which he labeled the *id,* the primitive, innate urges that exist at the unconscious level; the *ego,* the part of the personality that operates at the *conscious* level and responds to external conditions and consequences; and the *superego,* which is concerned with the morality of a particular action and which acts at the *preconscious* level. The id operates according to what Freud termed the *pleasure principle,* or the search for gratification of basic desires such as food and sex. The ego responds to the *reality principle,* or the external conditions and consequences that we face for our actions and behaviors. Freud suggested that one way in which the struggle between the id and the ego is manifested is in *Freudian slips,* or mistakes in speech that reveal our underlying desires and motivations.

Freud also posited that human beings pass through predictable *psychosexual stages of development,* summarized in the following chart. The chart summarizes the stages, the ages at which individuals normally encounter each stage, a brief description of the stage, plus Freud's theory of the *fixation* that could result from too much or too little gratification at a particular stage.

FLASH SUMMARY

Add to the chart any additional descriptions or examples that are provided by your instructor in lectures or that you encounter in your reading.

Freud's Psychosexual Stages of Development

Stage	Age	Description	Fixation
Oral	Birth–18 months	Pleasure centers on the mouth	Dependency/hostility
Anal	18 months–3 years	Pleasure centers on elimination process	Compulsive/impulsive
Phallic	3 years–7 years	Pleasure centers on genitals	*Oedipus complex*

Latency	7 years–11 years	Sexual urges minimal	
Genital	11 years–adult	Pleasure again centers on genitals	

While psychologists agree that Freud's theories had a profound impact on the development of psychology, his theory of personality development is today not accepted by most psychologists. For one thing, his theory cannot be subjected to any type of testing or systematic study; for another, many of his theories, such as his theories about the meaning of dreams, are not consistent with modern research findings. And, Freud's theories reflect his own values and upbringing, such as Freud's theory of *penis envy,* that girls are envious of boys' penises because they perceive them as superior to their own genitalia. In many of his theories, Freud assumed that men are the appropriate model for human behavior, and that women fail to "measure up" to this male model; his theories are also ethnocentric, in that they take Western European cultural standards as the model for all cultures.

Many of the followers of Freud developed differences with him, and several developed their own theories and schools of thought, which are generally termed *neo-Freudian.* One such neo-Freudian was *Carl Jung,* a Swiss psychologist, who believed Freud's theories put too much emphasis on sexual motivations. Jung called his approach *analytic,* as distinguished from Freud's psychoanalytic approach. Today his school of thought is referred to as *Jungian.* Jung developed the concept of a *collective unconscious* that is a shared storehouse of primitive ideas and images inherited from one's ancestors; *archetypes* are the emotion-laden symbols and images from the collective unconscious. As with Freud's theories, however, Jung's theories cannot be subjected to verification, and while they had an important impact on the development of psychology, they are not widely accepted today.

Another neo-Freudian is *Alfred Adler,* who differed from Freud in that he viewed humans as attempting to fulfill themselves rather than simply trying to find pleasure. He also considered social behaviors as more important than did Freud. According to Adler, people are motivated by feelings of inferiority, which lead them to strive for superiority and completion. Adler posited the importance of *birth order* among one's siblings as a determining factor in personality. Birth order is still considered a factor in personality development.

Karen Horney, another contemporary of Freud and one of the few women in the field of psychology or psychoanalysis, disagreed with Freud's interpretation of male and female differences. Horney felt that inferiority feelings in women were the result of the way women are treated by society. She viewed human conflicts as resulting not from the fixations Freud described but rather from *basic anxiety* resulting from childhood fears of abandonment.

In contrast to Freud's emphasis on unconscious factors and unacceptable impulses, other psychologists developed theories that are called the *humanistic theories* for their emphasis on growth, dignity, and self-determination. *Carl Rogers* developed a theory that human beings strive, over the course of their lives, to become *fully functioning persons.* Rogers theorized that the barriers to our full self-development develop when we experience inconsistencies between our *self-concept* and messages from outside ourselves. In order to reduce the inconsistency and consequent anxiety, individuals utilize defense mechanisms such as distortion and denial. Roger's suggested treatment to help individuals deal with unhappiness caused by such inconsistencies was to receive *unconditional positive regard* from the therapist. *Client-centered therapy* became an accepted form of therapy treatment.

Another humanistic theory of personality, proposed by *Abraham Maslow,* posited a *hierarchy of needs.* According to Maslow, lower-order needs must be satisfied in order for the individual to proceed to higher-order needs. Maslow felt that individuals are striving to become *self-actualized,* in order to attain their true potential. Self-actualized persons occasional attain *peak experiences,* in which they have powerful feelings of unity with the universe. Maslow described individuals like Thomas Jefferson and Eleanor Roosevelt as fully self-actualized. While some aspects of humanistic theories have been subjected to scientific research, such as research into the formation of self-concept and how self-concept is influenced by culture, other concepts are difficult to define and measure. Humanistic theories are acknowledged as having influenced the development of psychology, but are only partially accepted today as descriptive of the reality of personality and personality development.

Personality is often described by means of specific personality *traits,* or stable dimensions of personality which can be measured on a scale from low to high; thus, corresponding schools called *trait theories* developed. One of the first psychologists to identify key human traits was *Gordon Allport.* Allport distinguished *secondary traits,* which are less important, from *central traits,* about five to ten traits that together account for an individual's personality. He also noted that some individuals are dominated by a single all-important *cardinal trait;* for example, Napoleon was dominated by the trait of ambition. Allport also developed a theory of *functional autonomy,* which holds that patterns of behavior that are acquired in one set of circumstances may later be performed in very different circumstances.

Another trait theory was proposed by *Raymond Cattell,* who conducted extensive research to reveal patterns of traits. Cattell then identified sixteen *source traits,* or dimensions of personality that are the sources of other, less important *surface traits.* Cattell identified traits in pairs, such as cool versus warm, calm versus easily upset, and so on. Another variant on trait theory is *type theory,* which examines groupings of traits. *Hans Eysenck* focused on three basic dimensions of personality: emotional stability, *introversion* or *extraversion,* and *psychoticism.*

Some of the research on personality traits has seemed to indicate that there are five major dimensions of personality, termed the "big five," which include:

1. *Extraversion versus introversion,* or whether someone is outgoing, energetic, enthusiastic, or more retiring, sober, and reserved

2. *Agreeableness versus antagonism,* or whether someone is good-natured, cooperative, and trusting, or irritable, suspicious, and uncooperative

3. *Conscientiousness versus undirectedness,* or whether someone is well-organized, careful, and well-disciplined, versus impulsive, careless, and undependable

4. *Emotional stability versus instability* (also termed *neuroticism*), or whether someone is poised, calm, and not hypochondriacal, or nervous, high-strung, and hypochondriacal

5. *Openness to experience,* or whether someone is open to new experiences, imaginative, and has many interests; or whether they are closed, conforming, and uncreative

Studies have found that ratings on these basic traits are linked to important outcomes, such as people's success in performing many types of jobs. However, critics of trait theory point out that the trait approach is primarily descriptive and does not explain how traits develop and influence behavior.

Another school of personality theory is termed the *learning approach,* because it emphasizes the role of learning and experience in the formation of personality. Learning approaches include the *social-cognitive theory* of personality described by *Albert Bandura,* which emphasizes the *self-system,* or processes by which a person perceives, evaluates, and regulates his or her behavior. People also display *self-efficacy,* or the belief that they can perform some task or behavior successfully, and engage in *self-reinforcement,* or positive self-praise, when they achieve an objective. Bandura also emphasizes *observational learning,* a process in which individuals acquire information and new forms of behavior by observing others.

A related theory by *Julian Rotter,* the *social learning theory,* suggests that an individual's expectations about whether a given behavior will produce desired outcomes, and the reinforcement value attached to those outcomes, determine behaviors. Rotter distinguishes between those who strongly believe that they can shape their own destinies, or *internals* and those who believe that their destinies are the result of external forces, or *externals.*

The learning approaches are based on established principles of psychology and have also had practical application in therapy. In one example, people who had lost their jobs were taught techniques for restoring self-efficacy in the job search process, and almost two-thirds of them were able to find reemployment.

Psychobiological Studies of Personality Development

FLASH SUMMARY

Some studies have shown that personality traits are strongly heritable. Scientists have particularly used twin studies, studies of identical twins who are genetically identical, but who have been raised in different environments, to test the strength of genetic factors on personality. One study compiled by *M. Zuckerman* showed that identical twins were more similar in personality than were fraternal twins (who do not share the same genetic makeup, but are like any other brothers and sisters). Another conclusion was that hereditary factors probably play a large role in determining the nature of the family environment; in other words, a child who is more sociable to begin with will receive more social interaction. So far, scientists have concluded that heredity and environment interact to produce different personalities.

Mechanisms in the brain are also responsible for some of the differences in personality. This has been demonstrated by people who have experienced brain injuries that have caused dramatic personality changes. Zuckerman posited that the personality dimensions of extraversion, neuroticism, and psychoticism are determined by the neural systems responsible for reinforcement, punishment, and arousal. People who score high on the extraversion measure seem to be particularly sensitive to reinforcement, and as adults they seek out more reinforcement than do introverts. People who score high on the neuroticism–stability measure are particularly sensitive to the punishing effects of adversive stimuli; these people tend to be anxious and fearful. And people who score high on the psychoticism measure have a low sensitivity to punishment, so they have difficulty learning to refrain from doing things for which they will be punished. They also have high tolerance for arousal and excitation, which might make them more likely to seek out exciting or challenging situations.

Other research has been done in personality measures such as shyness in children. Researchers found that childhood shyness seems to be related to a low level of extraversion and a high level of neuroticism. Shyness also persisted from a very early age into childhood, and shy children exhibited higher rates of the hormones that are produced in reaction to stressful situations (norepinephrine and cortisol). These studies seemed to indicate that there might be a biological basis for certain types of personality traits.

Researchers have also sought to measure differences in personality based on gender. Some measures of the "big five" traits indicate that boys are higher in aggression than are girls; however, these differences may vary in different cultures. For example, aggressiveness scores of girls in Israel were higher than those of boys in America, and in some other countries such as Mexico, girls in certain areas who join gangs are encouraged to fight and display aggressive behaviors.

FLASH SUMMARY

There are many different ways to measure or to *assess* personality. *Objective personality tests* are tests that include multiple-choice and true–false questions, such as the *Minnesota Multiphasic Personality Inventory (MMPI),* devised by *Hathaway* and *McKinley* in 1939. The MMPI was originally created to identify personality traits that are related to mental health; the tests were given to a number of patients in mental institutions, and scales were created to indicate a range of normal responses versus responses that indicated mental health problems. The current version of the MMPI, MMPI-2, has norms based on a sample of people who are more representative ethnically and geographically than were the original respondents. The four *validity scales* of the MMPI measure failure to answer, which may indicate that a person is evading issues or finding issues too painful to answer; the "L" scale (lie), which indicates whether the person answering the questions is telling the truth; the "F" scale (frequency), which indicates items that receive consistent responses from a large majority of people, and can indicate whether the person answering the questions may be experiencing mental problems or is just suffering from an inability to correctly read and respond to the questions; and the "K" scale (defensiveness), which is supposed to identify people who are trying to hide their feelings. The MMPI has adherents as well as critics, but is not as widely used as it was at one time.

Projective personality tests are deliberately ambiguous, so that an individual will have to respond in what is intended to be a revealing manner. The best known example of a projective personality test is the *Rorschach Inkblot Test,* devised in 1921 by Swiss psychiatrist *Hermann Rorschach.* The inkblots are randomly created by spilling ink onto a piece of paper that is then folded in half; the subject is shown each card and asked to describe what it is. The interpretation of the inkblot test was originally based on psychoanalytic theory, but today is more likely to be based on empirical scoring methods.

Another projective test is the *Thematic Apperception Test (TAT),* developed in 1938 by American psychologists *Henry Murray* and *C. D. Morgan* to measure psychological needs. In this test, people are shown a picture that is ambiguous and then asked to tell a story about what is happening in the picture. Interpretation of the results of the test is very subjective. Many empirical studies have found that tests such as the Rorschach and TAT have poor reliability and little validity; one researcher found no perceivable differences in perception tests between groups of mental patients and groups of college students. However, many clinical psychologists and psychiatrists continue to use the tests, probably due to tradition.

The "big five," or five-factor, model of personality traits led to the creation of the *Neuroticism, Extraversion, and Openness Personality Inventory (NEO-PI),* which was originally created before the factors of agreeableness and conscientiousness were added to the factors. The NEO-PI consists of 181 statements with which respondents can agree or disagree on a scale of 1 to 5. Another test, called the *Myers–Briggs Type Indicator (MBTI),* based on Jung's theory of personality, was devised by Peter Myers and Isabel Briggs in the 1960s and measures four dimensions of personality: Extraversion-Introversion, Sensing–Intuition, Thinking-Feeling, or Judging-Perceptive. The various combinations produce sixteen different personality types. These types have been widely used in some types of workplace and academic counseling, but they are often administered by unskilled examiners. Also, the test takes neither cultural factors nor the possibility of maladjustment of personality into account.

FLASH LINKS TO PERSONALITY THEORY

The following chart includes some web sites on major theories of personality.

1. www.wynja.com/personality/theorists.htmlGreat Ideas in Personality

2. www.nypsa.org/FreudNet

3. www.cgjung.com/cgjCarl Jung Site

4. http://web.utk.edu/%7Egwynne/maslow.htmlAbraham Maslow

FLASH REVIEW

Comparing Freudian and Jungian Approaches to Personality

Go to the website www.cgjung.com/cgjung/ for Jung and www.nypsa.org/ for Freud. After exploring the sites, answer the following questions:

1. How did Freud and Jung differ in their approach to personality?

2. How did Freud and Jung agree in their approach to personality?

3. What aspect of each psychologist's theories did you find most interesting?

From Brian M. Kelley, *Psychology on the Net 2001.* Copyright 2001 by Allyn & Bacon, Boston. Reprinted by permission.

FLASH TEST

Review the Core Concepts for this chapter. Then take the Practice Test for Chapter 9 on the following pages and rate your performance.

PRACTICE TEST

(Chapter 9—Personality)

Multiple Choice (3 points each)

1. The definition of the term *personality* in psychology includes
   a. idiosyncratic characteristics that change over time.
   b. features for which no measurement devices exist.
   c. unique and relatively stable features.
   d. inconsistent features that change with environmental pressures.

2. Today, most psychologists agree that people exhibit a considerable degree of consistency in their behavior, but their behavior is also strongly influenced by
   a. heredity.
   b. situational/external factors.
   c. unconscious motivations.
   d. archetypes.

3. The term "personality type" refers to
   a. a particular pattern of thinking and behaving that prevails across time and situations, differentiating one person from another.
   b. the different categories into which personality characteristics can be assigned.
   c. an enduring personal characteristic that reveals itself in a particular pattern of behavior across a variety of situations.
   d. individual differences in cognition and behavior.

4. According to Freud, the _____ is made up of the thoughts, desires, and impulses of which we are largely unaware.
   a. conscious
   b. subconscious
   c. preconscious
   d. unconscious

5. According to Freud, the psychic entity that serves as the self and operates according to the reality principle is the
   a. id.

      b. ego.

      c. ego-ideal.

      d. superego.

6. The id, located in the unconscious, operates according to the _____ principle.

      a. pleasure

      b. reality

      c. catharsis

      d. equilibrium

7. A child experiencing the Oedipus complex is in the _____ stage of development.

      a. oral

      b. anal

      c. genital

      d. phallic

8. Carl Jung, Alfred Adler, and Karen Horney are all classified as

      a. Freudians.

      b. neo-Freudians.

      c. learning theorists.

      d. behaviorists.

9. According to Jung, memories and ideas that we have inherited from our ancestors are stored in the _____ as _____.

      a. libido, urges

      b. unconscious, drives

      c. collective unconscious, archetypes

      d. preconscious, ethical rules.

10. According to Alfred Adler, people are motivated by feelings of

      a. competitiveness.

      b. aggressiveness.

      c. superiority.

      d. inferiority.

11. Adler believed in the importance of _____ in the development of personality, which is still considered a factor in personality development.

      a. emotions

      b. traits

      c. birth order

      d. heredity

12. The neurotic personality and feminine psychology were two of the main themes in the work of

      a. Karen Horney.

      b. Anna Freud.

      c. Alfred Adler.

      d. Marian Rotter.

13. A form of therapy developed by Carl Rogers is

      a. psychoanalysis.

      b. systematic desensitization.

      c. rational–emotive therapy.

      d. client-centered therapy.

14. In Maslow's theory of personality, a peak experience generally includes feelings of

      a. power, wonder, and unity with the universe.

      b. anxiety as id impulses threaten to break free.

      c. separation between the aspects of personality.

      d. power and control over other people.

15. To Maslow, historical figures like Thomas Jefferson and Eleanor Roosevelt were

      a. domineering.

b. fully self-actualized.

c. empowered.

d. subject to powerful feelings of inferiority.

16. To Gordon Allport, the most important five or ten traits that account for an individual's personality are the

a. secondary traits.

b. cardinal traits.

c. central traits.

d. hierarchy of needs.

17. Hans Eysenck focused on three basic dimensions of personality, including

a. emotional stability, introversion or extraversion, and psychoticism.

b. agreeableness, antagonism, and psychoticism.

c. openness, agreeableness, and psychoticism.

d. neuroticism, psychoticism, and agreeableness.

18. Joe is always worried about something, but his wife Erica remains calm. These two differ most strongly on which of the "big five" personality traits?

a. agreeableness–antagonism

b. neuroticism–stability

c. openness to experience

d. conscientiousness–undirectedness

19. In Bandura's learning theory, our perceived ability to carry out a desired action is called

a. self-reinforcement.

b. self-efficacy.

c. self-regulation.

d. self-esteem.

20. Julian Rotter distinguished between _____, or people who believe they can shape their own destiny, and _____, or people who believe their destinies are the result of external forces.

a. self-actualizing individuals, non-self-actualizing individuals

b. extroverts, introverts

c. internals, externals

d. positives, negatives

21. In psychobiological research, individuals who score high on the dimension of _____ are particularly sensitive to punishment.

a. agreeableness

b. conscientiousness

c. extraversion

d. neuroticism

22. Byron is a shy 2-year-old child. According to research on shyness, Byron will

a. eventually outgrow his shyness.

b. become less shy depending on his social experiences during adolescence.

c. have about a 50 percent chance of remaining shy as an adult.

d. grow up to be a shy child.

23. Which of the following is an example of a projective test of personality?

a. Rorschach Inkblot Test

b. California Psychological Inventory

c. Minnesota Multiphasic Personality Inventory

d. Sixteen Personality Factor Inventory

24. When a patient is being evaluated for psychiatric problems, the appropriate objective test the psychiatrist should use is the

a. Thematic Apperception Test (TAT).

b. Minnesota Multiphasic Personality Inventory (MMPI).

c. California Psychological Inventory.

d. Rorschach Inkblot Test.

25. Which personality test is based on Carl Jung's theory of personality and categorizes people into sixteen types based on such characteristics as extroversion, intuition, thinking, and judging?
    a. the MMPI
    b. the CPI
    c. the MBTI
    d. the TAT

Essay Questions (5 points each)

1. Describe Freud's theory of personality development and its place in modern psychological thought.

2. Describe trait theory, and compare and contrast at least two proponents of trait theory.

3. Name and describe the "big five" dimensions of personality.

4. Discuss Zuckerman's findings on personality and the brain.

5. Distinguish between objective personality tests and projective personality tests, and name some of the tests that are most frequently used.

ANSWER EXPLANATIONS

Multiple-Choice Questions

1. c

Personality in psychology is defined as the particular pattern of thinking and behavior that differentiates one person from another and persists over time.

2. b

Psychologists today agree that people can be consistent over time in their behavior, but that behavior is strongly influenced by situational/external factors.

3. b

Systems of personality classification involve the creation of personality types, or different categories into which personality characteristics can be assigned.

4. d

Freud believed that the unconscious includes the thoughts, desires, and impulses that are unacceptable to the conscious mind of which we are unaware.

5. b

According to Freud's psychoanalytic theory, the ego operates on the reality principle and serves as our conscious mind or self.

6. a

According to Freud's theory, the id, which exists in the unconscious, operates on the pleasure principle.

7. d

In Freud's theory of psychosexual development, children experience the Oedipus complex (or for girls the Electra complex) during the phallic stage of development.

8. b

Jung, Adler, and Horney were all at one time students or disciples of Freud's, but developed differences with him. Each developed his or her own approach to personality.

9. c

Jung theorized that humanity shares a collective unconscious inherited from our ancestors that contains archetypes, or forms and symbols.

10. d

According to Adler, people are motivated by feelings of inferiority and then strive for superiority and completion.

11. c

Adler believed that birth order, or one's position among one's siblings, is a determining factor in personality, a view that is still held by many psychologists today.

12. a

Karen Horney viewed human conflicts as resulting from basic anxiety over childhood fears of abandonment; she also disagreed with Freud's interpretation of male and female differences.

13. d

Carl Rogers, one of the proponents of humanistic theories of personality, developed client-centered therapy, in which clients receive unconditional positive regard from the therapist.

14. a

Maslow's humanistic theory described a peak experience as powerful feelings of wonder and unity with the universe.

15. b

Maslow saw individuals like Thomas Jefferson and Eleanor Roosevelt as fully self-actualized, or as having attained their true potential.

16. c

Allport considered each individual to have five to ten central traits that accounted for his or her personality and a number of secondary traits. He also saw some individuals as being dominated by a single all-important cardinal trait; for example, Napoleon was dominated by the trait of ambition.

17. a

Eysenck focused on three dimensions of personality including emotional stability, introversion verus extraversion, and psychoticism.

18. b

Joe and his wife Erica differ most strongly on the "big five" traits of neuroticism versus stability.

19. b

According to Bandura's learning theory, people display self-efficacy, or the belief that they can perform some task or behavior successfully.

20. c

Bandura distinguished between internals, people who believe that they control their own destinies; and externals, people who believe that their destinies are the result of external forces.

21. d

In psychobiological research, Zuckerman found that people who score high on the extraversion measure seem to be particularly sensitive to reinforcement, whereas people who score high on the neuroticism-stability measure are particularly sensitive to punishment.

22. d

Research on shyness indicates that the trait persists from early childhood into late childhood and that shy children produced higher rates of the hormones produced in reaction to stressful situations.

23. a

The Rorschach Inkblot Test is an example of a projective personality test, which relies on self-revelation by the individual.

24. b

The appropriate objective personality test for detection of psychiatric problems is the Minnesota Multiphasic Personality Inventory, which was created to identify personality traits that are related to mental health.

25. c

The MBTI, or Myers-Briggs Type Indicator, is based on Jung's theory of personality and measures four dimensions of personality: Extraversion-Introversion, Sensing-Intuition, Thinking-Feeling, and Judging-Perceptive.

Essay Questions

1. Describe Freud's theory of personality development and its place in modern psychological thought.

   Freud's theory included his observations about the three-part nature of the personality, consisting of the id, the ego, and the superego, which reside on the levels of the unconscious, conscious, and preconscious mind. He also posited five stages of psychosexual development, including the oral, anal, phallic, latency, and genital stages. At each of these stages, individuals are subject to fixations resulting from too much or too little gratification. He viewed individuals as being motivated by the pleasure principle to satisfy basic desires such as sex and food. Freud's theories are no longer accepted by most psychologists, but his work is considered ground-breaking for its attention to the unconscious motivations of behavior.

2. Describe trait theory, and compare and contrast at least two proponents of trait theory.

Trait theories consider personality as composed of specific traits, or stable dimensions of personality that can be measured on a scale from low to high. One of the first psychologists to posit a trait theory of personality was Gordon Allport, who identified central traits, secondary traits, and, in some extraordinary cases, one cardinal trait that dominates an individual such as Napoleon. Another trait theorist, Raymond Cattell, identified sixteen source traits along with a number of lesser surface traits. Type theory is a variant of trait theory, and one well-known proponent, Hans Eyseck, focused on three basic dimensions of personality: emotional stability, introversion or extraversion, and psychoticism.

3. Name and describe the "big five" dimensions of personality.

The "big five" dimensions of personality are extraversion versus introversion, or whether someone is outgoing, energetic, and enthusiastic or more retiring and serious; agreeableness versus antagonism, or whether someone is good-natured, cooperative, and trusting or irritable, suspicious, and uncooperative; conscientiousness versus undirectedness, or whether someone is well-organized, careful, and well-disciplined or impulsive, careless, and undependable; emotional stability versus instability, or whether someone is calm and poised or nervous and high-strung; and openness to experience, or whether someone is open to new experiences and imaginative or closed, conforming, and uncreative. The "big five" dimensions have been found to correlate to certain types of outcomes, such as people's success in performing jobs.

4. Discuss Zuckerman's findings on personality and the brain.

While there is no specific location for "personality" to reside in the brain, it has nonetheless been apparent that the brain and mechanisms of the brain affect personality. This has been dramatically demonstrated by people who have received brain injuries and whose personalities have undergone drastic change. Zuckerman's studies indicate that there is some correspondence between the personality dimensions of extraversion, neuroticism, and psychoticism, and the neural systems of the brain. He found that people who score high on the extraversion measure are particularly susceptible to reinforcement, and people who score high on the neuroticism-stability measure are particularly susceptible to punishment. Also, people who score high on the psychoticism measure have a low sensitivity to punishment and a high tolerance for arousal and excitation. These findings seem to indicate that personality may be inborn and biologically based, although it is also undoubtedly affected by environmental factors.

5. Distinguish between objective personality tests and projective personality tests and name some of the tests that are most frequently used.

Objective personality tests include multiple choice and true-false questions. The best known of these tests, the Minnesota Multiphasic Personality Inventory (MMPI), included validity scales to provide some measure of objective evidence of evasion or falsehoods. The MMPI is no longer as widely used, even though it has been updated to include a more representative sample of individuals than when it was first devised.

Projective personality tests include the Rorschach Inkblot Test and the Thematic Apperception Test, which rely on the individual to interpret a picture or a meaningless inkblot. Interpretation of projective personality tests is highly subjective, and empirical studies have not shown either test to have much validity or reliability.

Other types of tests based on trait theory include the NEO-PI, which measures the "big five" or five-factor model of personality, and the Myers-Briggs Type Indicator (MBTI), which is based on Jung's theory of personality.

UNIT III: HUMAN DEVELOPMENT

CHAPTER 10—INTELLIGENCE, INTELLIGENCE TESTING, AND CREATIVITY

 FLASH FOCUS

When you complete this chapter, you will be able to:

✓ Define intelligence and describe the evolution of intelligence tests

✓ Compare and contrast at least three different theories of intelligence

✓ Discuss the controversies surrounding differences in intelligence scores

✓ Describe the components of emotional intelligence

✓ Discuss the concept of creativity and some of the different approaches to the analysis of creativity

Use a highlighter to identify ideas, terms, and people that your instructor refers to in lectures or emphasizes in the course. Add to the charts any other ideas, terms, or people that your instructor discusses.

Core Concepts in Intelligence, Intelligence Testing, and Creativity

Important Ideas	Key Terms	Important People
Intelligence	g factor	Charles Spearman
IQ/intelligence quotient	s factors	Louis L. Thurstone
Primary mental abilities	Primary mental abilities	Thelma G. Thurstone
Test	Savant syndrome	Howard Gardner
Triarchic theory of	Componential intelligence	Robert Sternberg
intelligence	Experiential intelligence	Raymond Cattell
Stanford–Binet test	Contextual intelligence	Alfred Binet
Wechsler Scales	Formal academic knowledge	Theodore Simon
Aptitude tests	Tacit knowledge	Lewis Terman
Achievement tests	Fluid intelligence	David Wechsler
Mentally challenged	Crystallized intelligence	Sir Francis Galton
Mental retardation	Wechsler Adult Intelligence Scale—Revised	Thomas Bouchard
Intellectually gifted	Down syndrome	Arthur Jensen
Nature–nurture controversy	Williams syndrome	Hernstein and Murray
Twin studies	Fraternal twins	Daniel Goleman
Cultural bias	Identical twins	
Emotional intelligence (EQ)	Mundane creativity	
Creativity	Exceptional creativity	
	Divergent thinking	
	Convergent thinking	
	Confluence approach	

The Nature of Intelligence

FLASH SUMMARY

Intelligence is defined as the overall capacity of a person to act purposefully, to think rationally, and to deal effectively with the environment. It is intuitively obvious to us that people differ in their levels of intelligence; some people are clearly capable of defining and analyzing complex issues that the rest of us can hardly grasp. The term that is used for the measure of an individual's intelligence is the *IQ* or *intelligence quotient*; but an IQ is not synonymous with intelligence. An IQ is merely a score derived from a test designed to measure intelligence.

Psychologists have many questions about intelligence, including whether it is merely one capability or a reflection of many unrelated capabilities. Psychologists and other scientists have devised many theories to explain what intelligence is, whether it is derived from our heredity or our environment, and how it can be measured. English psychologist *Charles Spearman* believed that people who are intelligent in one area are usually intelligent in other areas as well. He theorized that intelligence is a general ability, which he termed the *g factor*, that underlies all of the different functions of intelligence. However, people do vary in some of the subtests that make up a general intelligence test, so Spearman called these specific abilities the *s factors*.

Another early researcher, *Louis L. Thurstone*, rejected Spearman's theory of the g factor, and identified seven *primary mental abilities*, including verbal comprehension, numerical ability, spatial relations, perceptual speed, word fluency, memory, and reasoning. Thurstone and his wife, *Thelma G. Thurstone*, developed the *Primary Mental Abilities Test* to measure the seven abilities.

Modern theorists including *Howard Gardner* and *Robert Sternberg* have proposed that there are a number of different types of intelligence. Gardner proposed seven independent forms of intelligence including:

1. Linguistic (language skills)
2. Logical/mathematical (math and quantitative skills)
3. Musical
4. Spatial (forms and the manipulation of forms in space)
5. Bodily kinesthetic (body control and dexterity)
6. Interpersonal (the ability to understand and relate to others)
7. Intrapersonal (the ability to understand one's own feelings and behavior)

Gardner developed his theory by studying people who had had specific types of brain damage and also by studying the *savant syndrome*, or individuals who exhibit a combination of mental retardation and outstanding abilities for certain kinds of knowledge or calculations. Gardner's theory has been popular among educators, because it gives them some pathways to reach children who are not successful by traditional educational measures of linguistic or logical intelligence. However, his theory has been criticized for not being based on empirical evidence.

Sternberg formulated a *triarchic theory of intelligence*, which posits three kinds of intelligence: *componential* (analytic), *experiential* (creative), and *contextual* (practical). Componential intelligence is measured by conventional IQ and achievement tests; experiential intelligence is reflected in creative thinking and problem solving, contextual intelligence is equated to common sense. Sternberg felt that measures of "practical" intelligence are better predictors of things like job success than are traditional measures, and he distinguished *formal academic knowledge*, acquired in school, from *tacit knowledge*, or real-life expertise.

Raymond Cattell identified two major clusters of intelligence abilities: *fluid intelligence*, which refers to largely inherited abilities to think and reason, and *crystallized intelligence*, or accumulated knowledge. Cattell also noted that fluid intelligence seems to decrease with age, whereas crystallized intelligence stays the same or increases.

Measuring Intelligence

FLASH SUMMARY

In 1904, educators in Paris asked psychologist *Alfred Binet* if a standardized test could be devised that would identify children who are mentally retarded (as it was then termed), so they could receive special education. Binet and colleague *Theodore Simon* devised a test that included two types of items: one set of familiar questions that the children were likely to have encountered before and one set of new or unusual questions that they would never have seen before. The first version of their test included thirty items and did seem to be effective in identifying children in need of special help. Binet and Simon then broadened the scope of the test to include all children. The test was soon revised and adapted for use in many countries.

In the United States, psychologist *Lewis Terman* of Stanford University developed the *Stanford–Binet test,* which became commonly used and yielded the single numerical "IQ" score. To obtain a student's IQ, the examiner divided the student's mental age by his or her chronological age, and multiplied by 100; an equal measure of chronological and mental age gave a score of 100, whereas IQ's above 100 indicated that the person's mental age was higher than his or her chronological age, and IQ's below 100 indicated the opposite. However, since this calculation would yield IQ scores that decrease as a person ages, the IQ is now understood to measure a person's intelligence as against those of his or her peers, with an IQ of 100 being the average.

Since the Stanford–Binet test measured primarily verbal or linguistic intelligence, *David Wechsler* devised another measure that would include nonverbal as well as verbal items. The *Wechsler Adult Intelligence Scale–Revised* is currently among the most frequently used intelligence tests, even though there has been criticism that it is not clear that they actually do measure different aspects of intelligence. The components of the Wechsler Adult Intelligence Scale are summarized in the following.

Subtests of the Wechsler Adult Intelligence Scale

Test	Description
Verbal tests	
Information	General information questions, increasing in difficulty
Digit span	Repeat series of digits read aloud by the examiner
Vocabulary	Give definitions of thirty-five words
Arithmetic	Solve arithmetic problems
Comprehension	Answer questions requiring detailed answers
Similarities	Indicate in what way two items are alike
Performance tests	
Picture completion	Indicate what part of a picture is missing
Picture arrangement	Arrange pictures to create a story
Block design	Duplicate designs made with red and white blocks
Object assembly	Solve picture puzzles
Digit symbol	Fill in boxes with coded symbols corresponding to numbers above boxes

Adapted from Robert A. Baron, *Psychology,* Fifth Edition. Copyright Allyn and Bacon, Boston, 2001. Adapted by permission.

FLASH SUMMARY

Tests such as the Wechsler Intelligence Scale are called *aptitude tests*, since they are designed to measure the ability to acquire new information or skills, as compared with *achievement tests,* which measure what has already been learned.

Intelligence tests are still used, in part, to identify children who are *mentally challenged* or who might suffer from some type of *mental retardation* from children who are *intellectually gifted*. One type of mental retardation, *Down syndrome,* is caused by the presence of an extra chromosome in the individual's DNA. People with Down syndrome usually have an IQ of below 50. Mental retardation can also be caused by environmental factors, such as alcohol or drug use during pregnancy, infections, toxic agents, or traumas prior to or during birth. The American Psychiatric Association has categorized mental retardation as mild, moderate, severe, and profound, which is defined both by IQ and by practical abilities to function in the environment.

Some types of mental retardation are even more puzzling, such as *Williams syndrome*, which is a term for individuals who are born with specific physical features, like Down syndrome individuals and are mildly to moderately retarded, but who also display exceptional musical abilities, such as perfect pitch and the ability to memorize and play long musical pieces.

Differences in Intelligence Scores

FLASH SUMMARY

One of the key areas of dispute about the meaning of intelligence and intelligence testing is the issue of whether heredity or environment is more important in intelligence. Englishman *Sir Francis Galton* framed the *nature–nurture controversy* in 1874, when he tested a number of prominent families in England and concluded that intelligence is inherited. To answer these questions, researchers have again relied upon various types of *twin studies* of both *fraternal* and *identical* twins. One important site of twin research has been the Minnesota Center for Twin and Adoption Research, in which over 10,000 pairs of twins have been studied. Headed by *Thomas Bouchard*, the researchers have studied pairs of fraternal and identical twins who were raised together and apart. Their results indicated that, of all the traits studied, intelligence appeared to be the most heritable. While some psychologists dispute the results of Bouchard's studies, other studies have also shown that, while family environment has an effect on IQ early in life, that effect decreases with age, and the genetic influences seem to increase to a factor of heritability of 0.62 for general cognitive ability in later adulthood.

There are also controversies about intelligence measures among large groups of people. Some studies have shown that African Americans generally score about 15 points lower on standardized intelligence tests than do Whites, which one psychologist, *Arthur Jensen,* held is due to genetic differences between the races. In 1994, authors *Hernstein* and *Murray* published *The Bell Curve,* which also argued that low IQ is due to genetic differences and also predicts social status and social ills such as poverty, welfare dependency, crime, and illegitimacy. However, studies of African American and interracial children who were exposed to "enriched environments" scored above average for all races on IQ tests, indicating that environment plays a substantial role in intelligence.

Some critics have claimed that intelligence tests themselves suffer from *cultural bias,* because the items included on the tests may be more familiar to middle-class White children than they are to other races. Some observers feel that this unfamiliarity may serve to make the tests seem threatening to minority students.

Comparisons of Asian and American children have also consistently found the Asian children outscoring the Americans on math ability and achievement. Again, while racial comparisons can be made, some researchers looked to the children's environments. Within the Asian families, the parents considered academic achievement to be the most important pursuit of their children, whereas American parents did not see academic achievement as a central concern. Asian parents were seen to be instilling the importance of hard work and persistence, whereas the American parents gave more importance to innate ability.

While boys and girls as groups do not differ in overall measurements of intelligence, they do differ in some of the individual measurements. Females tend to score higher than males on tests that measure verbal abilities, whereas males score higher on visual–spatial tasks such as tracking a moving object through space. However, the differences are small, and while there is some debate about whether they reflect evolutionary differences (such as that men were required to find their way back to the home location from a distance after hunting, whereas women needed to be able to notice edible plants and pinpoint their location), there is no way at present of determining their cause.

Emotional Intelligence and Creativity

FLASH SUMMARY

Psychologists have long recognized differences between different types of abilities that comprise intelligence, but the separate study of *emotional intelligence* is more recent. Psychologist *Daniel Goleman* published a book called *Emotional Intelligence* in 1995, in which he argued that traditionally defined intelligence is separate from emotional intelligence (also called *EQ*), and that emotional intelligence may be the basis of many kinds of success in life. Emotional intelligence includes self-awareness, impulse control, persistence, motivation, and social factors like the ability to get along with others. Goleman also believes that individuals can be taught to recognize emotions, understand relationships, develop tolerance of frustration , and other skills related to emotional intelligence. However, at this point there is no empirical evidence supporting Goleman's theory.

Another factor that psychologists can identify but are unable to measure is *creativity*. Creativity has been defined as the ability to produce work that is novel or that solves problems. There is some correlation between IQ and creativity, although in the upper IQ ranges (over 120), there seems to be little correlation between IQ and creativity. Psychologists devised several ways of measuring creativity, including the Unusual Uses Test or a test that requires the individual to formulate as many ways of improving a product as possible, but none of them are completely satisfactory.

Psychologists have identified four common steps or stages in creativity, including:

1. Preparation, or searching for information that may help to solve the problem
2. Incubation, or letting the problem "sit" while information is digested
3. Illumination, the sudden realization of a solution to the problem
4. Translation, or putting the insight into action

Cognitive psychologists have distinguished between *mundane creativity,* or the creativity that people use everyday in creating new sentences, and *exceptional creativity,* or the emergence of something completely new. Distinctions have also been created between *divergent thinking,* or the ability to create multiple ideas or solutions for which there is no agreed-upon solution, and *convergent thinking,* or the type of intelligence measured by IQ and achievement tests. Social psychologists focus on the personality traits that make people creative and environmental conditions that may foster creativity.

One view, called the *confluence approach,* suggests that, in order for creativity to occur, several factors must come together: intellectual abilities, knowledge, a preference for thinking in novel ways, personality attributes such as willingness to risk, and an environment that is supportive of creative ideas. Some studies have seemed to confirm the confluence approach, in that they found that creativity in one domain was not necessarily related to creativity in another and that intellectual ability, thinking style, and personality are all significantly related to creativity.

FLASH LINKS TO INTELLIGENCE, INTELLIGENCE MEASURES, AND CREATIVITY

The following sites offer more information on intelligence, intelligence measures, and creativity.

1. www.2h.com/Tests/iqtrad.phtmlIQ Tests
2. www.2h.com/Tests/iqalt.phtmlAlternative IQ Tests
3. www.geocities.com/CapitolHill/1641/iqown.htmlTraditional Intelligence Test
4. http://ai.iit.nrc.ca/misc.htmlArtificial Intelligence Subject Index
5. www.brain.com/Braintainment Center
6. www.ozemail.com.au/~caveman/Creative/Creativity Web

FLASH REVIEW

Stimulating Creativity

The following steps are recommended for stimulating creativity:

1. "Tune in" to your own creativity and have confidence in it.
2. Challenge yourself to develop your special interests.
3. Broaden yourself.
4. Use problem finding as a stimulus to creativity.
5. Change your normal routine.
6. Spend more time with creative people.
7. Be flexible and open to new possibilities.
8. Avoid self-censorship.
9. Don't be afraid to make mistakes.
10. Capture your creative thoughts.
11. Relax.

Adapted from Samuel E. Wood and Ellen Green Wood, *The World of Psychology,* Fourth Edition. Copyright Allyn and Bacon, Boston, 2002. Adapted by permission.

FLASH TEST

Review the chart of Core Concepts at the beginning of this chapter. Then take the Practice Test for Chapter 10 on the following pages and rate your performance.

PRACTICE TEST

(Chapter 10—Intelligence, Intelligence Tests, and Creativity)

Multiple Choice (3 points each)

1. An individual's ability to understand complex ideas, to adapt effectively to the environment, to learn from experience, to engage in various forms of reasoning, and to overcome obstacles by careful thought is the definition of
   a. cognition.
   b. intelligence.
   c. development.
   d. personality.

2. Charles Spearman theorized that
   a. intelligence is a general ability that underlies different specific factors.
   b. there are seven primary mental abilities.
   c. an IQ is not a valid measure of intelligence.
   d. intelligence is made up of a number of specific abilities called s factors.

3. Which of the following is *not* one of the seven specific factors suggested by Thurstone as part of intelligence?
   a. number facility
   b. musical facility
   c. spatial visualization
   d. verbal fluency

4. Which of the following is *not* one of the three types of intelligence proposed by Sternberg?
   a. componential
   b. contextual
   c. crystallized
   d. experiential

5. According to Sternberg, the ability to deal effectively with new situations and to solve problems is called _____ intelligence.
   a. contextual
   b. componential
   c. performance
   d. experiential

6. _____ intelligence is described by Sternberg as the ability to adapt to one's environment.
   a. Contextual
   b. Componential
   c. Experiential
   d. Evolutionary

7. Raymond Cattell theorizes that _____ intelligence decreases with age, whereas _____ intelligence remains the same.
   a. crystallized, fluid
   b. fluid, crystallized
   c. experiential, componential
   d. contextual, experiential

8. The term *savant syndrome* refers to
   a. individuals with high IQ's.
   b. individuals with a combination of high IQ and low impulse control.
   c. individuals with a combination of mental retardation and outstanding ability for certain types of knowledge or calculations.
   d. individuals who are mildly mentally retarded.

9. The first intelligence test was developed in France by
   a. Wechsler.
   b. Binet.
   c. Goleman.
   d. Spearman.

10. The first intelligence test was devised in order to
    a. establish intellectual norms for the French population.
    b. identify children who could benefit from special academic instruction.
    c. measure the intelligence of preschoolers.
    d. identify gifted children.

11. Psychologist Lewis Terman adapted the Binet intelligence test for use in the United States, a test now known as
    a. Terman–Binet.
    b. Simon–Binet.

    c. Stanford–Binet.
    d. American IQ Measure.

12. To assess a child's intellectual ability, Binet and Simon
    a. administered several sensory discrimination tests to children of various ages.
    b. devised an overall point rating system ranging from below average to above average.
    c. formulated the IQ quotient.
    d. compared the child's performance relative to an established age-determined average.

13. Wilma is 10 and has a mental age of 8. What is her ratio IQ?
    a. 80
    b. 100
    c. 125
    d. 150

14. David Wechsler devised a different measure of intelligence that would measure more than just the _____ intelligence measured by the Binet test.
    a. standard
    b. IQ
    c. performance
    d. verbal-linguistic

15. If you received scores for subtests including similarities, picture completion, and vocabulary, you would be taking the
    a. Sanford–Binet.
    b. Wechsler Adult Intelligence Scale—Revised.
    c. Kaufman Assessment Battery.
    d. Goleman Test for Emotional Intelligence.

16. A multiple-choice test that you take for a college course is an _____ test.
    a. aptitude
    b. achievement
    c. applied
    d. acquisitions

17. The beginning of the nature–nurture controversy with regard to intelligence can be traced to
    a. Thomas Bouchard in the 1970s.
    b. Alfred Binet in 1904.
    c. Sir Francis Galton in 1874.
    d. Lewis Terman in the 1920s.

18. A syndrome that combines mild to moderate mental retardation, a combination of specific physical features, and unusual musical ability, is called
    a. Williams syndrome.
    b. Down syndrome.
    c. moderate mental retardation.
    d. Wechsler syndrome.

19. Twin studies conducted at the Minnesota Center for Twin and Adoption Research have concluded that
    a. intelligence is the result of environmental factors such as enriched learning experiences.
    b. intelligence is 100 percent inherited.
    c. intelligence is the most heritable of all the traits that were studied.
    d. fraternal twins are more similar in intelligence scores than identical twins.

20. According to *The Bell Curve*, the cause of social problems such as poverty and crime is
    a. low IQ.
    b. high IQ.
    c. poor powers of concentration.
    d. that poverty causes crime.

21. Comparisons of Asian and American children find that
    a. American children score higher on math ability and achievement.

b. Asian children are not rewarded for academic achievement.

c. American parents feel that academic achievement is all-important.

d. Asian children score higher on math ability and achievement.

22. Compared to girls, boys score higher on tests of
   a. spatial visualization.
   b. vocabulary.
   c. perceptual speed.
   d. spelling.

23. The type of intelligence that is concerned with the ability to recognize and manage emotions, restrain impulses, and handle interpersonal relationships effectively is called
   a. impulsive intelligence.
   b. interpersonal intelligence.
   c. emotional intelligence.
   d. cognitive intelligence.

24. The ability to create work that is novel and appropriate is called _____.
   a. creativity.
   b. productivity.
   c. originality.
   d. novelty.

25. The steps involved in creativity involve *all except one* of the following; which one should *not* be included?
   a. preparation
   b. cognition
   c. incubation
   d. illumination

Essay Questions (5 points each)

1. Discuss and differentiate between single-factor theories of intelligence and multiple-factor theories.

2. Describe the development of modern intelligence tests and the current thinking about their validity.

3. Describe the nature–nurture controversy as it is applied to intelligence.

4. What are the components of emotional intelligence, and what is emotional intelligence believed to predict?

5. Define creativity, and name some different types of creativity, the stages of creativity, and the most current theory of creativity.

ANSWER EXPLANATIONS

Multiple-Choice Questions

1. **b**
   Intelligence is defined as the overall capacity of a person to act purposefully, to think rationally, and to deal effectively with the environment.

2. **a**
   Spearman believed that there is one general ability, called the g factor, underlying different variables of intelligence. He also believed that individuals vary in their specific abilities, called the s factors.

3. **b**
   Thurstone identified seven primary abilities: verbal comprehension, numerical ability, spatial relations, perceptual speed, word fluency, memory, and reasoning.

4. **c**
   Sternberg proposed three types of intelligence: componential (analytic), experiential (creative), and contextual (practical).

5. **d**
   According to Sternberg, experiential intelligence is the ability to think creatively and solve problems.

6. a

Contextual intelligence, according to Sternberg, enables a person to adapt to his or her environment; it is also termed "common sense."

7. b

Cattell posited two different types of intelligence: fluid intelligence, which refers to inherited abilities to think and to reason, and crystallized intelligence, which refers to accumulated knowledge. Fluid intelligence seems to decrease with age, whereas crystallized intelligence stays the same or increases.

8. c

The term *savant syndrome* refers to individuals who are simultaneously mentally retarded and also exhibit amazing abilities to retain certain types of knowledge or make numerical calculations.

9. b

The first intelligence test was devised by Alfred Binet at the request of French educators.

10. b

The first intelligence test was devised by Binet and Simon in 1905 to help French educators identify children who had mental deficiencies, so that they could receive special education.

11. c

Lewis Terman was a professor at Stanford University in California, and his adaptation of the Binet–Simon intelligence test became known as the Stanford–Binet.

12. d

Binet and Simon compared a child's performance on their intelligence test to an established, age-determined average.

13. a

Wilma's IQ would be measured as 80, a figure obtained by dividing the student's mental age (8) by her chronological age (10), and multiplying by 100.

14. d

David Wechsler devised his Wechsler scale to include measures that would include nonverbal as well as verbal items.

15. b

The Wechsler Adult (as well as Child) intelligence scales include subtests such as similarities, picture completion, and vocabulary.

16. b

A test that you take during a college course is (usually) an achievement test, becuase it measures what you have learned.

17. c

Sir Francis Galton in 1874 tested a number of prominent families in England and concluded that intelligence is inherited.

18. a

The unusual combination of mental retardation, distinctive physical features, and unusual musical ability is called Williams syndrome. Down syndrome is another well-known type of mental retardation caused by the presence of an extra chromosome.

19. c

Studies conducted at the Minnesota Center for Twin and Adoption Research indicated that, of all the traits studied, intelligence is the most heritable; however, this does not rule out the importance of environmental factors.

20. a

In *The Bell Curve*, Hernstein and Murray argued that low IQ is due to genetic differences and also predicts social ills such as poverty, welfare dependency, crime, and illegitimacy.

21. d

Comparisons of Asian and American children find that Asian children score higher on measures of math ability and achievement. It has been posited that environmental factors, such as the high value placed on achievement by Asian parents, is partly responsible for these differences.

22. a

Boys score slightly higher than girls on measures of spatial perception, whereas girls score higher than boys on tests that measure verbal abilities.

23 c

Emotional intelligence has been defined as intelligence that includes self-awareness, impulse control, persistence, motivation, and social factors such as the ability to get along with others.

24. a

Creativity has been defined as the ability to produce work that is novel or that solves problems.

25. b

The steps that have been identified in creativity include preparation, incubation, illumination, and translation.

Essay Questions

1. Discuss and differentiate between single-factor theories of intelligence and multiple-factor theories.

   English psychologist Charles Spearman believed that intelligence is a general ability, called the g factor, that underlies all of the different components of intelligence. However, even Spearman acknowledged that there are different, specific abilities that can be individually tested, which he called s factors.

   Multiple theories of intelligence have been more numerous and include Louis and Thelma Thurstone's seven primary mental abilities, Howard Gardner's seven forms of intelligence, and Robert Sternberg's triarchic theory of intelligence which posits three kinds of intelligence. Raymond Cattell distinguished two major clusters of intelligence abilities.

2. Describe the development of modern intelligence tests, and current thinking about their validity.

   The first standardized measure of intelligence was undertaken by Alfred Binet and Theodore Simon, in response to a request from French educators who wanted to identify mentally challenged children for special education. Binet and Simon devised a test that was effective at identifying children with special learning needs. They then expanded their test to include all children. However, the test's measure of IQ was changed not only to reflect not mental versus chronological age (since older people would then necessarily lose IQ points as they aged) but also to reflect a person's intelligence as compared to that of his or her peers. The Binet test (or Stanford–Binet in the United States) has been found useful to indicate verbal or linguistic ability, but it does not measure some of the other aspects of intelligence.

   The Wechsler Child/Adult Intelligence Scale was devised by David Wechsler to address the measurement of multiple forms of intelligence, including spatial relations, assembly and completion of forms, and other components of intelligence. The Wechsler Scales are still widely used, although there has been criticism that there is little or no evidence that they actually measure different aspects of intelligence.

   Intelligence tests are also open to the criticism that they are culturally biased and may produce better results for middle-class children who are more familiar with the material being tested.

3. Describe the nature–nurture controversy as it is applied to intelligence.

   The nature–nurture controversy refers to the debate over whether intelligence is inherited, or is a product of the environment. From the earliest days of the debate, in 1874, when Sir Francis Galton concluded that intelligence is inherited, the evidence has been more in favor of inheritance than environment; however, there is no doubt that environment is important and that an enriched environment can raise IQ scores. Twin studies conducted at Minnesota's Center for Twin and Adoption Research have also concluded that intelligence was the "most heritable" of the traits that were studied in pairs of fraternal and identical twins who were raised together and apart.

4. What are the components of emotional intelligence, and what is emotional intelligence believed to predict?

   Emotional intelligence is a concept originated by Daniel Goleman in his book *Emotional Intelligence,* published in 1995. Goleman believes that emotional intelligence is separate from traditionally defined intelligence and consists of factors such as self-awareness, impulse control, persistence, motivation, and social factors such as the ability to get along with others. Goleman posited that emotional intelligence is the basis of many kinds of success in life and that individuals can be taught techniques of emotional intelligence such as recognizing emotions, understanding relationship, developing tolerance of frustration, and other skills. There is no empirical evidence at this point that supports Goleman's conclusions.

5. Define creativity, and name some different types of creativity, the stages of creativity, and the most current theory of creativity.

Creativity can be defined as the ability to produce work that is novel or that solves problems. Some psychologists have differentiated between mundane creativity, the type of creativity we use everyday in creating new sentences, and exceptional creativity, the type of creativity that produces novel ideas and products. Other scientists have distinguished between divergent thinking, the ability to create multiple ideas or solutions for problems for which there is no agreed-upon solution, and convergent thinking, the type of intelligence measured by standard IQ and achievement tests. A widely accepted theory called the convergence theory posits that creativity requires the coming together of several factors, including intellectual ability, knowledge, a preference for thinking in novel ways, personality attributes such as willingness to take risks, and an environment that is supportive of creative ideas.

Psychologists have listed four stages of the creative process: preparation, incubation, illumination, and translation.

UNIT IV: VARIATIONS ON NORMAL FUNCTIONING

CHAPTER 11—STRESS, COPING, AND HEALTH

FLASH FOCUS

When you complete this chapter, you will be able to:

✓ Define stress, and identify the physical and psychological processes that occur in response to stressors in the environment

✓ Describe some of the coping skills that can help individuals to adapt to stressful events and situations

✓ Discuss some of the links that have been identified between behavior and illness

✓ Name some fundamental lifestyle changes that have important impacts on health

Use a highlighter to identify ideas, terms, and people that your instructor refers to in lectures or emphasizes in the course. Add to the chart any other ideas, terms, or people that your instructor discusses.

Core Concepts in Stress, Coping, and Health

Important Ideas	Key Terms	Important People
Health psychology	Sympathetic nervous system	Walter Cannon
Behavioral medicine	Alarm stage	Hans Selye
Stress	Resistance stage	Richard Lazarus
Stressors	Exhaustion stage	Neal Miller
Fight-or-flight response	Primary appraisal	Thomas Holmes
General adaptation	Secondary appraisal	Richard Rahe
Syndrome (GAS)	Frustration	Talcott Parsons
Burnout	Conflict	Meyer Friedman
Post-traumatic stress	Pressure	Ray Rosenman
disorder (PTSD)	Approach–approach conflict	
Social Readjustment Rating	Avoidance–avoidance conflict	
Scale (SRRS)	Approach–avoidance conflict	
Resilience	Unpredictability	
Coping skills/strategies	Lack of control	
Health belief model	Social support	
Immune system	Defense-oriented coping	
Psychoneuroimmunology	Strategies	
Self-determination theory	Task-oriented coping	
Prevention strategies	Strategies	
	Proactive coping	
	Sick role	
	Type A behavior	
	Type B behavior	
	Lymphocytes	
	B cells	

T cells Antibodies Antigens Autoimmune diseases Human immunodeficiency Virus (HIV) Nicotine Arteriosclerosis Controlled motivation Autonomous motivation Primary prevention Secondary prevention	

The Effects of Stress

FLASH SUMMARY

Health psychology is the branch of psychology that studies the relationship between mind and body, or the relation between psychological variables and health. A related field called *behavioral medicine* combines behavioral and biomedical knowledge in the prevention and treatment of disorders. One major area in which behavior strongly impacts health is *stress,* or our responses to perceived threats in the environment. Various events and situations in life become *stressors,* or stimuli in the environment that provoke intense physical and psychological reactions.

When confronted with a stressor, human beings, as well as most other species, experience physiological reactions that include an increase in blood pressure, heart rate, and sweating. These reactions are part of the body's *fight-or-flight syndrome,* a term coined by *Walter Cannon* to describe how the *sympathetic nervous system* prepares the body for immediate action. This sequence of events was termed the *general adaptation syndrome (GAS)* by *Hans Selye.* Selye perceived this reaction as composed of three parts: the *alarm stage,* in which the body prepares for immediate action via the sympathetic nervous system, which releases hormones in preparation for meeting the stressor; the *resistance stage,* in which the body continues to draw upon resources at a rate above normal; and finally, the *exhaustion stage,* in which the body is drained of its resources and is consequently more liable to disease or injury.

Other psychologists and researchers have pointed out that, in addition to the physiological responses noted by Cannon and Selye, there is also a cognitive component to our reactions to stress. Psychologist *Richard Lazarus* pointed out that individuals often react very differently to the same stressor, depending on their evaluation of the seriousness of the threat. Lazarus distinguished between the initial evaluation of a threat and its potential seriousness as the *primary appraisal* and the evaluation of whether the individual's resources will suffice to meet that threat the *secondary appraisal.*

In modern life there are many different types of stressors that can produce either everyday, temporary stress, or chronic, intense stress. Sources of stress can include *frustration,* an emotional state that results from the inability to achieve a certain goal, and *conflict,* an emotional state that results from the need to make a difficult decision. Psychologist *Neal Miller* categorized different types of conflict as the *approach–approach conflict,* in which an individual must choose between two equally attractive alternatives; the *avoidance–avoidance conflict,* in which an individual must choose between distasteful alternatives; and the *approach–avoidance conflict,* in which the individual must choose between alternatives that have both pleasant and unpleasant aspects. Miller theorized that each of these situations leads to different degrees of stress.

Stress may also occur due to *pressure* experienced by individuals, particularly in workplace situations. Pressure can be defined as an emotional state created by the real or imagined expectations of other people concerning certain behaviors or results. Work that is either overstimulating or understimulating can produce stress, which can lead to physical symptoms including headaches, sleeplessness, overeating, and/or intestinal disorders. Stress at work can also affect the immune system, which can lead to illness and related health problems such as alcoholism. Positions shown to involve a high degree of stress include those of surgeons, inner-city school teachers, customer service agents, waiters and waitresses, and emergency workers. Job stress that is intense and unrelieved is called *burnout*, a condition in which people become dissatisfied, inefficient, and psychologically debilitated.

One key finding about stress is that *unpredictability* and *lack of control* increase the effects of stress. A study of individuals in a nursing home found that those who were able to exercise some measure of control over their lives, such as arranging their rooms and choosing when to view movies, actually had a lower death rate than did residents who had less control over their lives. Similarly, researchers have suggested that cancer patients do better when they exercise more control over their physical symptoms and emotional reactions.

Catastrophic life events can also create intense stress. These catastrophes can include war, accidents such as plane crashes, or natural events such as fire, flood, hurricanes, and earthquakes. The impact of such a major catastrophe can be long-lasting, and psychologists have coined the term *post-traumatic stress disorder (PTSD)* to describe the set of symptoms that commonly afflict those who have suffered traumatic stress. This syndrome was first specifically noted among veterans of the Vietnam War, many of whom suffered from disturbed sleep, the reliving of painful experiences either while awake or asleep, difficulty concentrating, and feelings of panic and alienation.

Other causes of severe stress are life-changing events such as the death of a relative, divorce, marriage, losing a job, pregnancy, and many other events. Psychologists *Thomas Holmes* and *Richard Rahe* constructed the *Social Readjustment Rating Scale (SRRS)* to attempt to measure the stressfulness of different life events; they ranked these events from most to least stressful. According to their scale, the most stressful life events is the death of a spouse, followed by a divorce or separation. Among the less stressful events are vacations, Christmas, changes in eating habits (such as going on a diet), and minor violations of the law. Holmes and Rahe conducted studies from which they concluded that there is a connection between degree of life stress and major health problems; other psychologists have not found reliable correlations between major life changes and subsequent illness.

Coping with Stress

FLASH SUMMARY

Resilience is the term used for the extent to which people are flexible and respond adaptively to external or internal demands. Psychologists believe that the development of *coping skills* or *coping strategies,* techniques to deal with stressful situations and events, can help people to become more resilient. One major factor affecting resilience and the ability to cope with stress is *social support,* or the comfort, recognition, approval, and encouragement of others. This support can be provided by family and friends, therapy groups, or even pets.

Richard Lazarus identified two types of coping strategies utilized by people: *defense-oriented coping strategies,* or psychological defense mechanisms that may enable people to cope with stressful events, and *task-oriented coping strategies,* which involve identifying the stressor, choosing an appropriate course of action, and then implementing the chosen plan. Since the defense-oriented strategies may involve distortions of reality such as rationalization or reaction formation (in which one behaves the opposite of how one feels), psychologists tend to recommend task-oriented strategies for coping with stress. Actions taken to combat or relieve stress may include relaxation techniques such as biofeedback or meditation, learning to defuse stress by reacting early rather than later *(proactive coping)*, and self-talk techniques such as imagery.

Other coping strategies include beginning or increasing exercise, eating a healthy diet, getting enough sleep, and trying to be flexible in the face of changing circumstances and demands.

Health and Disease

 FLASH SUMMARY

Physical and psychological responses to illness are closely linked; stress is only one example of a condition that may have both physical and psychological effects. In 1979, sociologist *Talcott Parsons* identified a *sick role,* an identifiable social role that is played by individuals who are either physically ill or believes they are physically ill. Individuals playing the "sick role" receive attention, sympathy, and concern, and little is expected of them. However, people often ignore symptoms of illness and do not seek needed medical attention. The *health belief model* suggests that willingness to seek medical services depends on the extent to which a threat is perceived and the extent to which individuals believe that a particular behavior will reduce that threat. Studies have found that women are more likely than men to seek out health services, either because they are more sensitive to symptoms and bodily changes or because cultural norms and expectations give them more permission than men to access health care services. After health services have been obtained, it has been found that only 50 percent of individuals will actually follow the advice of a physician, even among patients with chronic disorders. As many as 97 percent of patients do not adhere fully to recommended changes in lifestyles, such as increasing exercise or changing diet.

The leading cause of death in the United States is heart disease, which accounts for about 33 percent of all deaths. Physicians *Meyer Friedman* and *Ray Rosenman* identified a pattern of behavior that they believed contributed to heart disease, which they termed *Type A behavior.* People who exhibit Type A behavior are competitive, impatient, hostile, and always pressed for time. People who exhibit *Type B behavior* are calmer, more patient, and less hurried. Research has supported a connection between Type A behavior in middle-aged men and increased risk of heart disease; however, further research has suggested that the negative health effects of Type A behavior come from feelings of anger and hostility. One study found that anger is associated not only with increased risk of heart disease but also with ill health in general. Research among women has indicated that women who suppress their emotions may be at increased risk of heart disease.

The second leading cause of death in the United States is cancer, which is responsible for 23.4 percent of deaths. It is estimated that some 30 percent of Americans will develop cancer at some point in their lives. Cancer diagnosis and treatment are incredibly stressful, and researchers now believe that cancer patients need help with psychological and behavioral factors as well as physical treatment. Some studies have indicated that those who retain a positive outlook and a sense of humor experience less distress than those who have denial or negative thoughts about the disease and its treatment. One study indicated that the most effective elements of a strategy for coping with cancer included support groups, a focus on the positive, and distraction. Reactions such as fantasizing, denial, and social withdrawal were associated with greater emotional distress.

Health risks also vary according to one's cultural and ethnic background and socioeconomic status. Low socioeconomic status has been shown to be linked to higher mortality rates from all causes. Among U.S. ethnic groups, African Americans have higher rates of diabetes, arthritis, and high blood pressure, three times the risk of contracting AIDS, and twice the rate of infant mortality as White Americans. Hispanic Americans have higher rates of hypertension and diabetes, higher rates of cigarette smoking and alcohol abuse, but lower rates of heart disease than white non-Hispanic Americans. Hispanic Americans also have higher rates of death from accidental injuries, homicide, cirrhosis and chronic liver diseases, and AIDS, than do white non-Hispanics. Native Americans have far lower life expectancies than do White Americans and higher rates of alcoholism, homicide, and suicide. Obesity is also common among Native Americans and contributes to a high rate of diabetes.

Women also experience disparities in access to health care and in treatment for disease. The American Medical Association (AMA) has even acknowledged that physicians have been more likely to view women's symptoms as "emotional" than as due to physical causes. One study showed that, following abnormal heart scans, more than 40 percent of men, but only 4 percent of women, were referred for further testing and possible by-pass surgery. Women are also less likely to receive kidney dialysis or kidney transplants. With increased awareness of the disparities in diagnosis and treatment, women and minority groups are now more likely to be included in major studies and receive appropriate treatment for physical conditions.

The *immune system* has been found to be key in resisting disease. The key components of the immune system are white blood cells called *lymphocytes,* which include *B cells* and *T cells.* These white blood cells carry *antibodies,* which can attack and destroy *antigens,* or foreign cells such as bacteria and viruses. However, this process can backfire when antibodies turn on healthy cells or organs of the body, causing *autoimmune diseases* such as juvenile diabetes, multiple sclerosis, rheumatoid arthritis, lupus, and AIDS. AIDS is caused by the *human immunodeficiency virus, HIV.* HIV attacks the body's T cells and gradually weakens the immune system until it is virtually nonfunctional.

A relatively new field of study, *psychoneuroimmunology,* focuses on the effects of psychological factors on the immune system. It is now apparent that psychological factors including emotions and stress are linked to the functioning of the immune system. Some studies have shown that maintenance of a positive social support network, made up of family, friends, and other close social ties, aids immune system functioning; whereas periods of prolonged stress, poor marital relationships, sleep deprivation, and even academic pressure are all linked to lowered immune response.

Life Styles and Health

FLASH SUMMARY

Studies have shown that 53.5 percent of all deaths in the United States are attributable to unhealthy behavior or lifestyles. These behaviors include lack of exercise, overeating, poor nutrition, too little sleep, and alcohol or drug abuse. Smoking is the number-one greatest cause of preventable illness and premature death in the United States. It is the leading cause of several types of cancer, including cancer of the lung, larynx, bladder, and cervix, and it also causes cardiovascular disease and emphysema (a progressive deterioration of the ability of the lungs to function). Smoking has deleterious effects on the fetus during pregnancy, and second-hand smoke (exposure to the smoke produced by the individual smoker) causes lung cancer and respiratory tract infections.

Even with all of the proven health risks, up to 25 percent of the U.S. population still smoke cigarettes, and that figure is even higher in other parts of the world. The *nicotine* contained in cigarettes is physically addicting, acting as a stimulant on the central nervous system. Cigarettes create not only physical dependence but also psychological dependence, or a craving to use the drug for its pleasurable effects. The percentage of individuals who smoke has declined in the United States from a high of 50 percent in 1965 to the current 25 percent; however, smoking is increasing among high school students and pregnant teens.

Poor diet and nutrition and overeating are factors that are linked to increased risk of heart disease and cancer. Rates of colorectal cancer (cancer of the colon and rectum) have been linked to poor diet; a diet rich in fruits and vegetables has been associated with a decreased risk of colorectal cancer. *Arteriosclerosis*, the leading cause of heart disease, is caused by a buildup of cholesterol on artery walls and a narrowing of blood vessels; arteriosclerosis is strongly influenced by diet. Overeating and eating a high-fat diet may have evolutionary origins; high-fat foods contain more calories, produce more energy, and elevate natural opiate levels in the body. Weight loss is a continuous struggle for many in the United States. *Self-determination theory* posits that individuals who lose weight at the urging of others (called *controlled motivation*) are less likely to be able to sustain the weight loss than if the loss is triggered by their own wishes (called *autonomous motivation*).

Alcohol consumption and risky behaviors linked to alcohol such as drunk driving also influence health. While some studies have shown that moderate amounts of alcohol, particularly wine, are associated with decreased rates of coronary heart disease, chronic excessive alcohol consumption can cause learning and memory problems, affect problem-solving as well as perceptual and motor skills, and lead to stomach disease, cirrhosis of the liver, cancer, impotence, and fetal alcohol syndrome in unborn children. Genetic studies have indicated that a propensity for alcoholism may be inherited; however, social and environmental factors also strongly influence alcohol use (or abuse).

Many health professionals and psychologists have adopted an approach to public health that is based on *prevention strategies,* or techniques designed to reduce the occurrence of illness. *Primary prevention* is designed to reduce or eliminate the incidence of preventable illness and injury; it can be undertaken through education programs and direct behavioral interventions. *Secondary prevention* focuses on early detection to discover and treat illnesses at an early stage. Education campaigns have been found to be of limited effect. The most effective campaigns are those that are targeted to individuals or specific population groups, such as a card that was mailed out to African Americans with a message about the negative effects of smoking on the African American population. Also, health promotion messages seem to be more effective when they emphasize the gains that can be obtained from a specific health practice rather than emphasize the potential negative effects of risky behaviors.

FLASH LINKS FOR HEALTH, STRESS, AND DISEASE

The following sites provide information on stress, health, and disease.

1. Health and health psychology:
   http://healthpsych.com/index.html
   www.youfirst.com/index.asp
   www.goaskalice.Columbia.edu/

2. Stress:
   www.stress.org/
   www.ivf.com/stress.html
   www.sidran.org/

3. Disease:
   www.unspeakable.com/

FLASH REVIEW

Visit the self-assessment site at www.psychtests.com, and visit the "lifestyles" section of that site. Take the self-assessment test on lifestyle and health, then answer the following questions:

1. What was your score on the self-assessment test?

2. What advice or changes in behavior were recommended?

3. What is your response to the advice? Do you intend to implement any changes in your behavior? Why or why not?

FLASH TEST

Review the chart of Core Concepts for this chapter. Then take the Practice Test for Chapter 11 on the following pages and rate your performance.

PRACTICE TEST

(Chapter 11—Stress, Coping, and Health)

Multiple Choice (3 points each)

1. Health psychology is the subfield of psychology that focuses on
   a. the applicability of psychological variables to issues of health.
   b. the appropriate psychological training for medical doctors.
   c. understanding unconscious motivations that make people ill.
   d. developing better organizational structures for hospitals.

2. In the "fight-or-flight" response, the bodily system that prepares the body for immediate action is
   a. the heart and lungs.
   b. the sympathetic nervous system.
   c. the sensory system.
   d. the lymphatic system.

3. Walter Cannon considered the fight-or-flight response to be adaptive because it
   a. helps the organism respond rapidly to threats.
   b. increases the heart rate, providing added health benefits.
   c. survives in so many species.
   d. occurs in a completely reflexive manner.

4. The "general adaptation syndrome" (GAS) was proposed by
   a. Charles Darwin.
   b. Sigmund Freud.
   c. Richard Lazarus.
   d. Hans Selye.

5. The stage of the general adaptation syndrome in which the organism may experience shock is called the _____ stage.
   a. alarm
   b. adaptation
   c. resistance
   d. exhaustion

6. The stage of the general adaptation syndrome in which the organism's body returns to more normal levels of functioning is called the _____ stage.
   a. alarm
   b. adaptation
   c. resistance
   d. exhaustion

7. The stage of the general adaptation syndrome in which the organism is most susceptible to illness is called the _____ stage.
   a. alarm
   b. adaptation
   c. resistance
   d. exhaustion

8. The view of stress proposed by Richard Lazarus emphasizes the role of _____ in determining stress.

a. behavior
b. genetics
c. cognition
d. the environment

9. The evaluation of whether one's resources are sufficient to meet an impending threat is termed the _____ according to Lazarus.
   a. primary appraisal
   b. secondary appraisal
   c. fight-or-flight decision
   d. resistance stage

10. Renaldo can't decide which course to take next. He loves biology and would like to take a course with his friend, but his best friend is in calculus. Renaldo is experiencing
    a. avoidance–approach conflict.
    b. approach–avoidance conflict.
    c. approach–approach conflict.
    d. avoidance–avoidance conflict.

11. Physical symptoms of stress include *all except one* of the following. Which symptom should *not* be included?
    a. headaches
    b. sleeplessness
    c. intestinal disorders
    d. irritability

12. After 2 years of work as a paramedic, Mike feels a sense of exhaustion and hopelessness and is becoming convinced that his hard work doesn't really help anyone. Mike is probably suffering from
    a. an approach–avoidance conflict.
    b. an avoidance–avoidance conflict.
    c. burnout.
    d. frustration.

13. The effects of stress can be mediated somewhat by providing some mechanism for _____ of the situation.
    a. avoidance
    b. control
    c. prevention
    d. an optimistic view

14. Which of the following stressors rates as most severe according to the Holmes–Rahe stressful life events scale?
    a. divorce
    b. losing a job
    c. death of a close family member
    d. death of a spouse

15. Several months after having her home destroyed by a fire, Gwen begins to have horrible nightmares and vivid recollections regarding the fire. Gwen may be experiencing a disorder that psychologists call
    a. agoraphobia
    b. post-traumatic stress syndrome
    c. anxiety
    d. manic depression

16. The term for the extent to which people are flexible and respond adaptively to internal or external demands is
    a. resilience.
    b. resistance.
    c. optimism.
    d. defensiveness.

17. A coping strategy that involves a set of specific steps for identifying the stressor, choosing a method of stress reduction, implementing the method, and evaluating its success is called the _____ strategy.
    a. external
    b. internal
    c. defense-oriented
    d. task-oriented

18. According to the health belief model, our willingness to seek medical help depends on the
    a. amount of role conflict in our lives.
    b. extent to which we perceive a threat to our health.
    c. stage of the general adaptation syndrome.
    d. level of education earned.

19. Individuals who are competitive, impatient, hostile, and constantly trying to do more in less time demonstrate _____ behavior.
    a. Type A
    b. Type B
    c. Type C
    d. Type D

20. The study of the interactions between the immune system and behavior is called
    a. psychoneuroimmunology.
    b. psychoimmunoassay.
    c. neuroimmofluorescence.
    d. socioimmunology.

21. The _____ of an individual involves the overall pattern of decisions and behaviors that determine health and quality of life.
    a. cognitive structure
    b. genetic makeup
    c. lifestyle
    d. experience

22. Male survivors of heart attacks are at greater risk of dying from heart disease if they are _____, and female survivors are at greater risk if they _____.
    a. high in hostility; suppress anger and resentment
    b. high in hostility; are high in hostility
    c. low in hostility; express anger and resentment
    d. low in hostility; have a sense of time urgency

23. According to _____, long-term weight loss maintenance is dependent on whether there is the perception of autonomous control or external control of the motivation to lose weight.
    a. self-control theory
    b. self-concept theory
    c. self-determination theory
    d. self-actualization theory

24. Which substance improves mental alertness, sharpens memory, and reduces tention by increasing the release of neurotransmitters in the brain?
    a. cocaine
    b. nicotine
    c. carbohydrates
    d. alcohol

25. Prevention strategies that are designed to increase early detection of disease are called
    a. preliminary.
    b. tertiary.
    c. primary.
    d. secondary.

Essay Questions (5 points each)

1. Differentiate between the major physiological and cognitive theories that explain an organism's reactions to stress.

2. Define post-traumatic stress disorder (PTSD) and describe some of the symptoms of the disorder.

3. Describe some of the different coping strategies that can be used to deal with stress and which strategies are most likely to be successful.

4. Discuss the relationship between heart disease and behavior and how that relationship is different for men and women.

5. Describe different types of primary prevention strategies that you have observed or experienced and discuss whether you felt they were effective in changing your behavior.

ANSWER EXPLANATIONS

Multiple-Choice Questions

1. a
Health psychology is the branch of psychology that studies the relation between psychological variables and health.

2. b
The "fight-or-flight" syndrome involves the sympathetic nervous system, which prepares the body for immediate action.

3. a
Cannon considered the fight-or-flight response to be adaptive, because it helps the organism to respond rapidly to threats in the environment.

4. d
The general adaptation syndrome, or GAS, was proposed by Hans Selye.

5. a
The organism may experience shock during the alarm stage of the general adaptation syndrome.

6. c
During the resistance stage of the general adaptation syndrome, the body's functions return to a more normal (though still somewhat above normal) level.

7. d
During the exhaustion stage of the general adaptation syndrome, the organism is more susceptible to illness due to depletion of the body's resources.

8. c
Richard Lazarus noted that there is a cognitive component to our reactions to stress.

9. b
According to Lazarus, during the primary appraisal, one evaluates the potential seriousness of a threat; in the secondary appraisal, one evaluates whether one's own resources are sufficient to meet the threat.

10. c
Renaldo is facing an approach–approach conflict, in which both choices have pleasant and positive aspects.

11. d
Irritability is not a physical symptom, although it can be a reaction to stress; the other symptoms, headaches, sleeplessness, and intestinal disorders, can all result from stress.

12. c
Burnout is the term used for a condition in which people become dissatisfied, inefficient, and psychologically debilitated.

13. b

Studies have shown that individuals who have some predictability and control over a stressful situation can decrease the effects of stress.

14. d

On the Holmes–Rahe scale, the death of a spouse is the most stressful life event that is experienced.

15. b

Post-traumatic stress disorder (PTSD) is a set of symptoms that commonly afflict those who have suffered traumatic stress, such as a war or catastrophe; symptoms can include disturbed sleep, the reliving of painful experiences, difficulty concentrating, and feelings of panic and alienation.

16. a

Resilience is the term used to describe the extent to which people are flexible and respond adaptively to stressful situations or events.

17. d

A coping strategy that involves several steps that are taken to identify and reduce the effect of the stressor is called a task-oriented strategy.

18. b

According to the health belief model, our willingness to seek medical services depends on both the extent to which a threat to health is perceived and the extent to which individuals believe that a particular behavior will reduce that threat.

19. a

Impatience, anger, hostility, and competitiveness are all characteristics of Type A behavior.

20. a

The study of the interactions between the immune system and behavior is called psychoneuroimmunology.

21. c

An individual's lifestyle is the pattern of decisions and behaviors that determine both health and quality of life.

22. a

Male survivors of heart attack are more likely to die of heart disease if they are high in hostility; and female survivors are at greater risk if they suppress their emotions of anger and resentment.

23. c

Self-determination theory posits that individuals who lose weight at the urging of others (controlled motivation) are less likely to be able to sustain the weight loss than if the loss is triggered by their own wishes (autonomous motivation).

24. b

Nicotine has physiological as well as psychological effects that include stimulation of the central nervous system, thus creating both physiological and psychological dependence on smoking.

25. d

Prevention strategies that are designed to increase early detection of disease are called secondary strategies; primary strategies attempt to reduce or eliminate the incidence of preventable illness or injury through education or behavioral intervention.

Essay Questions

1. Differentiate between the major physiological and cognitive theories that explain an organism's reactions to stress.

   The physiological theories that explain how living organisms react to stress include the fight-or-flight response, a term coined by Walter Cannon to describe the changes that occur in the sympathetic nervous system as a result of stressors in the environment; and the general adaptation syndrome (GAS) described by Hans Selye. The general adaptation syndrome consists of three stages: alarm, resistance, and exhaustion.

The major cognitive theory proposed by Richard Lazarus posits that organisms react to stressors with a primary appraisal, in which the seriousness of the threat is evaluated, and a secondary appraisal to assess whether the individual organism can cope with the threat.

2. Define post-traumatic stress disorder (PTSD) and describe some of the symptoms of the disorder.

Post-traumatic stress disorder (PTSD) is a response to traumatic stress, caused by war or environmental catastrophes such as fires or earthquakes. Symptoms of PTSD can include sleep disturbance, painful reliving of traumatic experiences either awake or asleep, difficulty concentrating, and feelings of panic and alienation. PTSD was first named and identified as veterans of the Vietnam War returned home with these symptoms; however, the disorder itself has been manifested after many conflicts (including World Wars I and II) and after traumatic experiences such as rape, relocation of populations, and natural catastrophes.

3. Describe some of the different coping strategies that can be used to deal with stress, and which strategies are most likely to be successful.

Richard Lazarus identified two different types of coping strategies: defense-oriented coping strategies are responses such as rationalization and reaction formation; task-oriented coping strategies are planned strategies that involve identifying the stressor, choosing an appropriate course of action, implementing the action, and evaluating the results. Task-oriented coping strategies are preferred, because they are a healthier and more proactive means of reacting to stress. Other strategies for coping with stress include using relaxation techniques, self-talk, or imagery.

4. Discuss the relationship between accident and illness and behavior, and how that relationship is different for men and women.

Many accidents and diseases or illnesses are associated with unhealthy behaviors; for example, the decision to drink and drive may become a life-threatening type of unhealthy behavior. Heart disease is influenced by behavior; studies have shown that feelings of anger and hostility may be associated with an increased risk of death from heart disease. In women, an association exists between suppression of emotions and increased risk of death from heart disease. While behavior does not influence contracting diseases such as cancer, certain types of attitudes, such as optimism and a sense of humor, can have an effect on the amount of distress that is experienced during cancer treatment. The study of psychoneuroimmunology studies the relationship between psychological factors and the immune system, which is responsible for fighting off bacteria and viruses that can cause illness.

5. Describe different types of primary prevention strategies that you have observed or experienced; and discuss whether you felt they were effective in changing your behavior.

You may have been exposed to education campaigns designed to alert you to the danger of contracting AIDS/HIV, the dangers of smoking or drinking, and the effects of overweight (or, conversely, the dangers of anorexia and bulimia). Research has shown that the most effective education campaigns are those directed to a specific target audience. Have recent anti-smoking commercials on television affected your behavior with regard to smoking cigarettes? Why or why not? What do you think could be done to make those campaigns more effective?

UNIT IV: VARIATIONS ON NORMAL FUNCTIONING

CHAPTER 12—PSYCHOLOGICAL DISORDERS

FLASH FOCUS

When you complete this chapter, you will be able to:

✓ Discuss the concept of "abnormality," and give an overview of the DSM-IV classification scheme

✓ Distinguish and describe anxiety, somatoform, and dissociative disorders

✓ Name and describe several types of personality disorders and mood disorders

✓ Discuss the disease of schizophrenia, including early symptoms, possible causes, and types of schizophrenia

✓ Describe some substance-related disorders and disorders of sexual and gender identity

Use a highlighter to identify ideas, terms, and people that your instructor refers to in lectures or emphasizes in the course. Add to the chart any other ideas, terms, or people that your instructor discusses.

Core Concepts in Psychological Disorders

Important Ideas	Key Terms	Important People
Abnormal psychology	Biological perspective	Sigmund Freud
Abnormal behavior	Psychodynamic perspective	Emil Kraepelin
Maladaptive behavior	Learning perspective	Eugen Bleuler
Mental disorders	Cognitive perspective	
Electroconvulsive therapy	Humanistic perspective	
(shock treatment)	Generalized anxiety disorder	
Psychoanalysis	Panic disorder	
American Psychiatric	Social phobia	
Association (APA)	Agoraphobia	
Diagnostic and Statistical	Obsessive–compulsive disorder	
Manual of Mental Disorders	Post-traumatic stress disorder	
(DSM-IV)	(PTSD)	
Neurosis	Dissociative amnesia	
Psychosis	Dissociative fugue	
Anxiety	Depersonalization disorder	
Anxiety disorders	Dissociative identity disorder	
Phobias	Somatization disorder	
Dissociative disorders	Hypochondriasis	
Somatoform disorders	Munchausen's syndrome	
Personality disorders	Conversion disorder	
Mood disorders	Paranoid personality disorder	
Schizophrenic disorders	Schizoid personality disorder	

Positive symptoms
Negative symptoms
Externalizing problems
Internalizing problems
Disruptive behaviors
Attention-deficit/hyperactivity
disorders (ADHD)
Pervasive developmental
disorders
Autistic disorder/autism
Eating disorders
Substance-related disorders
Substance abuse
Sexual dysfunctions
Paraphilias
Gender identity disorders

Schizotypal personality disorder
Borderline personality disorder
Histrionic personality disorder
Narcissistic personality disorder
Antisocial personality disorder
Avoidant personality disorder
Obsessive–compulsive
personality disorder
Dependent personality disorder
Bipolar disorder
Mania
Major depression
Dysthymic disorder
Cyclothymic disorder
Norepinephrine
Serotonin
Seasonal affective disorder (SAD)
Thought disorders
Delusions
Delusions of persecution
Delusions of grandeur
Delusions of control
Hallucinations
Undifferentiated Schizophrenia
Catatonic schizophrenia
Catatonic postures
Paranoid schizophrenia
Disorganized schizophrenia
Reactive schizophrenia
Process schizophrenia
Dopamine
Dopamine hypothesis
Chlorpromazine
Oppositional defiant disorder
Conduct disorder
Ritalin
Anorexia nervosa
Bulimia nervosa
Substance-induced disorders
Substance-use disorders
Sexual desire disorders
Sexual arousal disorders
Orgasm disorders
Premature ejaculation
Fetishes
Frotteurism
Pedophilia
Sexual sadism
Sexual masochism
Sex-change operations

FLASH SUMMARY

The field of *abnormal psychology* focuses on the assessment, treatment, and prevention of mental disorders. How do psychologists distinguish "normal" from "abnormal" behavior? Some people exhibit markedly strange behaviors, like Jack Nicholson in the movie "As Good As It Gets," but most people exhibit so-called normal behavior for most of their lives. Questions that help psychologists and psychiatrists to determine whether behavior is truly abnormal include:

✓ Is the behavior considered abnormal within the person's own culture? Some behaviors that may seem strange in one culture are perfectly acceptable within another.

✓ Does the behavior cause personal distress? Many (but not all) people with psychological or mental disorders suffer from anxiety, fear, agitation, or other states of discomfort.

✓ Does the behavior cause distress in others? The family, friends, and neighbors of someone with a psychological or mental disorder may experience distress from their perception of the individual's problems.

✓ Is the person a danger to self or others? If an individual is likely to injure themself or anyone else, that individual is definitely in need of care.

If behavior is *maladaptive;* in other words, if it interferes with a person's ability to lead a useful, productive life, then it may be judged to be abnormal. However, social and cultural considerations may define one type of behavior as abnormal and another as merely odd. For example, survivalists or fundamentalists may live in a manner that most Americans would find odd or unusual, but which would not necessarily be considered evidence of a psychological or mental disorder. Today, *mental disorders* are defined as disturbances of behavioral or psychological functioning that are not culturally accepted and lead to psychological distress, behavioral disability, and/or impaired overall functioning.

There are a number of perspectives on the causes of psychological disorders. The *biological perspective* looks for biological or physical causes of mental disorders, such as inheritance, biochemical abnormalities or imbalances, structural abnormalities, infections or accidents. Those holding the biological perspective tend to favor biological treatments, such as drugs, surgery, or *electroconvulsive therapy (shock treatments)*. The *psychodynamic perspective,* based on the work of *Sigmund Freud,* holds that psychological disorders stem from unresolved childhood conflicts; the cure favored by this perspective is *psychoanalysis*. The *learning perspective* holds that abnormal behavior is learned; behavior therapists seek to replace maladaptive behaviors with new and more appropriate behaviors. The *cognitive perspective* suggests that faulty thinking or perceptions contribute to some types of psychological disorders, and that changing the thinking and perceptions of individuals can lead to changes in behaviors. Finally, the *humanistic perspective* views psychological disorders as blocks in the natural process of self-actualization, which need to be identified and removed in order for the person to resume the self-actualization process.

The need for a comprehensive classification of mental disorders was recognized by *Emil Kraepelin,* who provided an early classification system in a textbook published in 1883. The Association of Medical Superintendents of American Institutions for the Insane, the predecessor of the *American Psychiatric Association (APA),* incorporated Kraepelin's concepts into a classification system of its own. This system developed into a manual that was published by the American Psychiatric Association in 1952, which is today called the *Diagnostic and Statistical Manual of Mental Disorders (DSM-IV),* now in its fourth edition. The major categories of disorders distinguished by DSM-IV are listed in the following table.

The APA originally distinguished between *neuroses,* or disorders that caused some distress and impairment in functioning, but without loss of contact with reality, and *psychoses,* or severe disorders that cause loss of contact with reality either entirely or in part, including delusions and hallucinations. These distinctions are no longer recognized, although some health professionals still use the term "psychosis" in referring to the most serious psychological disorder, schizophrenia.

 FLASH SUMMARY

The following table lists the major categories of mental disorders recognized by the DSM-IV classification. Add to the table any disorders, symptoms, or examples that may be mentioned by your instructor in class.

Major DSM–IV Categories of Mental Disorders

Disorder	Symptoms	Examples
Anxiety disorders	Disorders characterized by anxiety and avoidance behavior	Panic disorder Social phobia Obsessive–compulsive disorder Post-traumatic stress disorder
Somatoform disorders	Disorders in which physical symptoms are present that are psychological in origin rather than due to a medical condition	Hypochondriasis Conversion disorder
Dissociative disorders	Disorders in which one handles stress or conflict by either forgetting important personal information or one's whole identity or compartmentalizing the trauma or conflict into a split-off alter personality	Dissociative amnesia Dissociative fugue Dissociative identity disorder
Personality disorders	Disorders characterized by long-standing, inflexible, maladaptive patterns of behavior beginning early in life and causing personal distress or problems in social and occupational functioning	Antisocial personality disorder Histrionic personality disorder Narcissistic personality disorder Borderline personality disorder
Mood disorders	Disorders characterized by periods of extreme or prolonged depression or mania or both	Major depressive disorder Bipolar disorder
Eating disorders	Disorders characterized by severe disturbances in eating behavior	Anorexia nervosa Bulimia
Substance-related disorders	Disorders in which undesirable behavioral changes result from substance abuse, dependence, or intoxication	Alcohol abuse Cocaine abuse Cannabis dependence
Disorders usually first diagnosed in infancy, childhood, or adolescence	Disorders that include mental retardation, learning disorders, communication disorders, pervasive	Conduct disorder Autistic disorder Tourette's syndrome

	developmental disorders, attention-deficit and disruptive behavior disorders, tic disorders, and elimination disorders	Stuttering
Schizophrenia and other psychotic disorders	Disorders characterized by the presence of psychotic symptoms including hallucinations, delusions, disorganized speech, bizarre behavior, or loss of contact with reality	Schizophrenia, paranoid type Schizophrenia, disorganized type Schizophrenia, catatonic type Delusional disorder, jealous type

Adapted from Samuel E. Wood and Ellen Green Wood, *The World of Psychology*, Fourth Edition. Copyright Allyn and Bacon, Boston, 2002. Adapted with permission.

Anxiety, Somatoform, and Dissociative Disorders

FLASH SUMMARY

Anxiety is a state of dread or concern that something unpleasant may occur. If feelings of anxiety are frequent or unusually intense, they can become one of a number of different *anxiety disorders*. *Generalized anxiety disorder* is the experience of intense and excessive worry and anxiety, which may cause irritability and difficulty in concentrating or sleeping. It is estimated that as many as 5.1 percent of the population will suffer from generalized anxiety disorder at some point, and women are more likely to experience the disorder than are men. A related condition, *panic disorder*, is a condition characterized by periods of unexpected and intense anxiety; these attacks can cause physical symptoms such as sweating, a racing heart, dizziness, nausea, and palpitations.

Anxiety disorders include various kinds of *phobias*, or intense, irrational fears of specific situations or objects. The most common phobia is *social phobia*, or fear of being evaluated and possibly embarrassed by others; it is estimated that nearly 13 percent of Americans have had a social phobia at some point in their lives. *Agoraphobia* is a fear of situations in which an individual believes that help will not be available if needed. Agoraphobia can include fear of open spaces, fear of being in public, fear of traveling, or even fear of having a panic attack while away from home; thus, individuals who suffer from this disorder can become housebound. Other specific phobias can be categorized as (1) situational phobias, or fears of specific places like elevators, airplanes, or enclosed spaces; (2) fear of the natural environment, such as storms, water, or heights; (3) fear of animals, such as dogs, snakes, insects, or mice; or (4) fear of blood or injections.

Obsessive–compulsive disorder is a cycle of obsessive thoughts, which then compel the individual to engage in a series of rituals to allay the thoughts. Obsessive–compulsive disorders often center on thoughts of germs and disease, bodily waste or secretions, or concern about doing a task or job adequately. Individuals suffering from this disorder may wash their hands many times a day, check the locks on windows and doors repeatedly, or hoard old mail and newspapers. While the rate of this disorder is equal for males and females, females are much more likely to be compulsive hand-washers than are males.

Post-traumatic stress disorder (PTSD) is another type of anxiety disorder that is caused by a traumatic event such as war or catastrophe. Individuals suffering from PTSD persistently reexperience the traumatic event in their waking thoughts or in dreams; they may experience difficulty falling asleep, irritability, outbursts of anger, or difficulty concentrating.

Dissociative disorders are disorders involving disruptions in a person's memory, consciousness, or identity. *In dissociative amnesia,* individuals suddenly suffer a loss of memory and feelings of unreality and uncertainty about their own identity. In a *dissociative fugue,* a person may travel to a different location with no memory of their past. In *depersonalization disorder* a person feels detached from their life, as if they were acting in a movie. The best known dissociative disorder is *dissociative identity disorder,* once called "multiple personality disorder." In this disorder, the individual's identity has split into two or more separate but coexisting personalities, who have different traits, behaviors, memories, and emotions. While dissociative identity disorder is somewhat controversial and has been widely (and at times, erroneously) publicized, there is evidence that the disorder does exist; for example, one personality may be allergic to a particular substance, whereas another personality is not.

Somatoform disorders are disorders in which individuals have physical symptoms in the absence of identifiable causes for those symptoms. *Somatization disorder* is a disorder in which an individual has a history of physical symptoms that affect their social, occupational, or other important areas of life, such as back or abdominal pain, nausea and vomiting, or sexual symptoms. Symptoms can even include blindness or paralysis for which there is no discernible physical cause. *Hypochondriasis,* a related disorder, is preoccupation with or fear of disease. People with *Munchausen's syndrome* obtain unnecessary medical procedures that are often costly or painful. In *conversion disorder,* individuals experience deficits of the motor or sensory systems, with poor balance or coordination, paralysis, blindness, deafness, or loss of sensitivity to touch or pain. People who experience somatoform disorders tend to focus on their private sensations, perceive bodily sensations more intensely than do other people, and have high levels of pessimism, fear, guilt, and low self-esteem.

Personality Disorders

FLASH SUMMARY

Personality disorders are disorders that involve extreme and inflexible personality traits that cause problems for individuals in their work or personal lives. DSM-IV names three distinct groups of personality disorders: those characterized by odd or eccentric behavior (including *paranoid, schizoid,* and *schizotypal* disorders); those involving dramatic, emotional, and erratic forms of behavior (including *borderline personality disorder*); and those characterized by anxious and fearful behavior (including *obsessive–compulsive personality disorder* and *dependent personality disorder*).

The first group of disorders includes *paranoid personality disorder,* in which individuals are convinced that others are out to deceive or take advantage of them in some way. Those who suffer from *schizoid personality disorder* lack basic social skills and show little or no sign of emotion; these people often live isolated lives on the fringes of society. Those with *schizotypal personality disorder* are highly anxious in social situations and may act in bizarre ways, such as wearing out-of-date or mismatched clothes.

The second group of disorders includes *borderline personality disorder,* manifested in people who show tremendous instability in their interpersonal relationships, self-image, and moods. People with *histrionic personality disorder* have a tremendous need for attention and will dress or behave in unusual ways to attract attention. Those with *narcissistic personality disorder* have grandiose ideas of their own importance and abilities. People with *antisocial personality disorder* are callous and manipulative and lack guilt or remorse over misdeeds. Antisocial personality disorder was once termed "psychopathic inferiority," and those who exhibited the disorder were called "psychopaths." Those with antisocial personality disorder may become criminals or "scam artists." Tests have shown that people with antisocial personality disorder have reduced reactions to negative stimuli, so punishment is ineffective.

The third group of disorders, which involve anxious or fearful behavior, include *avoidant personality disorder,* in which an individual avoids social situations due to feelings of inadequacy and hypersensitivity; *obsessive–compulsive personality disorder,* in which an individual is preoccupied with cleanliness and exhibits perfectionism and the need for control; and *dependent personality disorder*, in which the individual exhibits a pervasive and excessive need to be taken care of by others.

Mood Disorders

FLASH SUMMARY

Mood disorders are significant shifts in mood that affect a person's normal perception, thought, and behavior. *Bipolar disorder* is characterized by alternating periods of *mania*, or wild excitement, and depression. *Major depression* is a sustained mood of sadness and feelings of hopelessness and worthlessness that may be accompanied by changes in appetite, sleeping, and behavior. Less severe forms of these disorders include *dysthymic disorder*, or low-level depression, and *cyclothymic disorder*, or a less severe form of bipolar disorder. During a manic phase in bipolar disorder, an individual may speak quickly, move about restlessly, and make grandiose plans. During a depressive phase, the same individual may have sad, hopeless thoughts, and feelings of guilt and worthlessness. Major depression can lead to suicide; the fatality rate for those with major depression is estimated at 15 percent.

Mood disorders may have a biological or genetic component; people with first-degree relatives with serious mood disorders are ten times more likely to develop the disorder than are others. Both electroconvulsive therapy and antidepressant drugs are used to treat severe depression. In searching for biological causes for mood disorders, and particularly depression, investigators have found that two transmitter substances, *norepinephrine* and *serotonin*, play important roles in experiencing moods. Scientists have also noted a connection between sleep and depression, and have posited that depression may be linked to disturbances in sleep cycles. For example, depression that is experienced by women during menopause has been linked to the disturbed sleep caused by "hot flashes," or varying body temperatures, due to lack of the hormone estrogen. A phenomenon called *seasonal affective disorder* or *SAD* is a type of depression that has been linked to lack of light during the winter months; SAD can be treated by exposing people to bright lights for several hours a day.

Schizophrenic Disorders

FLASH SUMMARY

Schizophrenia is a group of psychological disorders involving distortions of thought, perception, and emotion; bizarre behavior; and social withdrawal. Schizophrenic disorders affect an estimated .7 percent of the U.S. population, or over 2 million Americans at any one time. The term "schizophrenia," which means "split mind," refers to the break with reality associated with the disorders. Individuals with schizophrenia may require lifelong institutionalization (about one-third of diagnosed cases), may have periodic remissions, only to have the symptoms return at times throughout their lives (another one-third), or may have a permanent remission (a final one-third).

Symptoms of schizophrenia include *positive symptoms* such as thought disorders, hallucinations, and delusions. *Thought disorders* are patterns of disorganized, irrational thinking; schizophrenics may jump from topic to (apparently unrelated) topic and draw bizarre conclusions. *Delusions* are beliefs that are contrary to fact; they may include *delusions of persecution*, that individuals or groups are conspiring against the schizophrenic; *delusions of grandeur*, or false beliefs in the individual's power and importance; and *delusions of control*, in which the individual believes that they are being controlled by others, such as by radar or radio waves. In *hallucinations*, the individual perceives stimuli that are not actually present. Hallucinations are commonly auditory, but may involve any of the senses. A "typical" schizophrenic illusion involves voices that appear to be talking to the individual, scolding or giving commands. *Negative symptoms* of schizophrenia indicate the absence of normal behavior; for example, schizophrenics may lack emotional responsiveness, be unable to experience pleasure, and withdraw from other people.

Types of schizophrenia include *undifferentiated schizophrenia,* which simply means that there is a diagnosis of schizophrenia without the symptoms of one of the other types; *catatonic schizophrenia,* in which the individual may take *catatonic postures,* bizarre, rigid poses that may be held for hours; *paranoid schizophrenia,* characterized by delusions of persecution, grandeur, or control; and *disorganized schizophrenia,* a serious progressive and irreversible disorder often characterized by using rhyming words out of context (called a "word salad").

Eugen Bleuler pioneered the study of schizophrenia in the first half of the twentieth century. He distinguished between *reactive schizophrenia,* which he believed was a reaction to life experiences, and *process schizophrenia,* which had an early onset and was considered chronic. Later research has indicated that schizophrenia has a genetic component; children of parents with schizophrenia are more likely than others to become schizophrenic. Other investigations have also pointed to abnormal activity of neurons that use *dopamine* as their transmitter substance; this is called the *dopamine hypothesis.* The introduction of *chlorpromazine* (trade name Thorazine) was effective in alleviating the positive symptoms of schizophrenia. Brain scans of patients with schizophrenia have indicated that the disease causes some forms of brain damage, which may indicate that the disorders are caused by some type of disease or birth trauma. Other research has indicated that there may be cognitive and environmental factors involved in schizophrenia; some studies have shown that being raised in a "mentally healthy" family may protect against development of the disease. No matter what the causes, people with various types of schizophrenic disorders constitute the largest proportion of people in mental hospitals.

Other Types of Disorders

FLASH SUMMARY

Other types of mental disorders include disorders that appear in infancy, childhood, and adolescence; those that form around eating; those that can arise from the use of psychoactive substances; and those that are related to the formation of a sexual identity. Mental problems or disorders that are identified in childhood consist of *externalizing problems,* or disruptive behaviors such as aggression and hyperactivity, and *internalizing problems,* or deficits in desired behaviors such as interacting with others.

Disruptive behaviors are common, and are usually the reason that children are referred for psychological evaluation. The DSM-IV divides disruptive behaviors into *oppositional defiant disorder* and *conduct disorder.* In oppositional defiant disorder, children have poor control of their emotions and repeatedly come into conflict with parents, teachers, and other adults. Oppositional defiant disorder may begin as early as age 3, and can evolve into conduct disorder, often when children enter puberty. Conduct disorder involves serious antisocial behaviors that may be harmful to property or to others. Boys demonstrate disruptive behaviors more than girls, and it has been posited that the behaviors stem from sex hormones; however, it has also been shown that environmental factors, such as poverty, placement in foster care, and coercive child-raising practices, are involved.

Attention-deficit/hyperactivity disorder (ADHD) is a childhood mental disorder characterized by inability to pay attention as well as hyperactivity or impulsiveness. ADHD has been linked with physical factors such as low birth weight and oxygen deprivation at birth, as well as with alcohol consumption by expectant mothers. ADHD is treated with drugs, most frequently *Ritalin,* which amplifies the impact of noreprinephine and dopamine in the brain.

Pervasive developmental disorders are childhood disorders that involve lifelong impairment of mental or physical functioning; these disorders include *autistic disorder,* or *autism.* Autism is a term for children who do not respond normally to outside stimuli; they seem to be preoccupied with themselves (as in the Greek word *autos,* or self). Children with autism have marked impairments in establishing relationships with others, show poor or nonexistent language skills, and have stereotyped, repetitive patterns of behavior. Autism is thought to be caused by biological factors, and the brains of autistic children exhibit structural abnormalities such as frontal lobes that are less well-developed than those of normal children.

Eating disorders are most often manifested by children, usually girls, entering puberty, although the disorders can be manifested as early as age eight. *Anorexia nervosa* is the intense, excessive fear of gaining weight coupled with the refusal to eat; *bulimia nervosa* is a similar disorder that involves binging and then purging, either by vomiting or by self-administered laxatives and diuretics. Anorexia or bulimia can also be characterized by excessive exercising. Individuals with anorexia and bulimia have distorted self-perceptions and see themselves as much larger than they actually are. The frequency of eating disorders seems to decrease with age.

Substance-related disorders are mental disorders that are linked to the use of psychoactive substances, including alcohol, cocaine, marijuana, and even cigarettes. The DSM-IV divides these disorders into two types: *substance-induced disorders,* or impaired functioning as a direct result of repetitive use of the substance, and *substance-use disorders,* or harmful behaviors that affect personal, social, and occupational functioning as a result of frequent use of the substance. *Substance abuse* is defined as a maladaptive pattern of substance use that results in repeated, significant adverse effects such as failure to meet social or work obligations, behaving in hazardous ways (such as driving while drunk), and legal and other problems resulting from use of the substance. Alcohol is the most frequently abused substance in the United States, but cocaine, amphetamines, and nicotine are also widely used.

Finally, sexual and gender identity disorders include *sexual dysfunctions, paraphilias,* and *gender identity disorders.* Sexual dysfunctions are disturbances in sexual desire and/or arousal; *sexual desire disorders* involve a lack of interest in sex or active aversion to sexual activity; *sexual arousal disorders* involve the inability to attain or maintain sexual arousal. *Orgasm disorders* include *premature ejaculation* in males and the delay or absence of orgasms in either sex.

Paraphilias are dysfunctions that involve the need for bizarre imagery or acts in order to become sexually aroused. Paraphilias include *fetishes,* in which individuals are aroused by inanimate objects; *frotteurism,* or fantasies and urges to touch or rub against a nonconsenting person; and *pedophilia,* or sexual urges and fantasies involving children. Other paraphilias include *sexual sadism* and *sexual masochism,* in which an individual's sexual satisfaction is tied to giving or receiving pain.

Gender identity disorders are experienced by individuals who feel, from an early age, that they were born with the wrong sexual identity. They identify strongly with the opposite sex and have a preference for cross-dressing (wearing the clothing of the opposite sex). Such individuals can now receive *sex-change operations* to have their sex organs altered to approximate those of the opposite sex. Evidence indicates that individuals who have had sex-change operations report feeling happier than they were before the operations.

 FLASH REVIEW

Go to www.behavenet.com/capsules/disorders/dsm4classification.htm to view the exhaustive listing of DSM-IV classifications, then answer the following questions.

(Note. The fourth edition of DSM has been revised and is referred to as DSM-IV-TR; but for purposes of this exercise, use the DSM-IV categories listed at the previously mentioned website.)

1. How many different substances are listed under substance-related disorders?

2. How many disorders are related to the use of caffeine?

3. How many disorders are related to the use of amphetamines? Read the description of several of the disorders. What can you conclude about the dangers of amphetamine use?

4. Under the category of depressive disorders, read the descriptions of dysthymic disorder and major depressive disorder. How would you describe the differences between these disorders?

 FLASH TEST

Review the chart of Core Concepts for Chapter 12. Then take the Practice Test for Chapter 12 on the following pages and rate your performance.

PRACTICE TEST

(Chapter 12—Psychological Disorders)

Multiple Choice (3 points each)

1. Which field of psychology focuses on the assessment, treatment, and prevention of maladaptive behaviors?
   a. health psychology
   b. personality psychology
   c. community psychology
   d. abnormal psychology

2. According to the criteria for defining abnormal behavior, when a behavior interferes with the quality of a person's life, it is considered
   a. to be maladaptive.
   b. to be a symptom of insanity.
   c. to be dangerous to the person or to other people.
   d. to be unusual in all cultures around the world.

3. Which perspective on mental disorders focuses on the effects of unresolved childhood conflicts?
   a. the biological perspective
   b. the learning perspective
   c. the psychoanalytic perspective
   d. the cognitive perspective

4. Which of the perspectives on mental disorders is most likely to make use of electroconvulsive therapy (shock treatment), drugs, or surgery?
   a. the biological perspective
   b. the learning perspective
   c. the psychoanalytic perspective
   d. the cognitive perspective

5. Who is the originator of the classification system for mental disorders that eventually became the DSM-IV?
   a. Sigmund Freud
   b. Eugen Bleuler
   c. Emil Kraepelin
   d. Carl Jung

6. _____ is a sense of apprehension that something unpleasant may occur and is accompanied by physical symptoms that include increased heart rate and sweating.
   a. Fear
   b. Stress
   c. A psychosis
   d. Anxiety

7. Someone with a social phobia exhibits extreme fear and avoidance of
   a. situations that involve being observed by others.
   b. being alone or in public places that are hard to exit.
   c. any small, confined space with no obvious way out.
   d. any specific object or situation that is not really dangerous.

8. Kathy is afraid to leave her home. She rarely goes outside, not even to check the mail; her sister needs to drive her to the local supermarket to do her shopping. Given these symptoms, it appears that Kathy suffers from
   a. social phobia.
   b. agoraphobia.
   c. panic attacks.
   d. major depression.

9. The anxiety disorder that provokes a person to undertake repetitive behaviors is called
   a. phobic disorder.
   b. panic disorder.
   c. obsessive–compulsive disorder.
   d. generalized anxiety.

10. Which of the following is an example of a dissociative fugue state?
   a. Maria has five different personalities.
   b. Mark cannot remember anything about the traffic accident that he was in yesterday.
   c. Skip cannot remember his true identity and is now living in a different town under the name of Stan.
   d. Anne believes she hears God's voice telling her that the end is near.

11. When a person appears to have two or more distinct personalities, that person is said to have which disorder?
   a. schizophrenic disorder
   b. somatoform disorder
   c. conversion disorder
   d. dissociative identity disorder

12. A mental disorder characterized by physical problems for which there is no physiological basis is called a _____ disorder.
   a. somatoform
   b. dissociative
   c. psychogenic
   d. psychoneurological

13. Paranoid, narcissistic, and histrionic are three types of
   a. schizophrenias.
   b. dissociation disorders.
   c. personality disorders.
   d. paraphilias.

14. Shawn is 14 years old; he has been caught stealing seven times in the past year. He is impulsive and often finds himself in fights. He doesn't seem to respect the rights of others and shows no remorse when he is caught breaking the law. Shawn seems likely to have _____ personality disorder.
   a. paranoid
   b. antisocial
   c. schizoid
   d. histrionic

15. A person who is extremely sensitive to rejection and is not confident in social situations is exhibiting symptoms of _____ personality disorder.

a. narcissistic
b. avoidant
c. passive–aggressive
d. histrionic

16. Bipolar disorder and depressive disorders are considered to be _____ disorders.
    a. personality
    b. anxiety
    c. dissociative
    d. mood

17. An individual who has been diagnosed as having _____ would probably describe their life as empty, hopeless, miserable, and worthless.
    a. bipolar disorder
    b. schizophrenia
    c. major depression
    d. a dissociative disorder

18. Antidepressant drugs appear to have stimulating effects on synapses that involve the transmitter substances _____ and _____.
    a. epinephrine; serotonin
    b. acetylcholine; dopamine
    c. norepinephrine; serotonin
    d. reserpine; GABA

19. The treatment for seasonal affective disorder (SAD) involves
    a. total sleep deprivation.
    b. exposure to bright light for several hours a day.
    c. REM sleep deprivation.
    d. injections of lithium carbonate.

20. The most common perceptual distortion experienced by people suffering from schizophrenia are _____ hallucinations.
    a. visual
    b. auditory
    c. tactile
    d. olfactory

21. Negative symptoms of schizophrenia include *all except one* of the following. Which one should *not* be included?
    a. flat affect
    b. poverty of speech
    c. hallucinations
    d. lack of ability to experience pleasure

22. According to Bleuler, _____ schizophrenia has a rapid onset and a brief duration, whereas _____ schizophrenia has a gradual onset and an extended duration.
    a. reactive; process
    b. process; reactive
    c. catatonic; undifferentiated
    d. disorganized; undifferentiated

23. The positive symptoms of schizophrenia are alleviated by a drug called
    a. reserpine
    b. atropine
    c. benzodiazepine
    d. chlorpromazine

24. Someone who sustains brain damage as a result of alcohol abuse is said to suffer from a(n)
    a. substance-use disorder.
    b. substance-induced disorder.
    c. alcohol disorder.
    d. paraphilia.

25. Fetishes, frotteurism, pedophilia, sexual sadism, and sexual masochism belong to the category of disorders called
    a. sexual dysfunction.
    b. sexual desire disorders.
    c. paraphilias.
    d. fugues.

Essay Questions (5 points each)

1. Describe ways in which psychologists and psychiatrists distinguish "normal" from "abnormal" behavior, and discuss the development of the major diagnostic tool currently in use.

2. Distinguish anxiety disorders, somatoform disorders, and dissociative disorders, and provide examples of each type.

3. Compare and contrast personality and mood disorders, and provide examples of each.

4. What are the positive and negative symptoms of schizophrenia, and some possible causes and treatments?

5. Select and discuss one of the other types of disorders named (such as eating disorders, substance disorders, or sexual disorders).

ANSWER EXPLANATIONS

Multiple-Choice Questions

1. **d**
   Abnormal psychology is the field of psychology that focuses on the assessment, treatment, and prevention of maladaptive behaviors, or mental disorders.

2. **a**
   Behavior that interferes with the quality of a person's life is considered to be maladaptive, and therefore possibly abnormal.

3. **c**
   The psychoanalytic perspective of Sigmund Freud focuses on unresolved childhood conflicts as the possible cause of mental disorders.

4. **a**
   Adherents of the biological perspective are most likely to use electroconvulsive therapy (shock treatment), drugs, or surgery to treat mental disorders, which they view as originating in biochemical abnormalities or imbalances or structural defects.

5. **c**
   Emil Kraepelin proposed a system of classification of mental disorders in a textbook published in 1883, which eventually evolved into the Diagnostic and Statistical Manual of Mental Disorders (DSM-IV) published by the American Psychiatric Association.

6. **d**
   Anxiety is the feeling that something unpleasant will occur, and it is accompanied by physical symptoms including increased heart rate and sweating.

7. **a**
   Social phobias involve fear of being observed by others; this is the most common phobia, and it is estimated that it affects almost 13 percent of the U.S. population at some point in life.

8. **b**
   Kathy appears to suffer from agoraphobia, a fear of situations in which a person feels that help may not be available if needed, such as traveling or being away from home.

9. **c**
   Obsessive-compulsive disorder is an anxiety disorder that compels an individual to perform compulsive, ritualized behaviors in order to reduce his or her level of anxiety.

10. **c**
    In a dissociative fugue, a person may travel to a different location and have no memory of his or her past life.

11. d

Dissociative identity disorder is the term for a disorder in which an individual may demonstrate two or more distinct personalities.

12. a

Somatoform disorders are disorders in which the individual experiences physical symptoms in the absence of identifiable causes for those symptoms.

13. c

Personality disorders include paranoid, narcissistic, and histrionic personality disorders.

14. b

Symptoms of antisocial personality disorder include callous and manipulative behavior, little regard for the feelings of others, and a lack of guilt or remorse over misdeeds.

15. b

In avoidant personality disorder, an individual avoids social situations due to feelings of inadequacy and hypersensitivity.

16. d

Bipolar disorder and depressive disorders are both mood disorders.

17. c

Major depression is a sustained mood of sadness accompanied by feelings of hopelessness and worthlessness.

18. c

Antidepressant drugs involve the stimulation of the transmitter substances norepinephrine and serotonin.

19. b

Seasonal affective disorder (SAD) appears to be related to the length of the day, and exposure to bright lights seems to help in the treatment of the disorder.

20. b

The most common perceptual distortion suffered by people with schizophrenia are auditory hallucinations.

21. c

Negative symptoms of schizophrenia means the absence of normal behaviors, such as the lack of ability to experience pleasure. Symptoms that are experienced such as hallucinations are termed positive symptoms.

22. a

According to Bleuler, reactive schizophrenia has a rapid onset and a brief duration, whereas process schizophrenia has a gradual onset and an extended duration.

23. d

The positive symptoms of schizophrenia can be alleviated by a drug called chlorpromazine.

24. b

A substance-induced disorder is an actual physical effect of substance abuse, such as brain damage caused by alcohol abuse. A substance-use disorder refers to harmful behavior that affects personal, social, and occupational functioning as a result of excessive use of a substance.

25. c

Fetishes, frotteurism, pedophilia, sexual sadism, and sexual masochism are all classified as paraphilias.

Essay Questions

1. Describe ways in which psychologists and psychiatrists distinguish "normal" from "abnormal" behavior, and discuss the development of the major diagnostic tool currently in use.

Psychologists and psychiatrists question whether the particular behavior is considered abnormal within the individual's culture, whether the behavior causes personal distress to the individuals or to others who are close to the person, whether the person is a danger to themselves or to others, and, particularly, whether the behavior is maladaptive, or interfering with the person's ability to live a useful, productive life.

The major diagnostic tool for mental disorders is the DSM-IV (*Diagnostic and Statistical Manual of Mental Disorders,* Fourth Edition), published by the American Psychiatric Association. The DSM-IV evolved from an early classification system devised by Emil Kraepelin in 1883, which was incorporated by the predecessor of the APA, and which eventually became the original DSM.

2. Distinguish anxiety disorders, somatoform disorders, and dissociative disorders, and provide examples of each type.

Anxiety disorders are characterized by a sense of foreboding or dread, which can interfere with a person's normal life and cause physical symptoms such as difficulty sleeping. Generalized anxiety disorder is suffered by as much as 5 percent of the population at some time in their lives. Other types of anxiety disorders include phobias, or fear of specific things or situations, obsessive–compulsive disorder, or the need to engage in rituals in order to allay anxiety, and agoraphobia, or fear of being in public places or places in which the individual might be unable to get help.

Somatoform disorders are disorders in which individuals experience physical symptoms in the absence of an identifiable cause for those symptoms; the most commonly known form of somatoform disorder is hypochondriasis, the preoccupation with or fear of disease.

Dissociative disorders involve disruptions in a person's memory, consciousness, or identity. This category of disorder includes dissociative amnesia, as well as dissociative identity disorder, commonly called "multiple personalities." In dissociative identity disorder, an individual's identity splits into two or more separate and distinct personalities, who may have their own memories, traits, and emotions.

3. Compare and contrast personality and mood disorders, and provide examples of each.

Personality disorders are disorders involving extreme personality traits that cause problems for the individual. The major types of personality disorders include paranoid personality disorders, characterized by feelings of paranoia; borderline personality disorders, characterized by instability in interpersonal relationships and wide mood swings; and avoidant personality disorders, in which individuals avoid social situations due to feelings of inadequacy and hypersensitivity.

Mood disorders involve significant shifts in mood that affect a person's perceptions, thoughts, and behaviors. The most common mood disorder is depression, or feelings of hopelessness and worthlessness. Depression is one of the most common types of disorders experienced by individuals in the United States. Other mood disorders include bipolar disorder, characterized by periods of mania, or excitement, that alternate with depression, or sadness; and seasonal affective disorder (SAD), a depression that is influenced by the lack of light during the winter months.

4. What are the positive and negative symptoms of schizophrenia, and some possible causes and treatments?

Positive symptoms of schizophrenia include hallucinations, delusions, and thought disorders; negative symptoms indicate the absence of normal behaviors, such as a flat affect, lack of emotional responsiveness, and the inability to experience pleasure. It has been hypothesized that schizophrenia is caused by biochemical abnormalities, since certain chemicals, particularly chlorpromazine (Thorazine), are effective in relieving the positive symptoms of schizophrenia. Other research has indicated that cognitive and environmental factors may be involved, and still further research points to brain damage caused by some type of disease or brain trauma.

5. Select and discuss one of the other types of disorders named (such as eating disorders, substance disorders, or sexual disorders).

You may choose to discuss one of the disorders that is identified in infancy, childhood, or adolescence, such as disruptive behaviors including attention-deficit/hyperactivity disorder (ADHD), or developmental disorders such as autism. Another category of disorders are eating disorders, which are usually manifested by children (most often girls) entering puberty; these disorders are characterized by efforts to control eating or refusal to eat, sometimes accompanied by purging and/or excessive exercising. Substance-related disorders are disorders that arise from the use of psychoactive substances, which can include drugs, alcohol, and even cigarettes. Individuals who become dependent on substances manifest substance-induced disorders, or impaired functioning that results from the use of the substance (such as brain damage in alcoholics), or substance-use disorders, or harmful behaviors that affect the individual's personal, social, and occupational functioning.

A final category of disorders includes sexual and gender disorders; paraphilias are dysfunctions that involve the need for bizarre imagery or acts in order to become sexually aroused, such as fetishes or pedophilia. Gender identity disorder is experienced by individuals who feel that they were born the "wrong" sex; these individuals may be aided by a sex-change operation to enable them to live as the opposite sex.

UNIT IV: VARIATIONS ON NORMAL FUNCTIONING

CHAPTER 13—THERAPIES FOR TREATING MENTAL DISORDERS

 FLASH FOCUS

When you complete this chapter, you will be able to:

✓ Differentiate and describe the major types of insight therapies

✓ Describe various types of behavior therapy, including those based on classical conditioning, operant conditioning, and observational learning theory

✓ Discuss cognitive therapy techniques

✓ Outline the techniques of group therapy and community therapy, and distinguish between primary and secondary prevention

✓ Describe the major types of biological therapies

✓ Discuss some of the difficulties involved in the evaluation of different therapies, and some of the multicultural variables that exist, as well as recent attempts to address multicultural differences

Use a highlighter to identify ideas, terms, and people that your instructor refers to in lectures or emphasizes in the course. Add to the chart any other ideas, terms, or people that your instructor discusses.

Core Concepts in Psychotherapy

Important Ideas	Key Terms	Important People
Psychotherapy	Free association	Sigmund Freud
Insight therapies	Dream analysis	Abraham Maslow
Psychoanalysis	Analysis of resistance	Carl Rogers
Humanistic/person-centered therapy	Analysis of transference	Fritz Perls
Client-centered therapy	Self-actualization	Albert Bandura
Gestalt therapy	Nondirective therapy	Albert Ellis
Behavior therapies	Directive therapy	Aaron Beck
Behavior modification	"Empty chair" technique	Donald Meichenbaum
Counterconditioning	Classical conditioning	J. L. Moreno
Cognitive therapies	Operant conditioning	Egas Moniz
Rational–emotive therapy	Observational learning theory	D. Sue
Group therapy	Systematic desensitization	D. W. Sue
Self-help groups	Flooding	
Family therapy	Exposure and response	
Couples therapy	Prevention	
Community psychology	Aversion therapy	
Preventive psychology	Token economies	
Biological therapies	Time out	

Drug therapy Electroconvulsive therapy (ECT)/shock therapy Psychosurgery/brain surgery National Institute of Mental Health (NIMH)	Stimulus satiation Participant modeling Beck's approach Meichenbaum's approach Psychodrama Alcoholics Anonymous Community mental health centers Halfway houses Primary prevention Secondary prevention Antipsychotic drugs Neuroleptics/major Tranquilizers Tardive dyskinesia Antidepressant drugs Tricyclics Serotonin-selective reuptake inhibitors (SSRIs) Monoamine oxidase Inhibitors (MAO inhibitors) Lithium Minor tranquilizers/benzodiazepines Lobotomy Cingulotomy Cingulum	

Insight Therapies

FLASH SUMMARY

The term *psychotherapy* refers to all psychological (not biological) means to treat emotional and behavioral disorders. Some forms of psychotherapy are referred to as *insight therapies,* since they rely on the assumption that people need to understand their own behavior and motivations in order to maximize mental health and personal effectiveness. The major types of insight therapies are *psychoanalysis, person-centered therapy,* and *Gestalt therapy.*

Psychoanalysis was a treatment approach developed by *Sigmund Freud* that was based on his psychoanalytic theories. Freud felt that it was essential for mental health to uncover repressed memories and to bring unresolved childhood conflicts into consciousness. Freud and his school of Freudian analysts used techniques that included *free association,* or the free flow of thoughts and ideas without censoring them, and *dream analysis,* or the interpretation of the meaning of dreams, which Freud believed conveyed important messages from the unconscious mind. Other techniques included *analysis of resistance,* in which areas that patients refuse to share or unconsciously avoid discussing with the therapist *(resistance)* are believed to hold significance, and *analysis of transference,* in which the patient transfers deep-rooted feelings from the original objects of those feelings, usually the parents, to the therapist.

Humanistic or *person-centered therapies* are based on the view of human potential pioneered by psychologists like *Abraham Maslow.* Person-centered therapy (formerly termed *client-centered therapy*) was developed by *Carl Rogers;* Rogers believed that that psychological disorders result from blocks in the process of *self-actualization.* Person-centered therapy attempts to provide a warm, accepting climate in which clients feel valued; it is a *nondirective therapy,* because the therapist is only the facilitator of the client's growth.

Gestalt therapy was developed by *Fritz Perls* in the 1960s. Gestalt therapy involves experiencing feelings and thoughts in the present moment and taking responsibility for those thoughts and feelings. Gestalt therapy is a *directive therapy,* because the therapist takes an active role in determining the course of therapy. Gestalt therapy focuses on helping clients to resolve past conflicts that may be affecting present relationships. One technique used by Gestalt therapists, the *"empty chair" technique,* involves having the client address an empty chair which he or she imagines is occupied by the mother, father, or some other important individual with whom the client has unresolved issues.

Behavior Therapies

FLASH SUMMARY

Behavior therapies are forms of treatment based on the learning approach to psychological disorders; in other words, dysfunctional behavior is learned. Behavior therapies utilize the techniques of *classical conditioning* and *operant conditioning,* as well as *observational learning theory,* to eliminate maladaptive behaviors and replace them with more adaptive responses. Behavior therapy is also referred to as *behavior modification,* because it focuses on changing behavior rather than on reexperiencing conflicts.

Behavior therapies that are based on classical conditioning, sometimes called *counterconditioning,* involve retraining one's reactions to stimuli; for example, the client is conditioned to be rid of fears or phobias through *systematic densensitization.* In the process of systematic desensitization, clients learn to perform relaxation techniques while they are visualizing the fear-producing stimulus, such as speaking in public. Gradually, the client loses the conditioned fear and begins to associate the stimulus, speaking in public, with a new conditioned response, relaxation and enjoyment. Another technique, *flooding,* involves exposing the client to the feared object or event until the anxiety subsides. For example, someone who is afraid of the sound of balloons popping would be kept in a room full of balloons that are systematically popped, until the association between the sound and the fear is extinguished. *Exposure and response prevention* is a technique used with obsessive–compulsive behavior, in which patients are exposed to a stimulus that evokes a compulsive response, then resist performing their compulsive rituals. Patients gradually learn to tolerate the anxiety provoked by the stimulus, without succumbing to the compulsive response. *Aversion therapy* pairs a harmful or undesirable behavior with a negative response, such as unpleasant tastes or electric shocks. The individual is then conditioned to avoid the harmful or undesirable behavior.

Therapies based on operant conditioning include *token economies,* in which desired behavior is rewarded with tokens such as gold stars or poker chips; the tokens can be exchanged for desired goods or privileges. Token economies have been used with schizophrenic patients in mental hospitals with some success. Another operant conditioning method is *time out,* in which negative behavior receives the consequence of being forced to spend time in a place with no company, television, books, etc. This negative reinforcement, often used with children, is expected to extinguish the undesired behavior. In *stimulus satiation,* individuals are provided with an excess of a formerly positive stimulus, so that they no longer desire it; for example, if a dieter craves ice cream, they are encouraged to eat ice cream every day, for three meals a day, until they are sick of ice cream.

The best known therapy based on observational learning theory is called *participant modeling;* introduced by *Albert Bandura,* this method involves the step-by-step modeling of appropriate behavior by the therapist, who encourages the client to copy the behavior. For example, a client with a phobia about snakes can observe the therapist handling a snake, and is gradually encouraged to imitate the therapist's behavior.

Cognitive Therapies

FLASH SUMMARY

Cognitive therapy focuses on changing an individual's behavior by changing their thoughts and perceptions. Cognitive therapy focuses on current behavior and thoughts rather than trying to recreate or affect past conflicts. One type of cognitive therapy, developed by *Albert Ellis,* is called *rational–emotive therapy.* This therapy stresses the importance of logical, rational thought processes. Ellis believed that "irrational assumptions," such as that it is necessary to receive love and approval from everyone in your life, cause emotional problems and maladaptive behaviors. The therapy involves pointing out to the client the irrationality of their assumptions, and encouraging them to adopt different behaviors based on more rational assumptions.

Another type of cognitive therapy created by *Aaron Beck,* termed *Beck's approach,* is based on the theory that individuals form distorted beliefs about situations, which then create negative beliefs and behaviors. In Beck's approach, individuals are helped to develop realistic appraisals of the situations they encounter and change their behavior accordingly. Another approach created by *Donald Meichenbaum* is based on the theory that an individual's "self-talk" influences his or her behavior. In *Meichenbaum's approach,* the therapist helps the individual to create an internal monologue that encourages adaptive behaviors.

Group and Community Therapies

FLASH SUMMARY

Group therapy, in which a therapist meets with two or more individuals, became common during World War II as an economic necessity for treating veterans with combat stress disorders. The structure of group therapy can vary widely, as can the actual techniques of the therapy. One technique used in group therapy is *psychodrama,* originated by *J. L. Moreno* to enable individuals to act out problems or conflicts with the assistance and participation of other group members.

Another type of group therapy is that of the *self-help group,* which originated with *Alcoholics Anonymous* in the 1930s. Today, more than 12 million people in the United States participate in some 500,000 self-help groups, including groups to aid in overcoming addictive behaviors such as gambling, groups of people who are grieving a particular kind of loss, such as a death or divorce, and groups of people who support each other in recovering from a particular kind of trauma, such as rape. In self-help groups, members offer each other a sense of belonging, share support techniques and strategies, and provide useful information on dealing with their common issues.

In *family therapy,* family members visit a therapist who specializes in treating families by helping them with troublesome issues and situations. The therapist particularly notes the dynamics of the family unit, and tries to help the family improve communications among members and to change destructive behavior patterns. *Couples therapy* is used by partners in a relationship, or who are ending a relationship, to better assess their situation.

Community psychology is a form of education and treatment that tries to address psychological problems by evaluating their sociocultural context. Community treatment programs included the *community mental health center,* a form of treatment initiated by Congress in the early 1960s that was intended to supplement mental health hospitals by providing outpatient treatment within the community, and the *halfway house,* which was designed to assist patients returning from mental hospitals or treatment centers to reintegrate themselves into the community. Community psychologists have also focused on *preventive psychology,* which is aimed at early identification and treatment of individuals at risk for certain types of mental disorders, such as depression. *Primary prevention* is the effort to eliminate conditions responsible for mental disorders, such as education on the dangers of using drugs; *secondary prevention* is aimed at early detection and treatment of disorders.

Biological Therapies

FLASH SUMMARY

Biological therapies are those therapies that are based on the belief that psychological disorders are usually based on underlying physical causes; therefore, these therapies use physical or biological methods such as *drugs, electroconvulsive therapy,* and *psychosurgery.*

The most frequently used biological therapy is drug therapy. Drugs have been shown to be effective in the treatment of symptoms of schizophrenia, depression, bipolar disorder, and some anxiety disorders. *Antipsychotic drugs,* which can control some of the symptoms of schizophrenia, have enabled some individuals to lead near-normal lives, whereas formerly a diagnosis of schizophrenia often meant lifelong hospitalization. Antipsychotic drugs are also called *neuroleptics* or *major tranquilizers;* they include the brand names Thorazine, Compazine, and Mellaril, and work by inhibiting the action of the neurotransmitter dopamine. About 50 percent of patients are helped by antipsychotic drugs in controlling symptoms such as delusions and hallucinations; but the side effects of these drugs can be unpleasant, and include restlessness, muscle spasms and cramps, and tremors. Long-term use of antipsychotics can cause *tardive dyskinesia,* jerking and twitching movements of the face, tongue, and hands and trunk. However, new drugs are being developed that have fewer side effects and can treat both positive and negative symptoms of schizophrenia.

Antidepressant drugs, which were introduced shortly after antipsychotic drugs, can elevate mood and also help in the treatment of certain anxiety disorders. Among these drugs are *tricyclics,* which block the reabsorption of norepinephrine and serotonin into the neurons, and which have been shown to be effective for over 60 percent of depressed patients. Again, however, side effects, including drowsiness, dizziness, fatigue, dry mouth, and weight gain, led many people to discontinue their use of the drugs. A new category of antidepressants was created called *serotonin-selective reuptake inhibitors (SSRIs),* which block the reuptake (reabsorption) of serotonin. SSRIs have been used in the treatment of obsessive–compulsive disorder, social phobia, panic disorder, and binge eating. The brand name Prozac became the most widely used antidepressant by the mid-1990s, with more than 28 million people worldwide having used it. A side effect of Prozac is sexual dysfunction, and there has been some contention that Prozac increases the risk of suicide and/or violent behavior. Another type of antidepressant, *monoamine oxidase inhibitors (MAO inhibitors),* blocks the action of an enzyme that breaks down norepinephrine and serotonin in the synapses; MAO inhibitors have been used for patients who do not respond to SSRIs, and can be effective in treating panic disorder and social phobia. However, MAO inhibitors have many of the side effects of tricyclics, and also increase the risk of stroke.

Lithium, a salt that occurs naturally, has been found to be effective in treating bipolar disorder, reducing the incidence and intensity of both manic and depressive episodes. Patients and therapists need to carefully monitor the level of lithium in the system, since too much can lead to lithium poisoning and permanent damage to the nervous system. The *minor tranquilizers,* called *benzodiazepines,* include the brand name drugs Xanax, Valium, and Librium. These minor tranquilizers are used to treat anxiety, and are prescribed more often than any other type of psychoactive drug. However, Xanax can cause withdrawal symptoms, including intense anxiety.

Electroconvulsive therapy (ECT), commonly called *shock therapy,* was introduced in 1938 as a treatment for mental disorders. In electroconvulsive therapy, an electric shock is administered to a patient for several seconds, causing loss of consciousness and a seizure that lasts for a minute or less. ECT is usually given three times a week for 2 to 4 weeks. Although shock treatment is represented in the media as a horrifying experience, patients have no memory of the treatment, and there are few complications. It is believed that the seizure temporarily changes the biochemical balance in the brain, which helps to lift the depression. Some psychiatrists and neurologists believe that ECT causes brain damage and memory loss, but studies of MRI and CT scans show no structural brain damage following the procedure. There is some memory loss following the procedure, but in most cases it lasts for only a few weeks.

The most serious procedure, *psychosurgery* or *brain surgery,* is used only to alleviate serious psychological disorders. The technique of *lobotomy,* or severing the connections between the frontal lobes, was devised by Portugeuse neurologist *Egas Moniz* in 1935. Moniz was awarded the Nobel Prize in Medicine in 1949 for the technique. However, it became apparent that while the treatment did calm patients, it also left them in a deteriorated condition, with feelings of apathy, impaired intellect, loss of motivation, and changes in personality. After the mid-1950s and the arrival of effective drug therapies, the lobotomy technique was nearly abandoned; however, there are now less drastic techniques that can destroy small areas of brain tissue without the major impact of a lobotomy. In a *cingulotomy,* electric current is used to destroy the *cingulum,* a small bundle of nerves connecting the cortex to the emotional centers of the brain. This treatment has been deemed effective in treating some extreme cases of obsessive–compulsive disorder.

Evaluation of Therapies

FLASH SUMMARY

It is difficult to compare and recommend particular therapies. First, there is the problem of how to measure the results of a particular therapy; it is difficult to measure a person's dysfunction, and equally difficult to evaluate treatment outcomes. It would also be unethical to conduct experiments in which a control group received no treatment, while the experimental group received a particular form of therapy. Some studies have shown that nearly two-thirds of individuals who seek some kind of psychological treatment do experience improvements. One study was commissioned by the *National Institute of Mental Health (NIMH)* to compare the effectiveness of cognitive therapy, psychodynamic therapy, and drug treatment for depression; patients in all four groups (including a control group) experienced improvement, with the drug treatment group producing the most improvement, followed by the two types of psychotherapy.

Other studies have indicated that patient characteristics that influence the outcome of psychotherapy include the patient's underlying psychological health at the beginning of therapy; the patient's motivation to change; and the patient's level of intelligence, anxiety, education, and socioeconomic status. Characteristics of the therapist that were found to be correlated with treatment effectiveness included the number of years the therapist had been practicing, the similarity of personality of therapist and client, and the ability of the therapist to communicate empathy to the client.

Recently, there has been a growing awareness that it is important for therapists to consider multicultural variables in treatments; for example, in the Asian culture a high value is placed upon restraint of strong feelings, a trait that may be seen as dysfunctional by a therapist who has not taken this cultural preference into consideration. Psychologists *D. Sue* and *D. W. Sue* identified four cultural barriers to effective counseling, including cultural values, social class, language, and nonverbal communications. Race and gender differences can also be crucial in prescribing optimal therapeutic levels of certain drugs; for example, women usually need lower doses of most psychiatric drugs than do men. In an effort to counter some of these problems, the APA issued Guidelines for Providers of Psychological Services for Ethnic, Linguistic, and Culturally Diverse Populations in 1993, and the DSM-IV also includes a section called Specific Culture, Age, and Gender Features for most of the disorders described.

FLASH REVIEW

Diagnosing Mental Disorders

Go to www.mhsource.com/, a source designed primarily for mental health professionals and providers. Visit the site, and answer the following questions:

1. Click on "Clinical Puzzles," then select "Begin This Course Now." Read one or more of the cases.

2. What physical information did the physician request in each case? How did that affect the diagnosis?

3. Read the Discussion for each case. What issues are of concern to the mental health professionals commenting on the cases? How much do the diagnoses of each case vary?

4. What conclusions can you draw about the difficulty of diagnosing an individual's problems from the combination of physical and psychological symptoms that are presented? What can you conclude about the connection between physical and psychological problems?

FLASH TEST

Review the chart of Core Concepts at the beginning of this chapter. Then, take the Practice Test on the following pages and rate your performance.

PRACTICE TEST

(Chapter 13 —Therapies for Treating Mental Disorders)

Multiple Choice (3 points each)

1. Freudian psychoanalysis is considered to be a type of
   a. insight therapy.
   b. cognitive therapy.
   c. behavioral therapy.
   d. humanistic therapy.

2. During the course of psychoanalysis, the client will attempt to prevent further insight into their unconscious motivations and desires, because such insight is psychologically distressing. Freud called this process
   a. rationalization.
   b. repression.
   c. regression.
   d. resistance.

3. The tendency of clients in psychoanalysis to project their attitudes and emotions onto the therapist as a result of reliving some of their unpleasant childhood experiences is called
   a. projection.
   b. transference.
   c. displacement.
   d. sublimation.

4. Person-centered therapy was developed by
   a. Sigmund Freud.
   b. Abraham Maslow.
   c. Carl Rogers.
   d. Fritz Perls.

5. Person-centered therapy is _____; whereas Gestalt therapy is _____.
   a. directive; nondirective
   b. nondirective; directive
   c. effective; ineffective
   d. ineffective; effective

6. An example of a treatment that is based on classical conditioning is
   a. systematic desensitization.
   b. stimulus satiation.
   c. token economy.
   d. participant modeling.

7. A token economy would be *least* effective in treating
   a. weight problems.
   b. negative verbal behaviors.
   c. poor social skills.
   d. schizophrenic hallucinations.

8. The therapy procedure that involves pairing noxious stimuli with cues that elicit undesirable behaviors is called
   a. systematic desensitization.
   b. implosion therapy.
   c. modeling.
   d. aversion therapy.

9. The therapeutic procedure in which a client observes another person performing the appropriate behavior is called
   a. observational therapy.
   b. modeling.
   c. vicarious therapy.
   d. imitation therapy.

10. In cognitive therapy, an example of an irrational assumption is,
    a. "I may get a lower grade from time to time, but I can cope with it."
    b. "I can handle most problems that crop up."
    c. "Everyone should love me unconditionally, all the time."
    d. "I may not be able to meet everyone's expectations all the time."

11. One of the original models for self-help groups was
    a. halfway houses.
    b. Gamblers Anonymous.
    c. Alcoholics Anonymous.
    d. Overeaters Anonymous.

12. Today it is estimated that there are around _____ self-help groups in the United States.
    a. 100,000
    b. 250,000
    c. 500,000
    d. 1 million

13. The major aim of _____ psychology is to understand and treat psychological problems as they occur in their sociocultural contexts.
    a. family
    b. community
    c. preventive
    d. psychodynamic

14. A community treatment program that functions primarily to help make the transition from living in a mental hospital or institution to living in a regular community is the
    a. community mission.
    b. group home.
    c. halfway house.
    d. community mental health center.

15. Identification of a mental problem or disorder at an early stage and intervening to treat it promptly is referred to as _____ prevention, whereas education programs or the removal of conditions that are conducive to the development of psychological programs is referred to as _____ prevention.
    a. primary; secondary
    b. secondary; primary
    c. secondary; tertiary
    d. primary; tertiary

16. For the most part, advocates of biological therapies assume that mental disorders
    a. have psychological causes.
    b. result from learning.
    c. have physical causes.
    d. result from environmental pollutants.

17. Drugs that help to control the symptoms of schizophrenia are called
    a. antidepressants.
    b. antipsychotics.
    c. tricyclics.
    d. lithium.

18. One possible side effect of the extended use of antipsychotic drugs is _____, the loss of motor control, especially in the face.
    a. antithetic disorder.
    b. epiglottis distortion.
    c. phlanges dysfunction.
    d. tardive dyskinesia.

19. Prozac, a brand name SSRI drug, inhibits the reuptake of
    a. dopamine.
    b. norepinephrine.
    c. serotonin.
    d. acetylcholine.

20. Lithium is used to treat
    a. bipolar disorders.
    b. schizophrenia.
    c. obsessive–compulsive disorders.
    d. paranoid delusions.

21. The most commonly prescribed antianxiety drugs are
    a. lithium salts.
    b. benzodiazepines.
    c. phenothiazines.
    d. tricyclics.

22. The therapeutic effect of ECT (electroconvulsive therapy) rests in the _____ it produces.
    a. seizures
    b. memory loss

    c. unconsciousness

    d. changes in the electrical activity of the thalamus

23. Some researchers contend that a major negative side effect of ECT is
    a. the uncontrolled changes in consciousness that occur between mania and catatonia.
    b. extensive memory loss and possible brain damage.
    c. extensive loss of motor control.
    d. impairment of language use.

24. The surgical procedure that is occasionally used to eliminate the symptoms of obsessive–compulsive disorder is called a(n)
    a. amygdalectomy.
    b. cingulotomy.
    c. occipital lobotomy.
    d. prefrontal lobotomy.

25. According to Sue and Sue, which of the following is *not* one of the cultural barriers that can hinder effective counseling?
    a. cultural values
    b. social class
    c. gender
    d. language

Essay Questions (5 points each)

1. Differentiate and describe the various types of insight therapies.
2. Describe the main types of behavior and cognitive therapies.
3. How did group therapy evolve? How does it differ from community therapy?
4. Describe the three main types of biological therapies, and evaluate their effectiveness.
5. What factors (including sociocultural factors) should be taken into account in selecting therapies for mental disorders?

ANSWER EXPLANATIONS

Multiple-Choice Questions

1. **a**
Freudian psychotherapy is considered to be a type of insight therapy, since it focuses on unresolved conflicts and bringing them from the unconscious to the conscious mind.

2. **d**
Freud termed the process in which the client attempts to block or stall the therapy "resistance."

3. **b**
In Freudian psychotherapy, the tendency of clients to project their feelings onto the therapist is called transference.

4. **c**
Person-centered therapy was developed by Carl Rogers.

5. **b**
Person-centered therapy is nondirective, whereas Gestalt therapy is directive.

6. **a**
Systematic desensitization is a type of classical conditioning, because it attempts to replace one conditioned response (fear) with another (relaxation techniques).

7. **d**
A token economy is an example of operant conditioning and will help to motivate an individual to change their behavior; however, schizophrenic hallucinations are not a behavior that is within the control of the individual.

8. d

In aversion therapy, some noxious stimulus is paired with cues that elicit undesirable behaviors; for example, learning to associate drinking alcohol with becoming violently ill.

9. b

The term for the therapy based on observational learning theory is participant modeling, in which an observer watches an example of appropriate behavior and imitates it.

10. c

An irrational assumption is one that creates unhappiness for the individual, such as the assumption that "everyone should love me unconditionally all the time," which sets up an unrealistic and impossible dynamic.

11. c

The original model for self-help groups was Alcoholics Anonymous; various other types of self-help groups, such as Gamblers Anonymous and Overeaters Anonymous, are based on the same format and principles.

12. c

It is estimated that there around a half-million (500,000) self-help groups in the United States.

13. b

Community psychology attempts to understand and treat psychological problems within the community and in their sociocultural contexts.

14. c

The halfway house exists in order to help individuals with the transition from a treatment facility, such as a substance abuse facility or mental institution, to living within the community.

15. b

The early diagnosis and prompt treatment of a mental disorder is called secondary prevention, whereas education programs and the removal of conditions that are conducive to the development of psychological problems is called primary prevention.

16. c

For the most part, advocates of biological therapies assume that mental disorders have physical causes.

17. b

Antipsychotic drugs, also called major tranquilizers or neuroleptics, help to control the positive symptoms (hallucinations and delusions) of schizophrenia.

18. d

Tardive dyskinesia, or the loss of muscle control, especially in the face, is a possible side effect of the long-term use of antipsychotic drugs.

19. c

Prozac and other SSRIs create their mood-elevating effect by inhibiting the reuptake of serotonin, leaving serotonin available for a longer period of time.

20. a

Lithium is used to treat bipolar disorders, since it reduces the intensity and frequency of both depressive and manic phases of the illness.

21. b

The minor tranquilizers, called benzodiazepines, are most commonly prescribed to treat anxiety.

22. a

The seizures that are created by ECT seem to be crucial to the treatment process.

23. b

Some researchers contend that a major negative side effect of ECT is the memory loss that it causes.

24. b

A cingulotomy is (occasionally) used to eliminate symptoms of severe obsessive–compulsive disorder.

25. c

Gender was not identified by Sue and Sue as a cultural barrier that can hinder effective counseling.

Essay Questions

1. Differentiate and describe the various types of insight therapies.

   Insight therapies are based on the assumption that self-understanding will be helpful in treating mental disorders. One of the main types of insight therapies, psychoanalysis, was pioneered by Sigmund Freud, and is based on his theories of unconscious drives and motivations; it is now less prevalent than it was in the 1930s–1950s. Humanistic or person-centered therapy was created by Carl Rogers to facilitate clients' process of self-actualization. Rogers believed that the therapist should provide a warm and accepting environment in which the client feels valued. Gestalt therapy was developed by Fritz Perls in the 1960s; it focuses on experiencing one's feelings in the present moment, while helping clients to resolve past conflicts, using techniques such as the "empty chair."

2. Describe the main types of behavior and cognitive therapies.

   Behavior therapies are based on the different learning approaches to psychological disorders, including classical conditioning, operant conditioning, and observational learning theory. In behavior therapies, clients learn to substitute appropriate behaviors for maladaptive behaviors through a variety of techniques. Some of these techniques, such as systematic desensitization, are particularly helpful in treating phobias.

   Cognitive therapies focus on changing an individual's behavior by changing their thoughts and perceptions. Albert Ellis, who pioneered rational-emotive therapy, believed that "irrational assumptions" are the cause of many emotional problems. Ellis, as well as therapists Aaron Beck and Donald Meichenbaum, taught techniques of changing clients' assumptions about themselves and others, and adopting different behaviors based on different, more rational assumptions.

3. How did group therapy evolve? How does it differ from community therapy?

   Group therapy evolved during World War II, when the numbers of soldiers to be treated for combat fatigue and stress challenged mental health resources. Mental health professionals discovered that there were some advantages to group therapy, including providing a sense of belonging and sharing common experiences and strategies for dealing with problems. Self-help groups work on these same principles, and many self-help groups are based on the structure of Alcoholics Anonymous, which was founded in the 1930s.

   Community therapy attempts to address psychological problems in their sociocultural context, through community treatment programs (including the community mental health center) and the establishment of halfway houses, to assist individuals in reintegrating themselves into the community. Community psychology focuses on prevention of mental disorders, either through primary prevention methods such as education, or secondary prevention aimed at early diagnosis and prompt treatment of mental disorders.

4. Describe the three main types of biological therapies, and evaluate their effectiveness.

   The main types of biological therapies are drug therapy, electroconvulsive therapy (ECT), and psychosurgery. Drug therapy is by far the most prevalent treatment method today, due to discoveries of effective drug treatments which have fewer negative side effects. The main types of drugs used are antipsychotics, used in the treatment of schizophrenia; antidepressant drugs, including tricyclics, SSRIs, and MAO inhibitors; lithium, which is used in the treatment of bipolar disorder; and minor tranquilizers, which are used in the treatment of anxiety. While drug therapy is effective in alleviating symptoms, it does not cure the underlying causes of the disorder, and the disorder usually returns once drugs are discontinued; also, there are still some negative side effects to drug therapy. Drug therapy in combination with some form of psychotherapy is probably the preferred treatment for most mental disorders.

   ECT is still used for the treatment of major depression; it seems to affect the biochemical balance in the brain. The major drawback of ECT is varying amounts of memory loss; there is also some controversy about whether ECT causes brain damage. The third method, psychosurgery, is used infrequently; lobotomies, once the primary type of psychosurgery, are rarely performed, since they leave patients with major aftereffects such as apathy, lack of motivation, and changes in personality. Specific surgeries such as cingulotomy are still used to treat extreme cases of certain disorders, such as obsessive–compulsive disorder.

5. What factors (including sociocultural factors) should be taken into account in selecting therapies for mental disorders?

   There are no studies that provide decisive information on which therapies are most effective. Most types of psychotherapy seem to be equally effective, and their effectiveness seems to depend on both the patient's willingness to change and the therapist's experience and ability to communicate empathy. There is today a growing recognition of the importance of sociocultural factors in selecting a treatment, and the DSM-IV now includes a section on Specific Culture, Age, and Gender Factors for most disorders.

UNIT V: INTERACTING WITH OTHERS

CHAPTER 14—SOCIAL PSYCHOLOGY

 FLASH FOCUS

When you complete this chapter, you will be able to:

✓ Define social psychology, and describe the processes of cognition and attribution

✓ Describe how attitudes are formed and changed, and the how prejudices are developed

✓ Discuss group behavior, and how conformity and compliance arise, as well as prosocial behavior

✓ Describe the process of attraction and the phenomenon of aggression

Use a highlighter to identify ideas, terms, and people that your instructor refers to in lectures or emphasizes in the course. Add to the chart any other ideas, terms, or people that your instructor discusses.

Core Concepts in Social Psychology

Important Ideas	Key Terms	Important People
Social psychology	Self-concept	H. H. Kelley
Social cognition	Self-schema	Richard Petty
Attribution	Interdependent construal	John Cacioppo
Attitudes	Independent construal	Solomon Asch
Persuasion	Primacy effect	Stanley Milgram
Impression formation	Situational factors	Sigmund Freud
Fundamental attribution	Dispositional factors	Konrad Lorenz
Error/correspondence bias	Consensus/consensual	L. Berkowitz
Heuristics	Behavior	Albert Bandura
Stereotypes	Consistency	
Cognitive dissonance	Distinctiveness	
Prejudice	Actor–observer effect	
Discrimination	Belief in a just world	
Social learning theory	Self-serving bias	
Social cognition	False consensus	
Conformity	Representativeness heuristic	
Norms	Availability heuristic	
Obedience	Systematic processing/central	
Compliance	route	
Social facilitation	Heuristic processing/	
Prosocial behavior	peripheral route	
Altruism	Elaboration-likelihood	
Interpersonal attraction	Model (ELM)	
Aggression	Heuristic systematic model	

	Induced compliance Trivialization Less-is-more effect Hypocrisy Realistic conflict theory Us-versus-them In-group Out-group Contact hypothesis Foot-in-the-door technique Door-in-the-face technique Low-ball technique Audience effects Coaction effects Social loafing Group polarization Groupthink Bystander effect Diffusion of responsibility Proximity Mere-exposure effect Association Reciprocal liking Halo effect Matching hypothesis Equity theory Intimate relationships Instinct theory of aggression Frustration–aggression Hypothesis Scapegoating Cognitive-neoassociationistic model Crowding Density Personal space	

Cognition and Attribution

FLASH SUMMARY

Social psychology is the study of how people think about, interact with, influence, and are influenced by the thoughts, feelings, and behaviors of others. Social psychologists study *social cognition,* or the process of attending to, analyzing, and interpreting social information; *attribution,* or the process by which people infer the causes of others' behavior; and *attitudes,* or people's evaluations of persons, places, and things.

Social cognition begins with one's *self-concept,* or knowledge, feelings, and beliefs about oneself. One's self-concept is organized by the *self-schema,* a mental framework that organizes information about oneself. The self-concept is influenced by one's culture, and changes over time, as more or different information is received. Generally,

Eastern cultures foster an *interdependent construal*, or a view of oneself that emphasizes the interconnectedness of people, whereas Western cultures foster an *independent construal*, or a view of oneself as autonomous and self-reliant. Research supports these cultural differences, such as in studies in which students from Eastern cultures judged themselves as similar to others, whereas students from Western cultures viewed themselves as dissimilar.

Our views of others are similarly influenced by our culture and by our environment. Social psychologists study *impression formation*, or the ways in which people form impressions of others. The tendency to form an impression about another person based on the initial information received about the person is called the *primacy effect*.

Attribution is the term for the process by which people infer the causes of other people's behavior. In judging another person's behavior, we evaluate both *situational factors*, or factors in the environment, and *dispositional factors*, or individual personality characteristics. Sociologist *H. H. Kelley* has posited that our evaluation of whether others' behavior is attributable to situational (external) or dispositional (internal) factors depends on three factors: *consensus* or *consensual behavior, consistency*, and *distinctiveness*. Consensual behavior is behavior that is shared by a large number of people; it is what is normally expected of another person. Consistency is the perception of reliability over time; distinctiveness is the extent to which a person performs a particular behavior only in a given situation.

An observer of another person's behavior tends to overestimate the significance of dispositional (internal) factors, and to underestimate the significance of situational (external) factors; for example, if someone meets a person who seems sad and depressed, the first person is likely to conclude that the person has a sad disposition. This is called *fundamental attribution error*, also called *correspondence bias*. One is much more likely to make this error with reference to another person; when considering our own behavior, we are much more likely to attribute our behavior to situational factors. This is called the *actor–observer effect*. Another example of fundamental attribution error is called *belief in a just world*; this is the belief that people get what they deserve in life. Studies have shown that this belief is more common among people of higher socioeconomic status. A related bias is when we attribute our accomplishments and successes to internal factors and our failures to external factors, a phenomenon called the *self-serving bias*. Another attribution error is called *false consensus*, or the tendency to perceive one's own response as representative of a general consensus.

In making social judgments, people tend to follow general rules, called *heuristics*. The *representativeness heuristic* is a general rule that causes a person to classify something into a category to which it appears to be most similar; in social psychology, this means that we are likely to match individual characteristics to *stereotypes*, or beliefs about the attitudes and behaviors of members of various social groups. Another heuristic is the *availability heuristic*, which means that people are more likely to assess an event by using examples that are more important or that occur more frequently. For example, it is easy for most people to call up images of being mugged when they are walking through a large city; other images of events that occur more rarely are not as easy to call to mind.

Attitudes

FLASH SUMMARY

Attitudes are lasting evaluations of any aspect of the social world, including ideas, issues, people, or groups. They are composed of three elements: an emotional or affective component, a cognitive component (beliefs), and a behavioral component (actions). Attitudes are formed through some of the basic learning processes such as operant conditioning (when children are rewarded for expressing "correct" attitudes) or observational learning, from modeling the attitudes of those around us. Advertisers and businesses are particularly interested in *persuasion*, or attempting to influence or change people's attitudes. Among other things psychologists have learned about persuasion are that experts are more persuasive than nonexperts; that people who do not seem to be trying to persuade are more convincing than those who are explicitly trying to affect our opinions; that attractive sources (such as models) are more effective than unattractive ones; and that persuasion can be enhanced by eliciting strong emotion from the intended audience.

One theory of how attitudes are formed and changed is the *elaboration likelihood model (ELM)*, proposed by *Richard Petty* and *John Cacioppo*. This theory suggests that people want to have attitudes and beliefs that will prove helpful in daily life. This model proposes two different cognitive paths to attitude change. One way, called *systematic processing*, or the *central route* to persuasion, involves a careful consideration of the message and its implications; the second way, called *heuristic processing*, or the *peripheral route*, involves the use of simple rules or shortcuts, such as the belief that an expert or trusted figure can be relied upon. The *elaboration likelihood model* posits that, when we have high motivation and our capacity for processing information is high, we are more likely to engage in systematic processing. The *heuristic systematic model* posits that when we care less or have less time for processing, we are more likely to engage in heuristic processing.

Attitudes are influenced by social considerations, such as the group we are with at a particular time. In certain situations, a person may voice an attitude they do not really believe, just to be "polite" or to fit in; this is called *induced compliance*. The term *cognitive dissonance* refers to the feeling that is experienced when an individual notices a gap between two contrasting attitudes, or between attitudes and behavior. To reduce this dissonance, individuals try to change attitudes or behaviors so they are more consistent; acquire new information to support the new attitudes or behavior; or engage in *trivialization*, or the conclusion that these attitudes or behaviors are not important. People are also (surprisingly) more apt to change attitudes when the reasons for engaging in contrary behavior are weaker. This is called the *less-is-more effect*, and is attributed to the fact that dissonance is stronger when the reasons for engaging in contradictory behavior are weaker, and so there is more pressure to change one's attitudes.

The effects of cognitive dissonance can be used to induce people to change their behaviors. For example, if a person who smokes is put into a position of advocating for nonsmoking, then they experience the difference between attitude and behavior as *hypocrisy*, and become more willing to reconsider the behavior.

Prejudice consists of (usually negative) attitudes toward others based upon characteristics such as race, gender, or membership in a particular group. *Discrimination* is the negative behavior in which prejudice is expressed. Various theories have been proposed to attempt to explain the basis of prejudice and discrimination. One, the *realistic conflict theory*, states that since there are not enough resources for all, competition for scarce resources among social groups creates conflict and hatred. Other theories posit that people tend to divide the world into *us-versus-them*, with an *in-group* composed of members who share a sense of togetherness from which others are excluded, and an *outgroup* that is specifically identified by the in-group as not belonging. *Social learning theory* holds that people learn attitudes of hatred and prejudice from those around them, and receive positive reinforcement for the expression of those prejudices. A theory based on principles of *social cognition*, or the ways in which people typically process information, posits that the process of simplifying and categorizing information leads to *stereotyping*.

Prejudice and discrimination can be unlearned through not only education but also direct contact between diverse groups. The theory that prejudices and stereotyping can be reduced through contact among diverse groups is called the *contact hypothesis*. Studies have shown that contact among diverse groups is most effective in combating prejudice if the groups are expected to share goals and to cooperate; if the groups are approximately equal in size and in economic status; and if the contact is informal, so group members come to know each other as individuals.

Group Behavior and Influence

FLASH SUMMARY

People's behavior in groups is an important area of study for social psychology. Social psychologists study the process of *conforming*, or adopting attitudes and behaviors that are consistent with the norms of a group; *norms* are the standards of behavior and attitudes expected of members of a particular group. A now-classic experiment performed by *Solomon Asch* asked participants to select two lines of the same length. Unknown to the experimental group, most of the group were individuals planted by Asch and instructed to select the incorrect line; the issue was whether the experimental group would feel the pressure to conform to the group's incorrect judgment. Asch found that 5 percent of the subjects conformed to the (incorrect) majority all of the time; 70 percent of the group conformed some of the time; 25 percent remained independent and were never swayed by the group opinion.

Another now-famous experiment was conducted by *Stanley Milgram*, in which participants were asked to administer an electric shock to another person if the person did not correctly answer a question. In the aftermath of World War II, Milgram wanted to see how far people would go in obeying an "order" of an authority figure. In Milgram's experiment, 65 percent of the participants continued to administer the supposed electric shocks even when the recipient pounded on the wall, screamed, and finally fell silent. However, the participants experienced extreme distress in complying with the directions of the authority figure. (Note that today such an experiment could not be conducted because of the questionable ethics involved in deceiving and causing great stress to the participants.)

When people act in response to the wishes or suggestions of another person, their actions are called *compliance*. Techniques that can be used by salespeople and others to induce compliance include the *foot-in-the-door technique*, in which an individual is persuaded to agree to a small request, which is then followed by a much greater request; the *door-in-the-face technique*, in which a large, unreasonable request is made first, followed by a smaller, more reasonable request; and the *low-ball technique*, in which an attractive initial offer is made, but after the individual agrees to the initial offer, the terms are then made less favorable.

Social facilitation refers to any effect on performance that can be attributed to the presence of others. Two types of effects are *audience effects*, or the effect on performance of having an audience, and *coaction effects*, or the effect of having other people also engaged in the same task. Research has indicated that, on tasks that individuals can easily complete or at which they are skilled, the presence of others has a positive effect of increasing performance effectiveness; however, on tasks that are difficult or which individuals are just learning, the presence of others causes a decline in performance. One effect of being required to work together is termed *social loafing*, or the tendency to work less diligently in groups than one would on one's own. Researchers have found that social loafing is more frequent in situations where individual performance cannot be distinguished, and in which individuals are neither praised nor blamed for their performance.

Psychologists who deal with workplace issues are well aware of the influence of the group on decision-making processes. One effect is *group polarization*, in which group members move to a more extreme position than they held initially during group discussions. Another, opposite effect is *groupthink*, a phenomenon in which tightly knit groups exclude possible alternatives in order to maintain the cohesiveness of the group. Groups can facilitate negative behaviors, such as the *bystander effect*. The bystander effect states that as the number of bystanders at an emergency grows, the probability of their giving aid to the victims decreases. This is probably due to a phenomenon termed *diffusion of responsibility*, in which everyone assumes that someone else will act. On the other hand, *prosocial behavior*, or behavior that helps and benefits others, is also common. There are many examples of *altruism*, or behavior that helps another, even at personal risk or cost to the helper.

Attraction and Aggression

FLASH SUMMARY

How do people begin and maintain relationships with others? *Interpersonal attraction* is the positive evaluation of another person that tends to draw people together. A major factor in such attraction is *proximity,* or geographic closeness. Proximity stimulates attraction in part because of the *mere-exposure effect,* or the tendency of people to feel more positively toward people or things with repeated contact. Other factors that influence attraction include *association,* or the tendency to associate people with either good or bad feelings or events that occurred when they were present, and *reciprocal liking,* or the tendency to like those people who express an attraction to oneself. Another factor is personal attractiveness; people of all ages, including 6-month-old infants, have a tendency to prefer people who are physically attractive. Researchers have found that people are considered more physically attractive the more their facial features approximate the average, as well as faces that are symmetrical. Physical attractiveness exerts a *halo effect,* in that people tend to associate other desirable qualities to people who are physically attractive. Smiling also increases the perceived attractiveness of others and makes them appear more sincere, sociable, and competent.

In addition to the effect of physical proximity, people are more attracted to others who share similar attitudes and beliefs. The *matching hypothesis* states that people are likely to enter into romantic relationships with others who are similar in attractiveness and other assets. Similarity in personality, physical characteristics, cognitive abilities, age, education, religion, ethnic background, attitudes and opinions, and socioeconomic status have all been found to be factors in selecting a romantic partner. The matching hypothesis also applies to friendships with individuals of the same sex. *Equity theory* states that individuals must also contribute approximately equally to the relationship in order for the relationship to be stable and consistent over time. *Intimate relationships* are those in which each person is willing to self-disclose and to express important feelings and information to the other person.

The opposite side of attraction is *aggression,* or the intentional infliction of physical or psychological harm on another person. The *instinct theory* of aggression holds that human beings are programmed for aggression due to evolutionary forces; this theory was proposed by both *Sigmund Freud* and *Konrad Lorenz.* Research has indicated that biological factors are involved in aggression to some degree, including a low arousal level of the autonomic nervous system. Researchers have posited that individuals with a low arousal level may seek stimulation and excitement from dangerous and aggressive activities. There is some correlation between high levels of testosterone and aggressiveness in both men and women, but there is also a correlation between aggression and very low levels of testosterone. Violent behavior has been correlated with low levels of the neurotransmitter serotonin. Brain damage can also lead to aggressive or violent behavior; studies have shown a correlation between severe head injuries and criminal behavior.

The *frustration–aggression hypothesis* suggests that frustration, the blocking of an impulse or interference with attainment of a goal, produces aggression. When frustration leads to the targeting of a specific group as the recipients of frustration and aggression, it is termed *scapegoating.* Another theory, the *cognitive-neoassociationistic model,* proposed by *L. Berkowitz,* suggests that aggression is a response to unpleasant events such as *crowding. Density* refers to the number of people occupying a given space, whereas crowding is a subjective response to the perception that there are "too many" people in a space. If an individual feels that their *personal space* is threatened, they are likely to perceive that there is crowding, and in some cases they respond with aggressive behavior. Negative events that lead to unpleasant emotional states, including exposure to pain, extreme heat, loud noise, and foul odors, have also been linked to increases in aggression.

Social learning theory, posited by *Albert Bandura,* holds that people learn aggressiveness, either by watching others and modeling their behavior and/or by having their aggressiveness reinforced by positive responses. Aggressive behavior is more common in groups and subcultures that condone and encourage violent behavior, and in which aggressiveness is correlated with higher social status. Bandura believes that aggressive models in culture, the family, and the media all contribute to increase the level of aggression in society. Some research indicates that both children and adults show higher levels of aggression after they view media violence.

 ## FLASH REVIEW

Go to www.influenceatwork.com/, a site about social influence, or the study of persuasion, compliance, and propaganda. Choose the link called "The Academic Side," and take the "Influence Quotient" quiz. Check your answers.

1. How well did you score on the quiz? Do you feel that learning the basic principles of social psychology helped you?

2. What conclusions can you draw from your exploration of this site about how the principles of social psychology are used in various commercial enterprises?

 ## FLASH TEST

Review the chart of Core Concepts for Chapter 14; then, take the Practice Test below, and rate your performance.

PRACTICE TEST

(Chapter 14—Social Psychology)

Multiple Choice (3 points each)

1. _____ is the study of how the thoughts, feelings, and behaviors of individuals are influenced by the actual, imagined, or implied presence of others.
   a. Social cognition
   b. Social perception
   c. Sociobiology
   d. Social psychology

2. Which of the following topics is of the *least* interest to social psychologists?
   a. attraction
   b. persuasion
   c. personality
   d. discrimination

3. The ways in which we attribute specific characteristics and traits to people is called
   a. social cognition.
   b. social perception.
   c. impression formation.
   d. a schema.

4. Generally, Western cultures foster a(n) _____ construal and Eastern cultures foster a(n) _____ construal or view of oneself.
   a. independent; interdependent
   b. interdependent; independent
   c. positive; negative
   d. negative; positive

5. According to the primacy effect,
    a. a foot-in-the-door increases compliance with requests for sales.
    b. a one-sided argument is more persuasive with most uninformed audiences.
    c. first impressions are more influential than information gained later.
    d. prejudice occurs when one racial group has more than its share of resources.

6. According to Juan, attribution is influenced by the following three factors:
    a. cognitive; emotional; and behavioral aspects.
    b. stimuli; behaviors; and outcomes.
    c. consensus; consistency, and distinctiveness.
    d. compliance; conformity, and obedience.

7. Our strong tendency to explain others' behavior in terms of internal causes rather than external causes is called the
    a. representative heuristic.
    b. self-serving bias.
    c. counterfactual thinking effect.
    d. correspondence bias.

8. The tendency of people to explain their own behavior in terms of situational factors and others' behavior in terms of dispositional factors is called
    a. belief in a just world.
    b. the actor–observer effect.
    c. the distinctiveness principle.
    d. self-serving bias.

9. The tendency to take credit for positive behaviors or outcomes by attributing them to internal causes but to blame negative outcomes on external causes is called the
    a. fundamental attribution error.
    b. self-serving bias.
    c. correspondence bias.
    d. social contagion effect.

10. Attitudes are composed of three dimensions, which are
    a. cognitive, affective, and behavioral.
    b. conscious, unconscious, and preconscious.
    c. internal, external, and conditional.
    d. primary, secondary, and tertiary.

11. The theory that attitude change takes one of two paths, either a central route or a peripheral route, is called the _____ of attitude change.
    a. foot-in-the-door technique
    b. Petty–Cacioppo model
    c. two-factor theory
    d. elaboration likelihood model

12. We are more likely to take the _____ route if we have less time, and if we care less about the subject.
    a. central
    b. peripheral
    c. heuristic
    d. elaboration likelihood

13. The notion that people seek to reduce anxiety when their cognitions and behaviors do not correspond is called
    a. the elaboration likelihood model.
    b. the fundamental attribution error.
    c. attribution theory.
    d. cognitive dissonance theory.

14. People engage in *all except one* of the following tactics in order to try to reduce cognitive dissonance:
    a. change attitudes or behaviors so they are consistent

b. acquire new information to support the new attitudes or behavior

c. voice an attitude in which the individual does not really believe, just to "fit in"

d. engage in trivialization, or the conclusion that the attitudes or behaviors are not important

15. An attitude or evaluation that is usually negative and that is focused on a particular group of people is called
    a. rationalization.
    b. bias.
    c. stereotype.
    d. prejudice.

16. The idea that prejudice stems from economic competition among social groups is a central tenet of
    a. realistic conflict theory.
    b. social categorization theory.
    c. social learning theory.
    d. group polarization theory.

17. The theory that prejudices and stereotypes can be reduced through contact is called the
    a. group polarization theory.
    b. contact hypothesis.
    c. social learning theory.
    d. realistic conflict theory.

18. Pressures toward acting or thinking like most other people refers to
    a. obedience.
    b. deindividualization.
    c. prosocial behavior.
    d. conformity.

19. The percentage of individuals who obeyed the orders to administer electric shocks to others in Stanley Milgram's experiment, even when they believed they were causing great harm, was _____ percent.
    a. 25
    b. 45
    c. 65
    d. 85

20. The compliance technique in which a person who agrees to a small request is then presented with a larger request is
    a. the door-in-the-face technique.
    b. the bandwagon technique.
    c. the skyrocket technique.
    d. the foot-in-the-door technique.

21. Performance on a(n) _____ task is likely to improve given the presence of others, whereas performance on a(n) _____ task is likely to become impaired given the presence of others.
    a. very simple; very difficult
    b. as yet unmastered; simple
    c. familiar; unfamiliar
    d. physically demanding; physically challenging

22. A decrease in performance exerted by a person who is performing a task with others is called
    a. deindividuation.
    b. social facilitation.
    c. social loafing.
    d. modulated compliance.

23. Kitty Genovese was murdered in front of her apartment while nearly forty people heard and did nothing to help. Social psychologists now believe that Kitty was not helped because
    a. people were afraid to become involved in the violence.
    b. the situation was too emotional for most people.
    c. in-group and out-group factors prevented anyone from responding.

d. too many people were around, so the sense of responsibility became too diffused.

24. The mere-exposure effect is most strongly related to
    a. discrimination.
    b. attraction.
    c. persuasion.
    d. prejudice.

25. People tend to end up with mates who are at about their same level of physical attractiveness; this phenomenon is known as the
    a. halo effect.
    b. similarity hypothesis.
    c. matching hypothesis.
    d. direct contact hypothesis.

Essay Questions (5 points each)

1. Differentiate and describe the processes of social cognition and attribution.

2. Define attitudes, and discuss the processes of persuasion and attitude change.

3. Define prejudice, and discuss some of the theories that explain prejudice and discrimination, as well as the theory of how prejudice and discrimination can be reduced.

4. Describe some of the dangers created by group behavior.

5. Discuss some of the mechanisms of attraction and aggression.

ANSWER EXPLANATIONS

Multiple-Choice Questions

1. **d**
   Social psychology is the study of how people think about, interact with, influence, and are influenced by the thoughts, feelings, and behaviors of others.

2. **c**
   Social psychologists study the topics of attraction, persuasion, and interaction with others, which includes discrimination.

3. **c**
   Impression formation is the term used for the ways in which people form impressions of others.

4. **a**
   Western cultures generally tend to foster an independent construal or view of oneself, whereas Eastern cultures generally tend to foster an interdependent construal.

5. **c**
   The primacy effect states that people tend to form impressions of each other based on the initial information received about the other.

6. **c**
   Juan posited that attribution is influenced by the factors of consensus, consistency, and distinctiveness.

7. **d**
   The tendency to attribute others' behavior to internal rather than external causes is called the fundamental attribution error, or correspondence bias.

8. **b**
   The actor–observer effect is the tendency to ascribe our own behavior to situational factors and others' behavior to dispositional factors.

9. **b**
   The tendency to attribute one's own accomplishments and successes to internal factors and one's failures to external factors is called the self-serving bias.

10. a

The three dimensions or components of attitudes are the emotional or affective component, a cognitive component (beliefs), and a behavioral component (actions).

11. d

The idea that attitude change takes either a central route (systematic processing) or a peripheral route (heuristic processing) is called the elaboration likelihood model.

12. b

The heuristic systematic model posits that when we have less time or care less about the subject, we are more likely to engage in heuristic, or peripheral, processing.

13. d

Cognitive dissonance theory posits that people feel anxiety when they realize that their attitudes and behaviors do not correspond.

14. c

Voicing an attitude in which one does not really believe in order to be polite or "fit in" is an example of induced compliance. The other behaviors (changing attitudes or behaviors to be consistent, acquiring new information to support new attitudes or behaviors or engaging in trivialization to minimize the importance of the attitudes or behaviors) are means of reducing cognitive dissonance.

15. d

An attitude or evaluation of a particular group of people that is generally negative is called prejudice. A stereotype is a generally negative belief about the attitudes and behaviors of members of various social groups.

16. a

The realistic conflict theory states that, since there are not enough resources for all, competition for these scarce resources among different social groups creates conflict and prejudice.

17. b

The theory that prejudice and stereotyping can be reduced by contact among diverse groups is called the contact hypothesis.

18. d

Pressure toward acting or thinking like most other people is called conformity.

19. c

In Stanley Milgram's experiment, 65 percent of individuals did continue to administer electric shocks to the subject, even when they believed that great harm was being caused.

20. d

In the foot-in-the-door technique, an individual is persuaded to agree to a small request, which is then followed by a much bigger request.

21. a

Performance on a very simple task is likely to improve in the presence of others, but performance on a very difficult task, or a task in which an individual has no experience, is likely to deteriorate in the presence of others.

22. c

Social loafing is the tendency to work less diligently in the presence of others than one would by oneself.

23. d

The bystander effect states that, as the number of bystanders at an emergency grows, the probability of their giving aid to the victims decreases, which social psychologists posit is due to diffusion of responsibility.

24. b

The mere-exposure effect posits that proximity stimulates attraction.

25. c

The matching hypothesis states that people are likely to enter into romantic relationships with others who are similar in attractiveness and other assets.

Essay Questions

1. Differentiate and describe the processes of social cognition and attribution.

   Social cognition is the process of attending to, analyzing, and interpreting social information; attribution is the process by which people infer the causes of others' behaviors. Social cognition begins with the self-concept, organized around a self-schema, or mental framework. Our view of ourselves, as well as our view of others, is influenced by our culture. Impression formation is the study of the ways in which people form impressions of each other. In observing others' behavior, people frequently fall into the fundamental attribution error, or correspondence error, of ascribing another's behavior to dispositional (internal) factors rather than situational (external) factors. However, in considering our own behavior, we are much more likely to attribute our own behavior to situational factors, called the actor–observer effect. Heuristics or general rules are often used as cognitive "shortcuts" to organize information about others; one example of such a heuristic is stereotypes, or beliefs about the attitudes and behaviors of members of various social groups.

2. Define attitudes, and discuss the processes of persuasion and attitude change.

   Attitudes are lasting evaluations of any aspect of the social world, including ideas, issues, people or groups. Attitudes have an emotional (affective) element, a cognitive element (beliefs), and a behavioral element (actions). Advertisers and businesses are particularly interested in techniques of persuasion, or attempting to change or influence others' attitudes. The elaboration likelihood model proposes that there are two main methods of attitude change; one, the systematic processing or central processing route to persuasion, involves a careful consideration of the message and its implications, and is performed when we have time, and when the information is important to us; the second method, heuristic processing or the peripheral route, involves the use of simple rules or shortcuts, and is used when we have little time or when the subject matter is of little importance.

3. Define prejudice, and discuss some of the theories that explain prejudice and discrimination, as well as the theory of how prejudice and discrimination can be reduced.

   Prejudice consists of attitudes (usually negative) toward others based on race, gender, or membership in a particular group. Discrimination is the behavior in which prejudice is expressed. There are several theories that attempt to explain the origin of prejudice, including the realistic conflict theory, which posits that groups must struggle for scarce resources, thus creating conflict and hatred; the us-versus-them theory, which describes the creation of in-groups, composed of members who share a sense of togetherness from which others are excluded, and out-groups, defined by the in-group as not belonging; and social learning theory, which holds that people learn attitudes of hatred and prejudice from those around them, and from receiving positive reinforcement for the expression of prejudice. The theory that prejudices and stereotyping can be reduced through contact among diverse groups is called the contact hypothesis.

4. Describe some of the dangers created by group behavior.

   Dangers of group behavior can include the pressures to conform to the attitudes and behaviors of a group, which can lead individuals to adopt beliefs that are not actually true, as demonstrated by Solomon Asch's experiments. Another danger is compliance, or acting in response to the wishes or suggestions of another person. Organizations use techniques to foster compliance, such as the foot-in-the-door technique (in which a small request leads to a larger request), the door-in-the-face technique (in which an unreasonable request is followed by a smaller, more manageable request), and low-balling (replacing an initial attractive offer with a less favorable offer). In group polarization, group members can move to more extreme positions than they held initially; and in groupthink, members of a group can exclude possible alternatives in order to maintain the cohesiveness of the group. In emergency situations, the larger the group, the less likely are individuals to come to the aid of others, due to diffusion of responsibility.

5. Discuss some of the mechanisms of attraction and aggression.

   Interpersonal attraction is the positive evaluation of another person that tends to draw people together. Social scientists have found that proximity is important in attraction due to the mere-exposure effect, or the tendency of people to feel more positively toward people and things with repeated contact. Personal attractiveness is an important feature of attraction, and tends to have a halo effect, by which attractive people are associated with other desirable qualities. The matching hypothesis states that people are likely to enter into romantic relationships with others who are similar in attractiveness and other assets, and equity theory states that individuals must contribute approximately equally to the relationship in order for the relationship to be stable and consistent over time.

Aggression, or the intentional infliction of physical or psychological harm on another person, has been posited as instinctive, due to evolutionary forces, and biological factors have also been explored, including levels of testosterone (in both men and women), levels of the neurotransmitter serotonin, and brain damage. The frustration–aggression hypothesis suggests that frustration (the blocking of an impulse or interference with the attainment of a goal) produces aggression; the cognitive-neoassociationistic model suggests that aggression is the result of unpleasant events such as crowding. Social learning theory posits that individuals learn aggressive behavior from others, and holds that aggressive models in culture, family, and the media all contribute to increase the level of aggression in society.

INDEX

NOTES

NOTES